D0934239

THE SECRETARIES OF STATE
FOR SCOTLAND, 1926-76

By the same Author

The Winning Counter
Muirfield and the Honourable Company
St Moritz; an Alpine Caprice
The Court of the Medici

THE SECRETARIES
OF STATE
FOR SCOTLAND
1926 – 76

FIFTY YEARS OF THE SCOTTISH OFFICE

GEORGE POTTINGER

SCOTTISH ACADEMIC PRESS
EDINBURGH

Published by
Scottish Academic Press Ltd,
33 Montgomery Street
Edinburgh EH7 5JX

SBN 7073 0230 7

Printed in Great Britain
by R. & R. Clark Ltd, Edinburgh

Contents

Thou shalt not worship projects nor
Shalt thou or thine bow down before
  Administration.
                    W. H. Auden

Author's Foreword

Seventeen Secretaries of State for Scotland, apart from Mr Bruce Millan the present Minister, have held office since the first appointment was made in 1926. This study gives some account of them. In order to set it in context earlier Ministers who have held the Scottish portfolio appear from time to time. Although this is a commentary, not a history, there are incidental reflections on the political temper of the twenties and thirties and, more recently, the events that have led to the Devolution Bill.

The individual Secretaries of State have differed greatly in character, capacity, and in what they achieved as the Scottish spokesman in the Cabinet. Over half a century it could scarcely be otherwise, but as my researches proceeded I was surprised to discover how acute the differences were. An assessment of their activities inevitably includes some astringent observations. No politician would expect a diet of marshmallow. But I have tried to be fair, and the comments that emerge from these pages do not detract from the conclusion that, in the period under review, Scotland has been well served by her Ministers. I believe that this verdict is also true of their advisers, although here too there are animadversions—not, I hope, unnecessarily captious—on the merits and demerits of the bureaucracy.

Tom Johnston and James Stuart published their memoirs. Walter Elliot wrote a short treatise, and has been the subject of a lucid biography. Otherwise, very little has been written about, and even less by, the Secretaries of State, and they appear only fitfully in the printed recollections of their peers. In my account I have relied principally on Cabinet Minutes and official papers now lodged in the Record Offices, *Hansard* which is more revealing with the passage of time, and material that has appeared in contemporary newspapers and periodicals. I have had the benefit of advice from those who knew, or served under, the Ministers, and many of the comments come from personal knowledge.

I am very grateful to all those who have assisted me. They are too numerous to identify, but I am glad to mention the relatives of Secretaries of State who kindly made papers available, suggested sources, and offered many helpful comments on my manuscript—Sir John Gilmour, M.P., Viscount Thurso, Mr J. W. H. Collins, Mrs Elspeth Barry, and Mrs Sheila McNeil. Mr John Imrie, the Keeper of the

Records of Scotland, and the staff of the Scottish Record Office sought out relevant files for me, and my thanks are also due to the staff at the Public Record Office at Kew, Cambridge University Library, the Archives at Churchill College, Cambridge, and the British Newspaper Library, Colindale.

Lastly, I am indebted to Mr J. G. Kellas of the Department of Politics at Glasgow University, and the Cambridge University Press for permission to quote the chronology which is set out in Appendix II.

BALSHAM, *June*, 1978

CHAPTER I

The Salted Haggis

In March, 1977, a public opinion poll showed that 17 per cent of those interviewed in Scotland did not know of the existence of the Scottish Office. If they had been asked to name past, or present, Scottish Ministers, the quotient of ignorance would no doubt have been higher. Does this point to a failure in communication, or does it reflect the unimportance of the office? It could scarcely be the latter.

The office of Secretary of State is the most significant political appointment in Scotland. When he is invited to serve, the new Minister, like other senior Ministers of the Crown, goes to Buckingham Palace to be received in audience by the Sovereign and kiss hands. As soon as possible thereafter he presents himself at the Court of Session in Edinburgh where the oath of allegiance and the official oath are administered by the Lord President, accompanied by a full bench of the Senators of the College of Justice. Witnesses to this historic ceremony have, however, been puzzled to observe that the Secretary of State is not required to speak, or otherwise indicate that he knows what is happening.

The Secretary of State is Keeper of Her Majesty's Seal, appointed by the Treaty of Union to be kept and made use of in Scotland in place of the Great Seal of Scotland. His own seal consists of the Royal Arms in Scottish form, bearing the Scottish lion in the first and fourth quarters, the English leopards in the second and the harp of Ireland in the third, and carries the title 'Secretary of State for Scotland'. Despite these heraldic trappings, references to him in the Statute Book are hard to find. Constitutionally all Secretaries of State in the Government— the number varies—hold one office deriving from the original one of King's Secretary. If need arises they can act or sign documents on each other's behalf, and in legislation the practice is to refer simply to 'The Secretary of State', leaving the lieges to deduce the identity of the Minister. There are only occasional exceptions to offend the purist where the parliamentary draftsman has nodded and allowed the Scottish Minister to be named, e.g. section 13 of the White Fish and

Herring Industry Act, 1951, and section 17 of the Transport Act, 1953.

In modern times the office of Secretary of State dates from 1926. The present devolution debate, however resolved, will almost certainly result in fundamental changes in his status. This affords a convenient opportunity to consider what use Scottish Ministers have made of their powers in the last fifty years, how far they have contributed to national wellbeing, and, conversely, the extent to which they can be arraigned for misgovernment. The present study is accordingly concerned to analyse the achievements and failures of the Secretaries of State, their reaction to Scottish opinion, and their relations with their advisers, over this period. Conclusions will be drawn about the place of a 'geographical' Minister, responsible for a part of the country which regards itself as a nation, in the government of the United Kingdom.

In order to set the study in perspective it is worth while looking briefly at the circumstances which led to the elevation of the principal Scottish Minister to the dignity of a Secretary of State, and before that to the creation of the Scottish Secretaryship in 1885. It would be ingenuous to suppose that these developments were a natural progression caused by the U.K. Government's sympathetic attitude to Scotland, or by the prompt acceptance of a vocal demand by the Scots to have more say in their own affairs. The truth is very different. Even a summary examination reveals a picture of intransigence and irresolution not unlike the present merry jockeying for position as the political parties try to decide, or not to decide, how Scottish business should be administered.

Before the Treaty of 1707 united the two Parliaments Scottish affairs were conducted by a Privy Council in Scotland. The leading members included the Lord Justice General, the Lord Justice Clerk, the Lord Advocate, and the Lord Clerk Register, whose offices survive although in a different form, and the Secretary. The Scottish Parliament included these Officers of State in its membership *ex officio*, but, mainly because it had two formidable rivals, it was never as authoritative as the Parliament in England. For much of its life its principal competitor was the Committee of the Lords of the Articles— according to Dicey and Rait 'by far the strangest and the most original creation to be found in the Scottish Constitution'.[1] The Lords of the Articles, about forty in number, were nominally elected by Parliament, but in practice they were appointed in accordance with the King's wishes. Parliament could not discuss or vote on any Bill which had not been brought forward by the 'Articles', as they came to be known, and even then its power was confined to simple acceptance or rejection. The Articles were in effect the legislative authority until they were abolished in 1690, at the time of the Revolution Settlement. This may seem irrelevant to our present enquiry, but as late as 1952, during the deliberations of the Royal Commission on Scottish Affairs, the distinguished lawyer Sir John Spencer Muirhead was attracted by the way in which the Articles acted as a quasi-Cabinet and was tempted to revive them as an efficient form of devolution. This reactionary idea did not, however, proceed beyond the theoretical stage.

In its last years, from 1690 to 1707, the Scottish Parliament exercised more authority in the passing of laws, and became more of a forum for public debate, but it was never considered to be the centre of the country's political existence, as happened in England. For it still had to coexist with the powerful General Assembly of the Church of Scotland. The General Assembly was not a purely clerical body: it included a lay element and it was democratically elected: it was widely representative at least so far as Scotland was a Presbyterian country: it promoted and regulated education: it supervised the distribution of poor relief: on secular matters parliamentary legislation was often passed at its prompting: and its undoubted moral influence transcended its own extensive powers. The relations between Church and State were aptly summarised as 'equal authority with coordinate jurisdiction'. This book is not concerned with these relations, as they continued, but it is significant that under the 1707 Union the Scottish National Church outlasted the Scottish Parliament.

In the years immediately before the Union friction between London and Edinburgh increased. The Earl of Seafield (remembered for his definition of the Treaty as 'the end of an auld sang') complained about the difficulties of commuting, and conducting Ministerial business, betwixt the two capitals. In this century Secretaries of State have said much the same thing as they rocked in their sleepers from King's Cross or fretted at airport delays.

The Treaty of Union, though safeguarding the Scottish legal system, did not preserve the office of Scottish Secretary or Secretary of State. The Scottish Privy Council was discontinued in 1708 (the Convention of Estates, which strengthened the actions of the Privy Council, did not meet after 1689) and in 1709 the Duke of Queensberry was appointed as a third United Kingdom Secretary of State and given the oversight of Scottish affairs. The decision to take formal cognisance of different conditions north of the border was not without its critics. The sinister government agent Daniel Defoe denounced the appointment in trenchant terms.

> Scotland No More Requires a Secretary than Yorkshire or Wales, Nor (the Clamour of Petitions Excepted) can it Supply bussiness for an Office with Two Clarks. . . .
> It keeps up a Faction in Scotland. . . .
> It Layes the Crown Under a Constant and Needless Expense.[2]

Defoe may have pre-empted the anti-devolution lobby, but the office of Secretary of State had few friends in either country. Sometimes the post was not even filled. Montrose, for example, was removed during the 1715 Rebellion and the Duke of Roxburghe was dismissed in 1725. The Duke of Newcastle's bland letter to the Lord Advocate exemplifies Westminster indifference.

> His Majesty, not intending for the future to have any particular Secretary of State for Scotland, has been pleased to remove the Duke of Roxburghe from that employment, and ordered his other Secretaries of State to take care of that department that his Grace had.[3]

Roxburghe probably suffered for agitating against the Malt Tax, always thought to be vexatious in Scotland. Walpole referred contemptuously to the Secretary of State as 'a public nuisance', but the office was restored with the appointment of Lord Selkirk and lasted until the Marquess of Tweeddale resigned in 1746. By then the most important man in Scotland was the Lord Advocate.

This shift in influence was partly due to the energy and striking personality of Lord Advocate Duncan Forbes, 'patron of the just, the dread of villains, and the good man's trust'. Forbes had a gift for carrying out unpopular policies without detriment to his own reputation. From the start, however, the Lord Advocate's duties extended beyond the statutory functions of a Law Officer of the Crown, and today they are still wider than those of his opposite number in England, the Attorney General. The relationship between the Lord Advocate and whoever exercises the political responsibility for Scottish affairs, whether it be one of the former U.K. Secretaries of State in Whitehall or in more recent times the Secretary of State for Scotland, remains ambivalent. Some Lord Advocates have been primarily interested in their profession and have been jealous to assert the rights and privileges of the Bar—a view that does not always command universal support. (The Bar have invariably resented the Secretary of State's right, albeit on the recommendation of the Lord Advocate, to submit names to the Sovereign for judicial preferment, maintaining that they alone are qualified to make the selection.) Other Lord Advocates have sought to impose their views on matters of general policy. The inherent tension does not make for harmony in administration, and not only eighteenth-century Ministers have resented the Lord Advocate's aspirations. This occurs in an acute form when a Secretary of State new to office, possibly lacking in forensic skill, finds himself at odds with a colleague learned in the law and adept at argument.

In the period following 1746, although the nominal responsibility for Scotland lay with one of the U.K. Secretaries of State, it was the influence of the Lord Advocate and, in an ill-defined way, the 'Scottish Manager' that counted. The qualifications for appointment as Scottish Manager were not prescribed, and in practice he was a Scot who happened to hold an office entitling him to a seat in the Cabinet. This informal arrangement, combined with the corrupt nature of Scottish representation at Westminster, enabled Henry Dundas, by far the most significant figure on the Scottish scene, to acquire alarming personal power. Appointed Solicitor General in 1766, he became Lord Advocate in 1775, and Keeper of the Signet with unlimited powers of patronage in 1782. His omnivorous appetite for office was still not satisfied, and in addition to his authority over Indian affairs he in time assumed the portfolios for the Home Office, the War Office, and the Admiralty.

The Scottish M.P.s, who normally voted as a clique to bolster the government of the day with a view to securing what they could for Scotland, and for themselves, from the English bounty, were elected not by the people or the Church but by a small number of aristocratic families. Scotland had a population of about one and a half millions, but the franchise extended to less than 4000 voters. Fox found the Scottish system 'so ridiculous and so revolting' that it served only to show that there was something worse than the, admittedly defective, English arrangements. 'In Scotland', he went on, 'there is no shadow even of representation. There is neither representation of property for the counties, nor of population for the towns.'[4] But, as Steven Watson has observed, the purpose was 'not to represent Scotland (which was very effectively done in the kirk) but to run an employment agency for the benefit of her surplus men of talent and the preservation of her great family connexions'.[5] Dundas exploited this situation more ruthlessly and efficiently than ever before and his approval was the essential preliminary to a seat in the House. At the 1802 General Election his army of adherents included all but 2 of the 45 Scottish M.P.s and he also had a decisive say in the election of Scottish representative Peers.

The Scots were by now beginning to chafe under the Lord Advocate's yoke, and discontent was exacerbated when Lord Advocate Hope assured the House of Commons that he possessed all the powers that before the Union had belonged to the Scottish Privy Council, together with a plethora of offices including that of public prosecutor and Home Secretary. Not surprisingly Lord Cockburn said that Hope's 'great defect was a want of tact'.[6] The peculiar intervention of the Scottish Manager was brought to an end by Prime Minister Canning in 1827, when Lord Melville (Henry Dundas's son) declined to serve under him. Canning then assigned Scottish affairs to the Home Office, but the Lord Advocate's effective influence was scarcely impaired. This was the age of the great Reform legislation. To meet the needs of the newly enfranchised classes, government activity grew in extent and complexity. By 1832 Lord Advocate Jeffrey, weary of the obloquy that his best-intentioned efforts produced, and Cockburn both concluded that Scotland required another parliamentary representative. Lord Althorp was appointed as a Scottish Lord of the Treasury, but this was no more than a sop. His duties were restricted and he could not expect to have any impact on Scottish administration.

No awkward questions of democratic election had so far disturbed the system of patronage. In the next twenty years, however, public opinion began to address itself more seriously to such mundane matters as local government, education, the poor law, and public health. Exchequer grants were introduced in new fields. The more pervasive government became, the more the governed questioned whether they were getting their fair share of attention. It was this reaction as much as any resurgence of national identity that led the Scots to become more sceptical at remote control from Westminster, but in time their disenchantment crystallised in the feeling that Scottish interests were, simply, disregarded. For good measure, the complaint—one that was to recur over the years—that Parliament did not find adequate time for Scottish legislation became more insistent.

In 1851 the Convention of Royal Burghs presented a Memorial to Parliament on Scottish grievances, and two years later disaffected interests combined to form a Society for the Vindication of Scottish Rights. The movement gathered impetus and on 15th June, 1858, Mr

Baxter, the Member for Dundee, tabled a motion in the House of Commons calling for the appointment of an Under Secretary for Scotland to take over the Lord Advocate's political duties.[7] The debate disclosed widespread concern. Scottish Members said they could not distinguish between the Lord Advocate's responsibility and that of the Home Secretary. They pointed to the conflict between the Lord Advocate's legal preoccupations in Edinburgh and his parliamentary duties in the South. Two recent Bills (Police and Lunacy) had been passed although defective in form because the Lord Advocate had to be in Edinburgh for the trial of Madeleine Smith. (Baxter also complained that lawyers monopolised patronage in Scotland and cited Cockburn's calculation that there were only 171 eligible advocates to compete for 78 public offices—one for every second man.) Lord Advocate Inglis, in a stubborn defence, played down his own authority and claimed that he did no more than tender advice to the Home Secretary. The motion was defeated by 174 votes to 47.

Another debate in 1864, initiated by Sir James Fergusson, resulted in little progress. Lord Palmerston did, however, cast a marbled eye across the Border to observe that if there was to be a transfer it should be to a Minister in charge of a Department. That was the sole crumb of comfort, and W. C. Smith noted in his learned monograph that 'the opinion of the leaders on both sides was at the time against the proposed change'.[8] Such is the fate of reformers, especially devolutionists. When Baxter raised the subject again in 1867 he failed to provoke a reply from the Government Bench.

The Scottish Members were not prepared to remain passive. In 1869 Sir Robert Anstruther and Mr Crawfurd wrote to Mr Gladstone on behalf of a majority of their colleagues urging that a Chief Secretary for Scotland should be appointed with powers similar to those of the Irish Secretary. They argued that the administration by the Scottish 'Boards' in Edinburgh (discussed in Chapter II) was unsatisfactory, and said once again that Scottish business was beyond the capacity of the Lord Advocate. Gladstone's response was to appoint a Commission of Enquiry under Lord Camperdown and Sir William Clerk. After a brief examination the Commission concluded that the Boards worked efficiently. Finding more to criticise at the Ministerial level, they recommended that the Home Secretary should be formally recognised as Minister for Scotland. This was not much of an advance, but their report did contain one proposal that bears all the marks of being improvised. This was that when wearing his Scottish hat the Home

Secretary should be assisted by a Civil Parliamentary Officer (c. 64). Nothing was done.

The weight of official opinion was still obstinately against any innovation and no pattern emerged in the perfunctory discussions over the next five years. Discontent continued to simmer, but it may have been mollified by the acceptance with which two Lord Advocates of some ability—Moncrieff and Young—performed their duties.

The Conservative Government which succeeded after the 1874 General Election was, if anything, more insensitive to Scottish requirements. The Home Office proceeded to display an affection for centralised arrangements which the Scots did not like. As a further affront, the Lord Advocate was put to the indignity of being moved to a 'very small and unwholesome room' in an attic in the Home Office itself.[9] In 1878, Mr Cross, reluctantly conceding the need for some improvement, introduced a Bill for the creation of an additional Under Secretary to deal with Scottish matters, but it had no high priority and was dropped from the Order Paper after Second Reading. In a Lords debate in 1881 Lord Rosebery, who had resigned from his post as Under Secretary at the Home Office, complained bitterly at the absurdity of trying to conduct Scottish business without a proper Department and permanent staff.[10] Despite the lack of any clear sign of purpose in Parliament, the Scottish question could not be buried, and Sir William Harcourt sponsored another Bill in 1883. Harcourt's speech was curiously apologetic, and though the Bill passed the Commons it was thrown out by the Lords.

Scottish indignation could no longer be appeased. A meeting held in Edinburgh on 16th January, 1884, under the chairmanship of Lord Lothian, attracted a widely representative attendance. From it went out a stern call for action. As the resolution submitted to the Prime Minister finally led to legislation, its terms are quoted.

> That in the opinion of this meeting more satisfactory arrangements for the administration of Scottish affairs are imperatively required; that the increasing wealth and population of Scotland make its proper administration most important to the empire, while its marked national characteristics and institutions, and separate legal and educational systems, render it impossible to govern Scotland solely through the Home Office and other existing departments of State; and that, therefore, Government should create a separate and independent department for the conduct of distinctively Scottish affairs, responsible to Parliament and the country for its administration.

That the department should be presided over by a Minister for Scotland of personal eminence and position in Parliament and the country; and it is suggested that this office should be conjoined with that of the Lord Privy Seal.

In May, 1884, Lord Dalhousie introduced a Bill in the Lords to create a Secretary for Scotland. It received a unanimous Second Reading but was then withdrawn in the course of a conflict between the two Houses on the Franchise and Redistribution Bills. The Bill was brought forward again in the following year by Lord Rosebery, and although Gladstone's administration had now been succeeded by that of Lord Salisbury it was treated as an agreed measure and passed. It will be noted that, not for the last time, no one party was prepared to take the lead in declaring itself in favour of devolutionary proposals. Only when the possibilities of evasion had been exhausted did Scotland acquire her own undisguised Minister. Sir Lyon Playfair pointed out in the House that 'A General Election is near. That induces both sides to throw a tub to the Scotch whale.'[11]

The Secretary for Scotland Act, 1885, did not in terms define the new Minister's powers and duties. Instead, it transferred the functions previously discharged in Scotland by the Home Office, the Privy Council, the Treasury, and the Local Government Board, under the forty-five statutes listed in the Schedule. The effect was to give the Scottish Secretary a very mixed bag of duties, ranging from prisons to fisheries, lunacy and vaccination. Lyon Playfair said the Minister would be 'mixed up like a Scottish haggis and then salted with education'.[12]

The Home Office did not pretend to like the new arrangements, as a petulant minute dated 14th October, 1885, by Cross indicates.

The office (of Scottish Secretary) only exists with certain statutory powers. The Secretary has no jurisdiction whatever beyond what is specially imposed on him by the Act. . . .[13]

In every other respect, Cross continued, until experience had shown the necessity of altering the law, and the law had been amended accordingly, the Home Secretary must remain responsible. But over the years Cross's dictum has not been observed, and today the duties of the Scottish Office are even more heterogeneous.

The Duke of Richmond and Gordon, who had privately opposed the Bill, became the first Scottish Secretary. There is a whiff of Wodehouse in the correspondence. Melbourne wrote to His Grace on 7th August, 1885.

> What are your feelings about the Secretaryship for Scotland? The work is not very heavy. . . . It really is a matter where the effulgence of two Dukedoms and the best salmon river in Scotland will go a long way.[14]

The Duke's reply two days later might have come from Blandings Castle.

> I am quite ready and willing to take the office of Secretary for Scotland if you would like me to do so. . . . You know my opinion of the office, and that it is quite unnecessary, but the Country and Parliament think otherwise—and the office has been created, and someone must fill it.[15]

With a salary of £2000 a year, the same as the Presidents of the Board of Trade and the English Local Government Board, the Duke set up office in Dover House, at one time Melbourne's town house and still the most agreeable building in Whitehall. Initially the post was not regarded as being of anything like the first rank, although an amending Act increased the Secretary's powers in 1887. In the first two years no fewer than five Secretaries—the Duke of Richmond and Gordon, Mr (later Sir G. O.) Trevelyan, the Earl of Dalhousie, Mr A. J. (later Earl of) Balfour, and the Marquess of Lothian—passed each other at the door of Dover House as they went in and out of office. Eventually there were complaints from the Commons if the Scottish Secretary sat in the Lords, and only three Peers were subsequently given the office. An important change in practice took place in 1892, and since then, except in wartime, the Scottish Minister has had a seat in the Cabinet.

The importance of this arrangement is not to be underrated. The Scottish Secretary, or nowadays the Secretary of State, may be in dispute with the corresponding English Minister. If the latter does not happen to be a member of the Cabinet he will be summoned for the item under discussion, but English departments have been known to complain that in the ensuing debate the Secretary has the edge as the resident member. This is a subject to which we will return.

In 1919 the Scottish Secretary was given the assistance of a Parliamentary Under-Secretary for Health. No further change was enacted till 1926 when the growing importance of the office in the control of domestic affairs in Scotland was given formal recognition. Paradoxically, it was abolished and the duties transferred to one of His Majesty's Principal Secretaries of State—the constitutional device for

promoting the holder to the full rank of Secretary of State. His
Parliamentary Under-Secretary automatically became a Parliamentary
Under-Secretary of State. No Minister can, however, be effective in
the in-fighting with his colleagues unless he is supported by a proper
department, and much of the past argument had centred on the lack
of suitable Scottish administrative arrangements. The Secretary of
State gradually took over the staff of the Scottish Boards, but the
Scottish Office was not organised as a major department of state until
1939. (These developments, and later accretions, are discussed in the
next chapter.) Meanwhile, in 1939 the Scottish Minister and his
advisers took station behind the impersonal façade of St Andrew's
House, the new government building which Tait had designed on the
site of the old Bridewell. There they were to stay until their most
recent move to the brutalised edifice that disfigures St James's Square.

A second Parliamentary Under-Secretary of State was added in
1940 to assist in the discharge of wartime regulations. Further changes
followed the 1951 General Election. The Conservative Party, which
could hardly ignore the growth in nationalist sentiment, made some
play in their manifesto with the need to give the Scots more scope to
settle their own affairs. They promised, if returned, to appoint a
Minister of State and a third Parliamentary Under-Secretary of State.
This they did, and the Scottish Office has since had a normal complement of five Ministers—the Secretary of State, a Minister of State, and
three Under-Secretaries. There have been occasional variations; at
one time there were two Ministers of State, and more recently there
has been an extra Under-Secretary. The two Scottish Law Officers
remain in the wings to give advice.

This stage has been reached after a halting, circuitous journey,
marked by indecision and confusion. No individual, and no one party,
can claim any great credit for recognising the case for appointing a
separate Scottish Minister, or for the eventual concentration of power
in his hands. A sense of national identity contributed, but no more than
the growth of government intervention in everyday matters. To come
back to Defoe, would Scotland ever have been given her own Minister
if the Treaty of Union had not left the Scottish institutions—the law,
the Church, the educational system—intact? It is not an easy question
to answer, and Defoe's jibe, his comparison with Yorkshire, is still
valid in the minds of many English M.P.s.

The analogue with Ireland is also worth a moment's reflection. The
1800 Union abolished the Irish Parliament, but though the legislature

was removed to Wesminster the 'Castle' at Dublin remained the centre of Irish political life. Moreover, the Lord Lieutenant and the Chief Secretary, though responsible to the U.K. government, still presided over a separate Irish executive. Scotland, though her institutions survived in 1707, and though her law was preserved in a way that Irish law was not, was given no vice-regal court and no separate administrative setup. There are two apparent reasons for this different treatment. First, there was the need to appease Irish sentiment following the troubled history of the immediately preceding years and at a time when a very vocal Parliament was being abolished. Second, and more important, the executive—in practice unchanged—continued to buttress the Protestant ascendancy. But the ultimate effect was to convey the impression that Ireland was not completely integrated in the United Kingdom, and, as hopes for Catholic emancipation, which was intended to follow the Union, were for long disappointed, to fan the flames of Home Rule.

The Scottish Minister has not confined himself to the functions set out in the 1885 schedule and later Acts. Sir David Milne, in his authoritative history of the Scottish Office, remarked that once the office had been created it tended to exert a magnetic attraction on other organisations concerned with Scotland. In short, it was natural that once there was a Scottish Minister he should be given other tasks, e.g. electricity or forestry, to be discharged either through his own office or through other instruments, and there has been a steady flow of additions. If the Scottish Office was a commercial body, even a holding company, the shareholders would feel that diversification had long exceeded the bounds of common sense. But the reaction to the spread of the Secretary of State's tentacles has been quite the reverse. In 1937 the Gilmour Committee on Scottish administration noted that there was an increasing tendency to appeal to him on all matters that have a Scottish aspect, even if on a strict view they are outside the province of his duties as statutorily defined (Cmd. 5563). Or, as Milne put it, 'the Secretary of State is popularly regarded as the Minister responsible for anything that happens in Scotland'.[16] In effect he is widely seen as 'Scotland's Minister'.

Some Ministers have played this rôle to the full. Tom Johnston, as we will see, interpreted it as enabling him to deliver a series of swingeing blows round Whitehall. Others have taken a narrower view, but no one has sought to circumscribe his right to intervene. The Royal Commission on Scottish Affairs reported in 1954 that his general responsibility, probably implicit from the outset, had been emphasised by the great extension of government activity since 1885. They found that although he was not personally accountable for the work of Great Britain Ministers (e.g. trade and employment) he was still vitally interested in the application of their policies to Scotland. The Royal Commission went on to record the evidence of the Scottish Council (Development and Industry) that

> that interest, and the effective action that successive Secretaries of State have repeatedly taken to safeguard and promote legitimate Scottish claims, have, to the direct knowledge of the Scottish Council, proved time and again to be of the utmost benefit to Scotland (Cmd 9212).

This is heady stuff, but if the Secretary of State has great power and influence he is also perpetually vulnerable. He may point with justifiable pride to progress with the housing programme, or to improvements in the health service, but there will be critics waiting to allege that he has not asserted Scotland's claims boldly enough when it comes to pit closures. In Whitehall the Home Office is regarded as the department where crises requiring the Minister's personal attention overlap. The Secretary of State's duties are infinitely more diverse. Can they be effectively and acceptably discharged by one man? The Royal Commission thought that they could, and recommended against dividing his functions between him and another Scottish Minister, a solution advocated at the time.

The verdict must depend on the assessment of good government. There is also a question whether any Secretary of State, however capable and well-intentioned, has done enough to still the apprehension voiced at the time of the Union. The fears in the anonymous ballad were not confined to the liturgy.

> From a new transubstantion
> Of the old Scots into ane English nation
> And from all the foes to Reformation
> Deliver us, Lord.[17]

Notes

1 A. V. Dicey and R. S. Rait, *Thoughts on the Union between England and Scotland*. London, 1920.
2 *Letters of Daniel Defoe*, ed. Healey. Oxford, 1955.
3 *Memoirs of Walpole*, vol. ii, Coxe. London, 1798.
4 *Parliamentary History*, xxxiii, 730 (1797), cited by J. Steven Watson in *The Reign of George III 1760–1815*. Oxford, 1960.
5 Watson.
6 Lord Cockburn, *Memorials of His Time*. Edinburgh, 1856.
7 *Hansard*, 15th June, 1858. Vol. cl, col. 2118.
8 W. C. Smith, *The Secretary for Scotland*. Edinburgh, 1885.
9 *Hansard*, 3rd August, 1883. 3rd series, vol. 282, col. 1490.
10 *Hansard*, 13th June, 1881. 3rd series, vol. 262, col. 319.
11 *Hansard*, 3rd August, 1885. 3rd series, vol. 300, col. 936.
12 *Ibid.*
13 HH I/816, Scottish Record Office.
14 Goodwood MS 871, West Sussex Record Office.
15 *Salisbury Papers*. (14 and 15 cited by Professor H. J. Hanham in the *Juridical Review*, 1965.)
16 Sir David Milne, *The Scottish Office*. London, 1957.
17 'A litanie anent the Union', *Penguin Book of Scottish Verse*. London, 1970.

CHAPTER II

The Bureaucrats

There is in some quarters an obstinate belief that Government Departments are wholly run by civil servants, and that Ministers are but transitory figures, going ever out by the same door that in they went. This is not so. Senior civil servants are infinitely happier working under a strong Minister, knowing that under his direction, and with his influence in the Cabinet and in Parliament, the policies on which they are engaged are more likely to come to fruition. Conversely, the Minister's reputation will eventually depend on the support which his officials give him. Ministerial memoirs are full of instances where political stars have waned following appointments, e.g. as Lord Privy Seal or as Chancellor of the Duchy of Lancaster, which do not have full-scale Departmental backing.

The growth of the Secretary of State's responsibilities has already been outlined. This chapter examines the parallel development of the machinery of the Scottish Office. It will be convenient to trace the path of the various Scottish Departments as they were set up, merged, or superseded, and then look at the nature and disposition of the civil servants and their relationship with Ministers.

The first Scottish Secretary did not assume only the functions itemised in the Schedule to the 1885 Act, together with a small nucleus of staff at Dover House. He also became answerable to Parliament for the independent Boards then existing in Scotland, and in time for those which were created in the following decades—although they retained their own legal identity. The cardinal dates in this process are 1928, when the Boards of Health and Agriculture and the Scottish Prison Commissioners were abolished and their work assigned to statutory Departments working under the Secretary of State's aegis, and 1939 when following the Gilmour Report the functions of all the main Scottish Departments were vested directly in him under the Re-organisation of Offices (Scotland) Act. The Departments then ceased to have a separate status of their own. But first the road to 1928.

In passing, the most curious of the old organisations was the Board of Manufactures. Set up in 1726 under two Acts promoted by the vigilant Lord Advocate Duncan Forbes, its remit was 'the improvement and encouragement of fishery and manufactures in that part of Great Britain called Scotland'. It was financed in part by a vestigial fund provided under the Treaty of Union to help the coarse-wool industry. Taking a liberal view of its duties, the Board applied subventions, imported weavers from Picardy, and also diversified into such unexpected activities as starting the Forth and Clyde canal in 1768. Latterly it concentrated on fostering industrial design and the fine arts. In 1906 the Board was replaced by the Trustees for the National Galleries—on the face of it an improbable sequence.

The other Boards pursued a more predictable course. Expansions or mergers were explained by the need to take account of public opinion in Scotland, or on the grounds of administrative efficiency. Sometimes the first apparent reason masked the second, and vice versa. The pre-1928 history will not detain us long.

The Fishery Board, originally part of the Board of Manufactures, was hived off in 1808 under the Herring Fishery (Scotland) Act; for some time its jurisdiction extended to England and the Isle of Man: and its powers were transferred to a new Board by the Fishery Board Act, 1882. This Board, which continued to act until 1939, was notably independent, and the Gilmour Committee observed with disapproval that it was in dispute with the Secretary of State over one of its by-laws which he refused to confirm.

The Board of Supervision for the Relief of the Poor in Scotland, which was set up in 1845, acquired duties in relation to public health under Acts of 1863 and 1867. It was the forerunner of the Scottish Board of Health (1919) which absorbed no less than three similar bodies of shorter duration—the Local Government Board for Scotland (1894), the Scottish Insurance Commissioners (1911), and the Highlands and Islands (Medical Services) Board (1913). The 1919 Board, which was noteworthy for the early appearance of a woman as a prescribed member, was replaced in 1928 by the Department of Health for Scotland.

The Board of Agriculture for Scotland was appointed under the Small Landholders Act, 1911, taking over the powers of the earlier Crofters Commission (1886) and the Congested Districts Board (1897), as well as most of the functions in Scotland previously exercised by the Great Britain Board of Agriculture. Like the other principal Scottish Boards it became a statutory Department in 1928. The Prisons Board, dating from 1840 (the Prison Commission from 1877) also became a statutory Department in 1928. (We may record that the versatile Dr Hill Burton at one time doubled as the Board's stipendiary manager and as Historiographer Royal.)

The pattern for Education was different and much of the parliamentary debate in 1885 centred on this topic. The sequence of non-events is mildly bizarre. From 1839 the Privy Council had exercised jurisdiction over education throughout Great Britain through a Committee of Council: but in 1872 the Education (Scotland) Act formed the 'Scotch Education Department' which was defined as 'the Lords of any Committee of the Privy Council appointed by Her Majesty on Education in Scotland', but was in effect a Government Department working under the Vice-President of this Committee. In 1885 the newly created Secretary for Scotland became Vice-President. There was no change (apart from amending 'Scotch' to 'Scottish' in 1918) until the Gilmour reforms in 1939, although the Committee did not meet after 1913.

It is tempting to regard the Boards that were set up in the last century and the beginning of this as an experiment in devolution. Certainly they carried out much government business in Scotland, and (except for the Education Department which lived in Dover House) they were located there. But their origin was not due to any devolutionary theory. There seem to have been two reasons for their proliferation. First, there were the practical difficulties in administering a country four hundred miles from Parliament. Second, the view prevailed that the Boards offered the best way of obtaining the expert knowledge that was needed for largely technical work. They were not like modern civil service departments. For example, the Fishery Board comprised a chairman, four representatives of sea-fishing interests, a sheriff and a scientist, and appointed its own staff. The Boards had their critics, and by 1914 Members of Parliament were becoming restive at the Secretary of State's lack of control over their operations. The Royal Commission on the Civil Service condemned the board system and proposed that the Boards should be replaced by the form of organisation that already existed in the Scottish Office—civil servants reporting direct to Ministers. Their case was that with the Boards it was difficult to pin down responsibility for official action and advice; that there were anomalies in the method of selecting Board members: and that the Boards and their staff, who owed their positions to patronage, often had to learn their duties in post. The Royal

Commission thought that the 'system affords no room for that type of selected and trained permanent official represented by the administrative class' (Cmd. 7338). This view was endorsed by the Haldane Committee on the Machinery of Government in 1918 (Cmd. 9320), but Parliament showed no great zeal for reform, and the Scottish Board of Health formed in 1919 followed the old model.

The illogical nature of the changes eventually adopted was equalled only by the delay in putting them into effect. A Bill to enact the Royal Commission's proposals failed in 1923, as did others in 1924 and 1927, and it was fourteen years after the original recommendations before the effective Bill was introduced in 1928. Under the Reorganisation of Offices (Scotland) Act, 1928 the new Departments of Health and Agriculture and the Prisons Department were to act 'under the control and direction' of the Secretary of State but were to retain their own statutory existence. The dangers of friction and confusion were at once evident.

So the Gilmour Committee found when they started their examination in 1937. Their thesis was that the fundamental objection to the Board system, as it survived in the statutory Departments, lay in the division of powers, the attempt to combine Ministerial responsibility with an assurance of some measure of independence for the Departments. It was, however, an overriding principle that some Minister must be responsible to Parliament for every action of government. The seeming independence of the Departments was therefore illusory, and there were difficulties in practice. If the Departments had a semblance of freedom of action the Minister could be embarrassed in defending them in the House. A Department established by statute was necessarily regarded as a separate entity. If officials acted and spoke in the name of the Board or Department this induced a nebulous belief that they were distinct and that it was possible to appeal to the Minister against their activities. The set-up also led to duplication and delay since the Departments and the Scottish Office (on behalf of the Secretary of State) often had to look at the same questions because of the Minister's ultimate responsibility.

The Gilmour Committee recommended that the statutory Departments should be abolished and their functions vested in the Secretary of State. As regards Education, they proposed that the link with the Privy Council should be ended and the Department's powers likewise transferred to him. For the future there should be four Departments of equal status—Health, Agriculture, Education, and Home (to include

Fisheries and Prisons)—deriving their responsibility from, and directly answerable to, the Secretary of State. In proposing four Departments, each under a Secretary who would be Accounting Officer for his unit and have direct access to the Minister, Gilmour rejected the idea that there should be a single Scottish Department on the somewhat timid ground that the separate designations were familiar to the public and that one office would be an 'unwieldy organism'.

They also proposed that there should be a Permanent Under-Secretary of State, senior to the Secretaries of the Departments, who would be free of departmental commitment. Their reasoning was that the work of the various Departments impinged on each other at many points and the Minister was entitled to have an adviser to whom he could turn when the views of the Departments differed. Otherwise he would tend to turn to one individual Secretary who would begin to dominate the office. (In the event, this sometimes happened.) Moreover —and here we come back to 'Scotland's Minister'—the well-defined functions of the Secretary of State were surrounded by 'a penumbra of other duties which may not require Departmental action and may well lie outside the recognised province of any of the four major departments'. In these circumstances the Minister could not expect all the advice he required from his four Secretaries. 'Penumbral' was to become a catchword at St Andrew's House.

The Reorganisation of Offices (Scotland) Act, 1939, enacted the Gilmour proposals and the staff of the new Departments moved into the recently completed building on the Calton Hill—though even then there was not room for them all. Only the Minister's secretariat and a small liaison detachment remained at Whitehall. The break was both symbolic and practical. (I have omitted from this summary various interim developments, e.g. the move of a part of the staff from Dover House to Edinburgh in the thirties and the recruitment in the same period of an administrative cadre in some of the Departments.) Scotland now had a full-scale Department based on Edinburgh and employing members of the same administrative class as in Whitehall. Many of the old habits persisted; the Departments kept their irritatingly individual office procedure; and the long-seated Treasury scepticism about Scottish aspirations was now directed towards the larger unit; but there is no disguising the importance of the 1939 Act.

Why have we followed the path to 1939 in such detail? A number of reasons suggest themselves. The tortuous history explains the federal structure of the Scottish Office, unique in major departments. Next, most senior civil servants in St Andrew's House were for long aware of the actual terms of the Gilmour Report and took to heart the strictures on purporting to act on behalf of the Department instead of on the Minister's account. Outside interests have not succeeded—though they often try—to drive a wedge between Scottish Office policy and that of the Minister.

There is a more significant point. When the Bill was before Parliament Tom Johnston, who had been a member of the Gilmour Committee, though that it did not go far enough. 'Things cannot go on as they are', he added.[1] The odd thing, as Professor Hanham detected in a penetrating essay, is that this is exactly what has happened.[2] The 1939 Act provided a flexible structure, enabling the Secretary of State by instrument to change Departments or reassign duties between them. There have been changes. New functions have been added; fisheries are now administered by the Department of Agriculture and Fisheries; the Home Department also lost child care to the Education Department; both the Health and Home Departments have been recast and renamed as the Development, and Home and Health, Departments respectively; a Department of Economic Planning has been added; and so on. But the basic pattern remains the one introduced in 1939. An excellent summary of the chronology of the Scottish Office, given in J. G. Kellas's *The Scottish Political System*, is reproduced as Appendix II.

One further word on structure, which affects both Ministerial responsibility and machinery. Since 1939 there have been transfers of functions to and from the Scottish Office. The Secretary of State has, for instance, been made responsible for the national health service, town and country planning, and electricity. He has also lost functions, e.g. national insurance. But the pieces do not fit neatly into either a Scottish Office or a Great Britain jigsaw. In 1968 the Department of Health and Social Security was formed to integrate health and social security administration in England. In Scotland there was no such unification: the health service remains under the Scottish Office, while D.H.H.S. administers cash benefits throughout Great Britain. The Scottish Education Department is in charge of schools and higher education—except for the Universities which come under the Department of Education and Science, although the Secretary of State has duties in connection with the four ancient universities. The Scottish Office is the authority for roads and bridges, but not for ports and only for fishery harbours. Airports come under the Department of

Trade. In energy the position is even more confused. Coal and gas come under the Department of Energy, but the Secretary of State is the Minister for electricity in Scotland. The Department of Energy is responsible for matters affecting North Sea oil, but the Scottish Office is inextricably involved in planning, infrastructure, etc., and under the Conservative government in 1973 Lord Polwarth was appointed as Minister of State with special responsibility for oil.

One would be justified in inferring a determination to make confusion worse confounded. The distribution is neither logical nor, it may be supposed, final. No crystal ball will show what will be the shape of things to come. There may be a tendency towards assimilation by Great Britain Departments to remove the most palpable anomalies. On the other hand, nationalism and the need to recognise Scottish peculiarities may lead to further transfers to a Scottish administration. But it can be argued that all the government's domestic business has a Scottish aspect, and if a G.B. Department can look after one function it can also administer the rest. Given the separate Scottish legal system, the main bulwark against assimilation, Scottish Ministers have a vested interest in preserving their jurisdiction, and even extending it where a case can be made. The same is true of their advisers in the Scottish Office (the collective term for the main Departments responsible to the Secretary of State), and it is to them that we now turn.

There are approximately 64,000 civil servants (43,000 non-industrial and 21,000 industrial) employed in Scotland. The figures used are as supplied by the Civil Service Department for the early seventies, rounded up for convenience. Later fluctuations do not alter the argument. Of these the Scottish Office employed 9300 (8300 non-industrial and 1000 industrial). The Scottish Office civil servants accordingly amount to less than one sixth of the bureaucracy in Scotland. We are not directly concerned in this study with the 54,700 who are engaged in the outstations of Great Britain Departments. This is not said in any derogatory sense, but they are for the most part concerned with the execution rather than the shaping of policy. They take their instructions from headquarters in Whitehall, but their senior officers also maintain close contact with the Scottish Office, particularly in the many matters which involve local authorities.

In 1885 the Secretary for Scotland had a staff of no more than a dozen: the Scottish Boards employed about 200: and the Scotch Education Department had 34 officers in London. Since then the present figure of 9300 has been reached in a steady progression—2400 in 1937; 5500 in 1953; and 8300 in 1970. This reflects the accretion of functions. It is the direct result of decisions taken by successive governments and approved by Parliament. It emphatically does not arise from the ambitions of the bureaucracy to acquire more subordinate staff to inflate their own importance. There is a proper sense of misgiving at the overall number of those who are now employed in Departments, but the issue has been succinctly put by a serving officer, Miss Anne Mueller, Deputy Secretary in the Department of Industry. 'If you want to do something about the size of the civil service you must stop shoving extra jobs on to it'.[3]

Within the Scottish Office there were in 1970 about 160 members of the administrative class, and the number is now slightly higher. (The administrative class was formally abolished in 1971 but the term is still apt for our purposes.) They comprise six grades. The Assistant Principals—now administration trainees—are cadets, just starting their careers. They will be given a variety of dogsbody jobs to learn how the machine works. In my time I was ordered to write notes on clauses in the Acquisition of Land (Authorisation Procedure) (Scotland) Bill before I knew what a clause was, but there is now a more rational system of training. The Assistant Principal will soon be brought into direct contact with Ministers, serving for a spell as Private Secretary to one of the Parliamentary Secretaries of State. He will then be promoted to Principal. This is the hardest worked grade in the service. The Principal is responsible for gathering much of the information on which policy is based and eventually for much of its execution. Next, the Assistant Secretary, in charge of a division with three or four Principals, will see that the material is beginning to take shape for submission to Ministers. The draft answer to a Parliamentary Question, or the first shot at a White Paper, will come from his desk. Proceeding up the hierarchy—and there is legitimate criticism that the hierarchic system is too rigid—the Under-Secretary imparts his own wisdom and will be in frequent touch with Junior Ministers. Next the Secretary of the Department (ranking with a Deputy Secretary in Whitehall) who is responsible for all the work of his office. He is directly answerable to two masters, the Secretary of State and, since he is the Accounting Officer, the Public Accounts Committee who may call on him to justify how the public funds under his control have been expended. Above the Secretaries sits the Permanent Under-Secretary of State, of which more later.

What kind of men, and women, are these administrators? First, they are mainly Scots. About four-fifths of them were born in Scotland. They are not, however, assigned to the Scottish Office on racial grounds. They are recruited as part of the Home Civil Service and successful entrants are asked by the Civil Service Department to state their preferences, which are not published. In practice most Scots who opted for the Scottish Office have found their way there. They were, for the most part, educated in Scotland, both at school and university. In 1968 only 20 per cent were 'Oxbridge' graduates: 28 per cent were non-graduates; and the remainder came from other, mainly Scottish, universities. It will be apparent that, with a predominantly Scottish background, Scottish Office civil servants find it congenial to spend their official careers in attempting to realise Scottish aspirations so far as the dictates of government allow. (Those who come from South Britain are allowed to forget the accident of their birth and tend to be even more zealous in the Scottish cause.) There is, however, the inherent danger that the Assistant Principal who goes straight to St Andrew's House after school and university in Scotland, probably in Edinburgh, without any leavening of experience elsewhere, will be infected with parochialism.

This danger is aggravated by the infrequency of interchange between Whitehall and Scottish Departments. From 1946 to 1970 there were 25 transfers from Edinburgh to Whitehall, 10 of them to very senior posts. In the same period movements in the opposite direction numbered 23, of which 10 were Assistant Secretary or above. But the Scottish civil servant will almost certainly serve in more than one of the St Andrew's House Departments, and on transfer he will take his expertise of the Scottish scene with him. He builds up a cumulative experience and in this respect has the edge over his Whitehall counterpart whose time in the Ministry of Defence will not be particularly relevant to the work of, say, the Customs and Excise. But in skirmishes with English Departments he may be at a disadvantage in that his knowledge is less specialised.

The Scottish administrator spends much of his time in passage between Edinburgh and London, to consult Ministers who have to be there while Parliament is sitting, or to attend the House if he is concerned with a Bill, or to engage in discussion in Whitehall. The teleprinter, telex, mufax, etc., ease the burden, but stamina is still tested. One result of this bifurcated existence is that, since most of the relevant files are kept in Scotland, submissions to Ministers have to be fully explanatory and self-contained. New Ministers usually arrive with the laudable ambition of insisting that matters for their decision should be summarised on a single sheet—sometimes quarto, double-spaced. A worthy thought, but it causes resort to lengthy appendices setting out the background. This is not as odd as might appear. The Minister has all the information at his disposal together with the point, or points, on which he has to take a view clearly identified. The civil servant has to think the whole thing out from beginning to end and ensure that his advice proceeds on demonstrable, logical grounds. This is not confined to Ministerial submissions. The Treasury say that the effect of distance from Whitehall is noticeable in their correspondence with the Scottish Office. They add somewhat wryly that letters from St Andrew's House are more precise, more didactic, and sometimes more rhetorical, than from elsewhere.

Ministers on taking up office normally regard their officials with healthy suspicion. On a change of government, incoming Con-servatives are convinced that they have landed in a bed of *New Statesman* addicts, left-wing sociologists, theoretical planners, or worse. New Labour Ministers have no doubt that they are surrounded by classicists and reactionary élitists. The bureaucrats in turn remember how recently the Minister, when in Opposition, denounced their activities. It takes a few months for these mutual suspicions to be dissolved, but the partnership becomes increasingly harmonious as time goes on.

Civil servants have no politics, but they are the most political of animals. They are relentlessly on the side of the Government. Ministers soon realise this, but they are always surprised to find that when the Government changes civil servants regard it as stimulating to look at the same problems from a different point of view. This does not, however, impair the impartiality or the objective nature of their advice. Criticisms that the bureaucracy has been obstructive, or occlusive, or has withheld vital information do not, it may be observed, come from Ministers. They have their origin in the ill-informed speculation of political journalists. Far from suppressing information, the reverse is likely to be true. Ministers may complain that they have been given too much detail, and the *reductio ad absurdum* is sometimes a necessary device to expose to the full the possible consequences of a particular action.

There is a fashionable demand for more 'open' government. It is, for example, suggested that civil servants should be called upon to explain in public the reasons for their activities. Curiosity about the working of the machine is perfectly understandable, but civil servants are the creatures of the government of the day. When a Minister has listened to what his advisers have to say and decided what he wants to do, it is his decision. If the civil service were then to embark on a programme of public justification, what would be left for the Minister to do? Ministers would soon resent bureaucrats usurping their position —especially when it came to announcing popular measures. The demand for more openness ignores the inquisitions already undertaken by the Public Accounts and Select Committees, whose proceedings are published.

An alternative, and even more damaging, proposal is that the advice that Departments tender to their Ministers should be patent to all. This would lead not to more open government, but to cynical, inefficient administration. If a Permanent Secretary knows that the minute which he submits to his Minister is to be open to the scrutiny of all and sundry, he will write it with this very much in mind. That will be the end of the frank, uninhibited advice on which the Minister relies. If the public appetite for further disclosures remains unsatisfied, the proper course is through a more vigorous use of Parliamentary Select Committees.

The relationship between the Secretary of State and his Permanent Under-Secretary of State is crucial—arising from the penumbral duties which accrue to Scotland's Minister, and the interlocking work of the Scottish Departments, where the P.U.S.'s job is surveillance but not interference. For long the P.U.S. was unique among Permanent Secretaries in the sense that he was relieved of direct responsibility for the day-to-day operation of the Scottish Office and was not the Accounting Officer. More recently this lofty isolation has been somewhat eroded. The Regional Development Division, created in 1964, reported directly to the P.U.S., and he later became the Accounting Officer for the Central Services organisation (mainly establishment matters) but the underlying theory remains. He is, in short, the Secretary of State's personal adviser, and, as a rule, he speaks with a long and intimate knowledge of Scottish problems. Only two of those who have held the office since 1939 have not had the benefit of previous experience in a Scottish Department.

Sir Edward (Lord) Bridges, while Permanent Secretary at the Treasury, once delivered a memorable lecture on the duties of the Higher civil service. Essentially, he said, the administrator must set out all the factors, political, financial, legal, social, etc., involved in a Ministerial decision. He should then be prepared—and this is the nub—to point out that though there are ten aspects to be considered, number seven is at the given time the one that matters and the one to which, in his view, the Minister should particularly address his mind. Adherence to these principles in submitting advice would probably have prevented the Crichel Down fiasco in 1952. On that occasion there was a public outcry concerning the Ministry of Agriculture's disposal of an estate acquired for Defence purposes with an obligation, not fulfilled, to return it to the original owner when the Defence requirement had lapsed. The Minister felt obliged to resign, although he had not been personally involved. Sir David Milne, the most sagacious of P.U.S.s at the Scottish Office, who made a point of rehearsing the Bridges philosophy, was determined that nothing like Crichel Down should happen at the Scottish Office. Nor did it.

The existence of the P.U.S. with a roving rôle as chief of staff is possibly one reason why the Scottish Office has not been much troubled with the current enthusiasm for Ministers to appoint 'political advisers' of their own. This development is worth more than a passing thought. In the past Ministers have seen some advantage in selecting someone from outside the public service, e.g. economists, agriculturists, industrialists, to add a further dimension to the advice they receive. When the great men from outside offer their own expertise this works admirably. Professors of Economics at the Scottish Universities have acted in this capacity since the mid-sixties. The political adviser is a different animal. He has no professional wisdom to add to the Department's store; he does not know how it works; but he claims audience on all aspects of the Minister's responsibility. This arrangement, which proceeds either from the Minister's feeling of insecurity, or more probably from envious pressure from Party organisations, has no logical, or efficiency, justification. Administration is an art learned over the years, and the intrusion of the political adviser is as sensible as the interpolation of a gardener in a symphony orchestra. If the P.U.S., and the Parliamentary Private Secretary who is meant to relay the views of government supporters on the back benches, are doing their job, the political adviser is no more than a cuckoo in the nest.

Lest this should appear to be an attempt to justify what would be, in effect, a closed shop, it is no part of the argument that the Minister should have to depend only on the advice of his administrators. He can also call on the experience of his chief professional and technical officers. The views of the Chief Medical Officer, the Chief Architect, etc., will be integrated in the final submission, and they will often be consulted in person. Although the Institute of Professional Civil Servants complain that professionals should have a higher status, and should be more frequently appointed to be head of their Department—a consideration which greatly exercised the Fulton Committee—it is doubtful whether the chief professional officers often aspire to change their existing rôle, supported as it is by their eminence in their own field. The Bridges template covers each of them, and the task of ensuring that the Minister when he makes up his mind is as omniscient as he can be inevitably falls to the senior administrator.

It remains to consider briefly how the geographical and structural conditions within which the Scottish Office civil servant works affects his performance. On one reckoning he is subject to a divided loyalty. He is part of the Great Britain service, and he is serving in an outpost of the Great Britain Government. But he has to conduct his activities in a way that will be acceptable to (often critical) Scottish opinion, and as a rule he sees his career in Scottish terms. His everyday relations with local authorities and other important bodies are much closer than is possible in the South. He ought to know what is happening on the spot. The combined effect of these circumstances, it is suggested, is that he has a more immediate sense of purpose, of direction, than his opposite number in Whitehall. (It is easier to identify with the Scottish scene than to give one's allegiance to one of several parts of England, all of which must be treated impartially by the Home Office.) Many of the proposals he puts forward, especially on the larger issues, have to be congruent with those in England, but, as we will see, there is also room for experiment. There is no yardstick to measure the efficiency of the Scottish Office against that of other Departments. If the total of government grants per capita were the criterion Scotland does better than the population ratio would support. But that is not the whole story, and it does not take into account the effect which individual Secretaries of State have had. This is now the subject of our enquiry.

NOTES

1 *Hansard*, 13th December, 1938. Vol. 342, col. 1858.
2 Article in *Government and Nationalism in Scotland*, ed. J. N. Wolfe. Edinburgh, 1969.
3 The *Daily Telegraph*, 28th January, 1978.

CHAPTER III

The Unobtrusive Architect

1926 is remembered for the General Strike. A less dramatic event in the summer of that year, but one still relevant to our study, was the swearing in of Sir John Gilmour as the first Secretary of State for Scotland. Gilmour had been Scottish Secretary since 1924, and as the man in post his claims to promotion when the dignity of the office was enhanced were unassailable. But the change in status had not been achieved without much hesitancy and faltering, and, regrettably, Gilmour was not paid the rate for the job.

Last century the Duke of Richmond and Gordon had agreed to be the first Scottish Secretary at a salary of £2000 a year, ranking him well below most Cabinet Ministers and the Lord Advocate, and the discrepancy had not been removed. There were mutterings from time to time that Scotland deserved better treatment, and in 1920 the Wilson Committee on the Remuneration of Ministers proposed that the Scottish Secretary should be 'raised to first class rank'.[1] The Cabinet seem to have accepted the Wilson view and there were promises of legislation. Lord Linlithgow kept raising the matter in the Lords, and in a Memorandum to the Cabinet on 11th March, 1921, Lord Chancellor Birkenhead urged that 'the Secretary for Scotland represents not a Department but a country'.[2] Birkenhead got authority to announce (7th June, 1921) that it was intended to equate the Scottish Secretary with other Secretaries of State 'both in status and emoluments'.[3] But English Members were not persuaded of the merits; the Bill was not forthcoming; and it was not till 17th December, 1925, that Baldwin gave an undertaking to upgrade the office in the following year—with the ungenerous rider that the salary would not be changed.[4] Under the Secretaries of State Act, 1926, the Scottish Secretary received his advancement, but he was still paid less than holders of equivalent office. Another ten years elapsed before all Cabinet Ministers were given the same salary of £5000 under the Ministers of the Crown Act, 1937, and the Secretary of State for Scotland at last reached parity. (I am indebted to Professor H. J. Hanham's painstaking research into this crepuscular problem.[5])

None of this worried Gilmour. The Prime Minister had had already told the Cabinet that the Secretary for Scotland had 'waived the question of any increase in emoluments in the case of the present holder of the office'.[6] In the long roll of Secretaries of State there is no more genial or conscientious Minister. A 'geographical' Minister is always subject to the disadvantage that he is known to be speaking for a special interest, but the Cabinet Minutes do not indicate that Gilmour was ever seriously frustrated when he brought proposals before his colleagues. It is also the case that *Hansard* and contemporary accounts, both in the daily press and in periodicals, disclose very few adverse comments on the manner in which he conducted Scottish affairs.

His early career gave few signs of things to come. Born in 1876, the eldest son of the first Baronet, he served in the South African War, 1900–1, winning the Queen's Medal with four clasps and being twice mentioned in despatches. In the 1914 War he again featured in despatches and was awarded the D.S.O. and Bar. He had contested East Fife unsuccessfully against Asquith in 1906 and sat for East Renfrewshire from 1910 to 1918. Thereafter he was Member for the Pollok Division of Glasgow. He held minor appointments as a Junior Lord of the Treasury in 1921 and as Scottish Unionist Whip in 1921–2 and in 1924. His progress so far had been orthodox but it would have taken an unusually prescient prophet to foresee that he would hold three major offices of state—at the Scottish Office from 1924 to 1929, as Minister of Agriculture in 1931–2, and as Home Secretary from 1932 to 1935. He was also Minister of Shipping at the start of the last war, although this appointment was greeted with modified enthusiasm by those who thought that a younger, more dynamic man should have been selected.

The question is how did he manage to fill all these offices with acceptance. Some factors might have been expected to tell against him. A former Master of Foxhounds, he was the only Scottish Minister who unashamedly entered his hobbies in *Who's Who* as hunting, shooting, fishing, and golf. He was also the only one to reach the eminence of being elected Captain of the Royal and Ancient Golf Club. A month after he became Secretary of State, appropriately dressed in tweed cap and plus fours, he played himself in as Captain and made a fair shot at the awe-inspiring ceremony, accompanied as it is by the firing of the ancient cannon. The press reported that the ranks of the caddies waiting to retrieve his ball in return for the customary sovereign were, on this occasion, swelled by unemployed Fifeshire miners. Critics found the contrast between the unmistakable Establishment figure on the tee and the underprivileged on the fairway somewhat symbolic of the times. One would not have expected that—in a troublous year when the General Strike was followed by an almost equally disastrous miners' stoppage—Gilmour would, with his background and interests, have been able to command the confidence of the country. But this he seems to have done. The evidence is not only the honours that were heaped on him—Freedoms, Honorary Degrees, and election as Lord Rector of Edinburgh University (where he defeated J. M. Keynes)—since some of these are the rewards of office. It is more remarkable that, even in the twenties, the parliamentary debates in which he took part were unusually free from personal bitterness. Invariably cheerful and courteous, Gilmour exemplified the belief that politeness pays, in politics as elsewhere.

On his first appearance as Secretary of State at the Despatch Box (Estimates Debate, 28th July, 1926) both sides of the House were complimentary. The press gallery were sorry for William Adamson having to move, even for form's sake, a reduction of the Secretary of State's salary by £100. 'I do not want his salary reduced', pleaded Adamson. Sir Robert Horne treated the House to an account of his recent discussion with an Indian prince who had thought the attendance in the Chamber had been very thin. 'Ah', he had replied, 'but you should see it when the Scottish Estimates are being discussed.' Now Sir Robert assured the thirty or so Scottish members present that Estimates Day was the time when the House exhibited its highest standard of intelligence. One reporter suggested that this was why there was so little criticism of Gilmour's administration.[7]

This may be going too far. But reviewing his first year of office Gilmour could point to some tangible achievements. There had been a rise in housebuilding, and, as Ministers do, he took credit for the increase in the number of houses built—4000 in 1924 had risen to 8600 in 1925, and 12-13,000 in 1926. The long-standing controversy about the erection of steel houses had been settled. There had been progress with the school medical services and a reduction in the size of classes. He acknowledged he had been helped by the formidable presence of another Scottish Member, the Duchess of Atholl, as Education Under-Secretary in England. Run-of-the-mill stuff, but not the least of the Minister's job is to facilitate the work of his Department and this was what Gilmour was doing. More important, the Scottish Rating Bill had reduced the number of rate-collecting authorities, a unification long considered desirable, but not previously attempted.

Gilmour was much concerned with the structure of the Office. Reorganisation, as we have seen in Chapter II, had long been pending, but nothing had been done. Gilmour, however, made progress. He persuaded the Cabinet that legislation would have to be introduced, and he persevered until the Bill was passed. The internal machinery of Departments is not a subject likely to engender a great deal of enthusiasm in Parliament, and little Ministerial kudos will be derived from it, but this did not deter Gilmour from mastering the details and advocating reform.

His first attempt was not successful. The Reorganisation of Offices (Scotland) Bill, 1927, proposed the replacement of the Scottish Boards by Departments acting under the control and direction of the Secretary of State, and staffed by administrative civil servants. It was only a limited reform, but the House did not like it. William Adamson feared that Government policy was to subordinate Scottish administration to Whitehall to a far greater extent than previously and 'to remove from Scotland practically the last vestige of independent Government and nationhood, and to have its centre in London'.[8]

The Bill did not proceed beyond Second Reading. A year later (28th February, 1928) Gilmour tried again. He emphasised the difficulty facing a Minister who received both minority and majority reports from the Boards. In order to dispel suspicion that it was intended to transfer the Scottish Departments from Edinburgh to Whitehall he had 'specifically inserted in the Bill a clause which declares that the Departments shall remain in Scotland'. Looking ahead, he said he intended, when the demands of economy were overcome, to centralise in Edinburgh under one roof all the Departments concerned with Scottish business.[9]

Tom Johnston in moving the rejection of the Bill was described as 'unusually hesitating'[10] and said petulantly that he could not understand why the Secretary of State persistently brought this Bill forward when there were other more pressing problems. He saw the proposals as an extension of bureaucracy. The Reverend James Barr was more trenchant, quoting Carlyle on the French Prime Minister during the Revolution.

And now nothing but a solid phlegmatic M. de Vergennes sits there in dull matter of fact, like some dull Public Clerk. In him is no remedy, only clerk-like despatch of business according to routine.

Barr likened Gilmour to Vergennes and refused to vote for 'a paltry measure of this kind'. The significance of this rhetoric is that it is one of the few unfavourable personal references to Gilmour.

There were others who criticised the Bill from different points of view. Sidney Webb suggested the abolition of the Boards was likely to 'subordinate in an altogether improper way' professional officers who had a range of knowledge and experience that the ordinary administrative secretariat could not properly have. Another Labour Member said that the whole language of the Bill gave the impression of taking away 'a little individuality so far as Scotland is concerned'. More surprisingly, the highly intelligent and greatly respected Noel Skelton saw no substance in the argument that the Boards were inefficient. He was convinced that this was not the time to take away from Scotland any Department that had any special Scottish features, and he joined the Opposition in voting against the Bill.

In the later stages of the proceedings Gilmour argued that he had even gone to Ireland to find out why they had replaced the Board system there. He added that because of impending retirements there had never been a time when the change should be made with less difficulty or disturbance. To keep the matter in perspective he added that, as Members seemed to have forgotten, the real controlling power remained with the House, whether Government policy was carried out by Boards or Departments.[11] Gilmour got his Bill. The reorganisation thus effected was only a halfway house, as Gilmour recognised when (no longer a Minister) he presided over the Committee whose report led to the next Reorganisation Bill ten years later. In short, Gilmour's personal intervention was highly influential in the development of the Scottish Office.

One commentator who had reservations about Gilmour's ability was the venerable Tom Jones, the doyen of the Cabinet Secretariat. In his *Whitehall Diary* he recalls Baldwin wondering whether Gilmour would be the right man to take over the India Office. 'I said no. He had no imagination and could not rise to the quality of a speech demanded in the House when big issues are at stake.'[12] Jones was a shrewd observer of Ministerial personalities, but this is a misjudgment, as can be seen from Gilmour's handling of his most important measure, the Local Government (Scotland) Bill.

The Bill was heralded by the publication of a White Paper (Cmd. 3135) in June, 1928. The White Paper's thesis was that the local government structure was out of date. There were too many, and too many different kinds, of authority, and the rating burden was unevenly spread. The reform envisaged was a radical one. It was proposed that in future all the major powers of local government should be entrusted to county councils, so far as the landward areas were concerned, and that in the burghs the councils should also exercise the more important functions. The duties entrusted to the small burghs (less than 20,000 population) would be drastically reduced. The four cities would remain all-purpose authorities, but parish and district councils would be abolished. Apart from structure, there were two other main proposals—the derating of agriculture and industrial subjects, and the introduction of an entirely new grant system. We return to local government reform, and in more detail to the relationship between the Scottish Office and local authorities, when we come to the most recent revision in the seventies. Meanwhile it may be noted that Gilmour's Bill as finally enacted set the pattern for the next forty years and was not altered till developments in the economic and planning tasks of local government made changes imperative.

The White Paper was not greeted with universal applause. The *ad hoc* Education Authorities were indignant at their impending extinction, and the parish and district councils found many supporters. But those who were not committed to the *status quo* were more favourable. Whatever might be said against the scheme it had the merit of courage. Reform was long overdue and changes in functions over the years had resulted in a patchwork structure. There were fewer complaints about the derating proposals, for which the authorities would be compensated. A new framework was needed to administer the new grants, and Scottish local government would benefit by substantial additional revenue.

The scheme was the product of years of preparation by the Scottish Departments, but it was Gilmour's achievement to ensure that it was logical and comprehensible, to secure Cabinet agreement, and to present the proposals as an acceptable package. This he did, first by an unusually detailed series of discussions with all those affected, and then —*pace* Mr Jones—by an eloquent speech on Second Reading. The conventions to be observed on introducing a major Bill, the need to expound the general principles and then itemise the provisions of the main clauses, normally restrict the Minister's room for manœuvre, but

Gilmour's delivery when he claimed that the Bill was designed 'to assist industry and agriculture, to relieve necessitous areas, and to simplify and strengthen the organisation of local government' was impressive.[13]

The Opposition's attitude was a classic example of being guided by the principle that their duty was to oppose. Tom Johnston's amendment moving the rejection of the Bill because it would attack the democratic foundations of local government, dissipate effective local interest, hinder necessary developments in the health service, and add to the burdens of tenants and shopkeepers, was a masterpiece of magniloquence, but little more. The same can be said of Mr Macpherson's dismissal of Gilmour as the Herod of the Scots, responsible for the massacre of the innocents in the shape of the smaller authorities. No feasible alternative was offered, and John Buchan congratulated Gilmour both on his speech and on his ingenious and conciliatory handling of the consultations since the White Paper was published.

As the lengthy proceedings in the Commons came to a close Tom Johnston's final criticism was that the Bill had been tabled in the last months of a dying Parliament, and had been 'crushed through this House' with the use of the 'Guillotine', though he admitted that Gilmour had given a 'clear and exhaustive account' of the Government's objectives. If all was not peace from Dan to Beersheba it was evident that abusive epithets were being hurled with more relish than rancour, and even the forthright Labour Member James Brown conceded that the Secretary of State had been 'so amenable to reason'. Gilmour, who had gone out of his way to meet reasonable criticism, then issued a further memorandum (Cmd. 3290) on the Bill as passed by the Commons, summarising the changes he had accepted. The small burghs were to retain more of their original functions, particularly housing; agriculture was more generously derated; and district councils were to remain in the landward areas. It was a workmanlike job. It made heavy demands on the Scottish Departments, and Gilmour confessed it had prevented progress with other legislation. But the Local Government (Scotland) Act, 1929, was not popular in the country, and together with the similar English Act passed at the same time it probably contributed to the Government's defeat at the 1929 General Election.

One more example of Gilmour's parliamentary expertise may be quoted. In July, 1927, Lloyd George surprisingly called for, and spoke in, a Fisheries debate. A visit to Aberdeen had provided him with statistics, and the local party managers may have urged that there was some electoral advantage to be gained from taking up the fishermen's case. The press, at any rate, thought Lloyd George's interest in the East Coast fishermen was likely to evaporate as quickly as it had developed.[14] His main proposal was that there should be more Exchequer credit for re-equipment. He was apparently unaware that only a small part of the fund set aside for this purpose by the last Labour Government had been used. It was true that manpower in the industry had declined. (Sir Archibald Sinclair asserted that the pre-war total of 38,000 men had shrunk to 26,000.) In a notably soothing speech Gilmour said that new methods were needed to reduce employment and pointed to experiments being made in building new craft. But he identified the real problem as the loss of world markets, especially the reduced value of Russian purchases. Lloyd George did not persist in his criticism.

Stirrings of nationalism were apparent towards the end of Gilmour's tenure. One of Labour's main misgivings about the Reorganisation of Offices Bill was that it would make an eventual transition to Home Rule more difficult. Noel Skelton thought that the abolition of the Scottish Boards would help the Nationalist cause. Gilmour was involved in a brush with the Nationalist John MacCormick when speaking from the platform during the 1928 Glasgow Rectorial Election which led to the founding of the National Party. But the contemporary mood is best seen in a peculiar debate on the Office of Works vote when Tom Johnston objected to one of the pictures in St Stephen's Hall depicting, as he put it, the Scottish Union Commissioners, probably with their pay tickets in their pockets, assenting to the 1707 Treaty. A discursive debate on the merits of the Union followed, John Buchan giving a historical review and Sir John Simon remarking acidly that 1707 saw the end of the English as well as the Scottish Parliament. The debate throughout was coy, but good-humoured. No one took it seriously.[15]

The difficulty in assessing Gilmour's time at the Scottish Office, and the clue to the assessment, lies in his unobtrusive character. He was not flamboyant. He proceeded by way of disarming reasonableness. At times it could be soporific. Speaking on the Consolidated Fund Bill in March, 1929, he covered everything from lifeboats to tuberculosis and tourism. Nothing spectacular, but a touch here and there demonstrated that the Office was alert to the demands made on it. His officials respected him and admired the manner in which he defused potentially explosive situations. There are no anti-Gilmour stories retained in the memories of the diminishing number of those who came into contact with him at Dover House. He was a skilled Parliamentarian. He was also, more than most of his successors, an integral figure in the Conservative hierarchy. From this the Scottish Office benefited, though its organisation was to prove susceptible to further change. When he handed over to William Adamson after the 1929 General Election he could be satisfied that he left behind the nucleus of a major Department which Whitehall would have to take seriously.

Notes

1 *Report of the Select Committee on the Remuneration of Ministers*, H.C. 241, 1920.
2 Cab. 24/121, Public Record Office.
3 *Hansard*, Lords, 7th June, 1921. Vol. 45, col. 464.
4 *Hansard*, 17th December, 1925. Vol. 189, col. 1612.
5 The Development of the Scottish Office, article by H. J. Hanham in *Government and Nationalism in Scotland*. Edinburgh, 1969.
6 Cab. 23/5.
7 The *Scotsman*, 29th July, 1926.
8 *Hansard*, 23rd March, 1927. Vol. 204, col. 474.
9 *Hansard*, 28th February, 1928. Vol. 214, col. 265.
10 The *Scotsman*, 29th February, 1928.
11 *Hansard*, 9th July, 1928. Vol. 219, cols. 1982–7.
12 Tom Jones, *Whitehall Diary*. London, 1969.
13 *Hansard*, 3rd December, 1928. Vol. 223, col. 859.
14 The *Scotsman*, 21st July, 1927.
15 The *Scotsman*, 20th July, 1927.

CHAPTER IV

Due Consideration

Pope Leo X, on his elevation to the Holy See, is credited with the splendid temporal remark that since God had been kind enough to give him the Papacy he intended to enjoy it. William Adamson equally intended to enjoy being Secretary of State. He told his Private Secretary that, compared with the Conservatives, the Labour Party were still in the boys' class when it came to exercising Ministerial power. But, he went on, that did not mean that the educative process which they were now starting should be disagreeable. He intended otherwise.

A portrait of Adamson by Tom Curr hangs in Dover House. It is a posthumous work, and not really a great painting, but it is still possible to identify the hard, chiselled lines that often dignify the faces of those who have endured the demanding physical exactions of life in the mines. The artist has also captured the gleam in his eye. For Adamson had a macabre sense of humour. Scottish Office folklore preserves the account of the occasion when Adamson sat down after one of his least effective speeches from the Despatch Box. It was clear from the number of M.P.s on both sides of the House who tried to catch the eye of the Chair that Adamson's case had not gone down well. As speaker after speaker monotonously denounced the Secretary of State's argument, so far as it could be understood, Adamson who was due to reply—with the permission of the House—at the end of the debate, made his way to the Official Box. What, he asked his advisers, was he to say now? The official on duty could only suggest that his Minister should say it all again, this time with more conviction. 'Ay, I see,' replied Adamson, 'and you're getting paid for this?' 'Not sufficiently, Secretary of State.' 'Ay, I see.' Adamson smiled grimly as he returned to the Front Bench.

Adamson's self-confidence was understandable. A miner's son, he had left school at the age of eleven. In one of his last speeches in the House he gave a moving account of his experience as a schoolboy in a mining village. He was one in a single room containing about 100 pupils of all ages from four to eleven, with a single heroic woman in charge. He had long learned the need to reduce the size of classes. When his schooldays were over there was nothing for Adamson but the pit, and for the next twenty-seven years he worked underground. With this notable record, and nineteen subsequent years as Member for West Fife, Adamson was, for his time, the archetypal figure of a Labour Minister. His Party had won the 1929 General Election, doing particularly well in Scotland where they now had 36 seats to the Conservatives' 20 and the Liberals' 13. They were in a stronger position than during the 1923–4 interlude (when Adamson had been Scottish Secretary), and given a chance they hoped to establish themselves as the new party in power. Events did not, however, allow this, and a bare two years later Ramsay MacDonald split the Labour ranks when he formed his National Government.

An inept intervention by Prime Minister MacDonald marked one of Adamson's earliest appearances as Secretary of State. In the last Parliament the Labour Party had vehemently opposed the passing of the Local Government (Scotland) Act, and in one of his election speeches MacDonald had committed himself, if elected, to its repeal. In the Debate on the Address (10th July, 1929) the Government were challenged to take early action to fulfil this promise. MacDonald, partly because he was quoted in person but also from his incurable tendency to interfere in the work of his Ministers, stepped in to make a woolly, rambling speech of self-exculpation. His commitment, he explained, was contingent on the Government having a reasonable period in office. Immediate, wholesale repeal was technically impossible because of the financial consequences for Scottish local authorities. He had, however, come to the view that it might be possible to introduce a short Bill suspending the operation of the sections of the Act that abolished the old education authorities (one of the most controversial parts) until further enquiry could be made. A Bill had been drafted and would be introduced without delay, but if it was to be effective it would have to be passed in the short time remaining before the Summer Recess. MacDonald must have known—certainly everyone else saw at once—that the Conservatives, having just passed the Act, were not likely to co-operate in the speedy banishment of one of its main proposals. The *Scotsman* observed that 'the art of Parliamentary pretence has seldom been carried further'.[1] The discomfited Adamson was left to wind up a thoroughly unsatisfactory debate.

The next day, during the business statement, MacDonald announced that the Second Reading of the Local Government (Amendment) (Scotland) Bill would take place the following Thursday 'if, as I announced yesterday, there is a wish to proceed with it'. Baldwin, with heavy sarcasm, asked if the Prime Minister could tell them 'the exact degree of ardour which would move the Government, and whether the ardour must be epidemic or only sporadic?' MacDonald said, rather pathetically, that he would do his best to find out if the House wanted the Bill.[2] A week later, (17th July) the Cabinet recorded resignedly that in view of 'the state of business in the House of Commons and the attitude adopted in some quarters to the Bill' it should be dropped.[3] On the same afternoon a somewhat crestfallen Prime Minister admitted in the House that he saw no prospect of the Bill passing all its stages in time to be effective and so did not propose to ask Parliament to consider it further.[4] The press comment was that the Bill had been disposed of 'like an unwanted kitten'.[5]

MacDonald's retreat did nothing to improve Adamson's prestige, or authority, in the House, and by the time of the summer adjournment the Lobby's view was that so far the Secretary of State had not been tested beyond his stolidity in refusing to answer supplementary questions. Before Parliament resumed in the autumn Adamson was being upbraided in the press for including too many Labour supporters in the Royal Commission on Licensing in Scotland. The temptation for Ministers to pack Commissions and Committees with Party sympathisers is always present, but on this occasion the charge does not appear to have been well founded. It would have been more apposite to object to the selection as chairman of Lord Mackay whose reputation as one of the primeval dunderheads of Parliament House was already well known.

Adamson was soon to be heavily attacked for his seeming inactivity following the East Anglian fishing disaster, and he got less credit than was his due. On 13th November, 1929, in answer to a Private Notice Question, Adamson had the painful task of reporting that two days earlier a serious disaster had befallen the Scottish fishing fleet off East Anglia. 'A gale of great fury' had swept the area when all the nets were out, and two drifters had sunk with loss of life. Some 200 vessels fishing from Lowestoft, and 400 from Yarmouth, had lost 31,000 nets, and the cost of replacement was meanwhile put at £150,000. Many of the Scottish ships had now no nets and might be compelled to abandon fishing and return home.[6] On 18th November Adamson asked the four Scottish Lord Provosts to launch a National Appeal Fund, but made no offer of a government contribution.

This attracted much unfavourable comment, and on 20th November he made a poor attempt to wind up a Great Britain fisheries debate. Scottish M.P.s were incensed that he allowed both the English Minister of Agriculture and his Under-Secretary to speak before him, allowing himself only a bare minimum of time to reply. Even then he was described as 'panting through his notes, with not a minute to spare for interruption'.[7] Adamson continued to be castigated in the House and the press for not providing government aid to the Relief Fund. There was the awkward precedent of the recent Exchequer contribution to the miners, and Adamson's desperate attempt to distinguish between a subvention to save part of the community from starvation and a proposal to pay for the replacement of the tools of the trade (fishing nets) did not win him many friends. Nor did the conventional argument about the undesirability of setting a pattern, etc. Meanwhile the Lord Provosts' Fund barely topped £20,000, and there was renewed anger when Adamson—questioned again by M.P.s—was reported as shaking his head, laughing, and refusing to answer. The general opinion by now was that Adamson had been ineffective in pleading the fishermen's case with his colleagues.

Ineffective he may have been, but he had tried. He brought the fisherman's plight to the notice of the Cabinet on 20th November, but Ministers, in Adamson's own words 'while feeling the fullest sympathy with the victims of this misfortune, felt unable, as a matter of principle, to make a contribution to the Relief Fund'.[8] Adamson wrote to Snowden, the Chancellor of the Exchequer, on 17th December saying in effect that this would not do. The Scottish fishing fleet had met a disaster of 'unparalleled magnitude' and he urged that £50,000 should be made available at once to be disbursed in interest-free loans for the replacement of gear. Snowden replied the next day in terse terms.

> I very much dislike the idea of surrendering to the clamours of Boothby, Brown, Hamilton, Mackenzie Wood and Duncan Miller— all Opposition members. You immediately put them in a position to boast to their constituents that they have forced an unwilling Government to make concessions which otherwise they would never have done.[9]

After this generous preamble he reluctantly agreed to the £50,000 fund, but insisted that loans from it should bear interest at the rate of 5 per cent. This niggling was too much for Adamson, and a manuscript note in his handwriting records that he sought out the Chancellor in his room and succeeded in getting the interest rate down to 3 per cent.[10] Those who have been engaged in similar negotiations with the Treasury would agree that he had not done badly. But it had taken too long.

One of the things that his officials most admired about Adamson was the resolute way he refused to be hustled at Question Time. When he had grasped the drift of the answers submitted to him he read them out in ringing Doric, and the House soon learned that even the most enticing supplementaries would provoke nothing more than a promise of 'due consideration'—which became something of a watchword. Otherwise, he would not budge. For example, when asked by McElwee about the injurious effects of drinking red biddy, Adamson replied that he was having enquiries made. Jocular supplementaries suggesting that this red movement was strongly entrenched in all parts of the House; that even Members drank this peculiar beverage; and enquiring who was the lady who went by the name of Red Biddy, all produced no reply.[11] A fortnight later Adamson said his enquiries showed that red biddy was a mixture of red wine and methylated spirits, with the surprising addendum that a lot of red wine was made in Leith. Ernest Brown ('Leith is famous for its rejection of inferior red articles'), Lady Astor, and others could not move Adamson further.[12]

There were, however, times when he could not avoid improvising, and this was not often successful. A typical Adamson answer was the one he gave to George Buchanan who asked about a case in the Glasgow Sheriff Court. Buchanan had earlier had interviews with both Adamson and his Parliamentary Secretary, but he had to be content with a singularly unhelpful reply.

> All I can say is that the matter has been engaging my attention for some time past and has been engaging my attention this evening, but I am not in a position to say what will eventuate. I am giving it close attention from all points of view, in the hope, if possible, of remedying the evil of which the hon. Member complains.[13]

The *Hansard* editor allows Private Secretaries considerable licence to correct their masters' utterances before they appear in the Official Report. In Adamson's case this tolerance was sometimes severely stretched.

Adamson's taciturnity got him into trouble in an agricultural debate on 22nd May, 1930. He had nothing new to say and was sternly taken to task by Robert Boothby for assuring the House that he had been 'hatching out an agricultural policy' for the past year, but refusing to say what it was. Boothby concluded that Adamson had been 'sitting unwittingly and in good faith on a china egg, because nothing productive has happened'.[14] This can be discounted as good Boothby rhetoric, but two months later, speaking on the Health and Education estimates, Adamson's survey did no more than cover ground already traversed by the Departmental reports without adding much of interest or value. Officials can, if required, import some specious eloquence into the Minister's brief, but Adamson seemed quite content to recite a catalogue of facts and rely on his Under-Secretary Tom Johnston to undertake the much more difficult job of answering the points made in debate. (Incidentally, Scottish Members were reproved for their poor attendance at both the May and July debates. In May an attempt was made to count out the House, and the debate was adjourned an hour early.)

The odd thing is that Adamson usually got away with it. Sir John Gilmour, for the Opposition, gave him a much easier passage than would be afforded today, often saying that from his own experience as Secretary of State he knew the difficulties and complexities of the office. Only once did Gilmour sharpen his criticism. After Adamson had opened on the, admittedly fairly minor, Small Landholders and Agricultural Holdings (Scotland) Bill, Gilmour confessed he was completely at a loss to understand many of the reasons and arguments with which he had introduced the Bill. Adamson had said that Tom Johnston would answer in detail and invited Members to refrain from intensive criticism until the Committee stage. It was evident that to Gilmour's mind this was not good enough.[15]

A year later, however, the educative process that Adamson had mentioned to his Private Secretary seemed to be producing results. During a fisheries debate Mackenzie Wood congratulated the Secretary of State on his interest in the fishing community. Adamson, he said, had gone out of his way to learn for himself something of the fishermen's life and work, and now knew their difficulties much better than he did two years ago. Similarly, on the ticklish question of agricultural credit, when Adamson announced that four of the Scottish Banks had agreed to find the capital to set up an Agricultural Security Company in Scotland, Gilmour, who had taken part in earlier abortive negotiations, was warm with his praise.

In his two years at Dover House Adamson demonstrated, if nothing else, the capacity to retain office, but it would be unfair, and certainly fruitless, to look for any constructive philosophy in his approach. It was for him a day-to-day business. Reviewing Adamson's time, the press took the view that while some useful Scottish Bills had been passed, dealing with such matters as urban and rural housing and land drainage, the real progress had been made administratively. There had been an increase in land settlement. An interesting school scheme had given 10,000 children a daily ration of Grade 'A' (T.T.) milk. The results of what was claimed to be the biggest dietetic experiment attempted provided evidence of the value of milk from tubercle-free herds. More housing plans were approved. Adamson took credit for restoring the Conservative cuts in housing subsidies, but his construction figures depended more on expectation than on performance. Grants for piers and harbours had been increased. Fishery loans had been remitted, and so on.

This record of modest achievement poses the question how the Scottish Departments were able to continue their duties with apparent acceptance despite the lack of any clear guidance from the Secretary of State. It seems fairly clear that they did so. Unusually in a parliamentary debate, Mr Scott commenting on Adamson's review of Departmental activity said that his report would not have been so favourable 'if it were not for the services, devoted and energetic, of all those in the Department of Health who are under his supervision'. Adamson also appeared satisfied with the service he got. Asked by the same Mr Scott if he would transfer the staff of the Scottish Education Department from London to Edinburgh, Adamson replied tartly that the existing arrangements were most effective.[16] How did these arrangements work so surprisingly well? The answer is perhaps that a well-trained crew can keep the ship on course, even without an authoritative skipper, provided the First Mate is capable of taking charge and issuing instructions. Tom Johnston was certainly an effective First Mate, and we record later how much he enjoyed the scope that Adamson gave him.

The verdict on Adamson's administration must be that more than any other Secretary of State he relied on his Under-Secretary to direct the office for him. Officials took their cue accordingly, and while loyally supporting the Secretary of State, looked to Johnston to see how the wind was blowing. How Adamson would have fared eventually when Johnston, promoted to be Lord Privy Seal, was succeeded by Joseph Westwood, remains a matter of conjecture. There

is an inevitable comparison between Adamson and Westwood as
Secretary of State. They had similar backgrounds, but Adamson had
a stronger, more engaging, character, and counting his earlier stint as
Scottish Secretary he survived two spells of office. Westwood, as we
will see, had a much more precarious tenure.

NOTES

1 The *Scotsman*, 11th July, 1929.
2 *Hansard*, 11th July, 1929. Vol. 231, col. 1080.
3 Cab. 23/61, Public Record Office.
4 *Hansard*, 18th July, 1929. Vol. 232, col. 630.
5 The *Scotsman*, 19th July, 1929.
6 *Hansard*, 13th July, 1929. Vol. 231, col. 2043.
7 The *Scotsman*, 21st November, 1929.
8 Scottish Office Papers AF 56/903 in the Scottish Record Office.
9 *Ibid.*
10 *Ibid.*
11 *Hansard*, 11th February, 1930. Vol. 235, col. 196.
12 *Hansard*, 25th February, 1930. Vol. 235, col. 2043.
13 *Hansard*, 20th December, 1929. Vol. 233, col. 1779.
14 *Hansard*, 22nd May, 1930. Vol. 239, col. 644.
15 *Hansard*, 10th November, 1930. Vol. 244, col. 1390.
16 *Hansard*, 20th April, 1931. Vol. 251, col. 608.

CHAPTER V

Style

Sir Archibald Sinclair's political career covered much more than his time at the Scottish Office. He was a very individual leader of his Party and a distinguished Air Minister. To get the measure of the man we have to look at the whole picture.

Born in 1890, he succeeded his grandfather as the fourth baronet in 1912. He was commissioned in the Life Guards, but unlike most of his generation he showed a keen interest in aeronautics, and before the 1914 War he had his own experimental aircraft. The war brought him for the first time into close contact with Churchill. Though both were cavalry officers by origin, they found themselves on dismounted service in the same battalion of the Royal Scots Fusiliers, Sinclair as second-in-command, and the empathy that developed between them coloured the rest of Sinclair's career. After the war he was Churchill's personal military secretary at the War Office, and followed him to the Colonial Office as private secretary in 1922—an exhilarating start for an aspiring politician.

He was returned as Member of Parliament for Caithness and Sutherland in 1922, survived the ensuing spate of elections, and held the seat till 1945. Most M.P.s are, to my knowledge, zealous in looking after the interests of their constituents, investigating complaints, and taking up their grievances with the relevant Minister. (This is the M.P.'s lifeline, and sometimes, if he is not prominent in debate, his main occupation.) It is, however, clear from Sinclair's papers, now appropriately lodged in the archives of Churchill College, Cambridge, that there were no local matters in which he did not concern himself, and it seemed that he knew all his constituents in the vast expanse of the two counties. Few M.P.s can have been so meticulous. Moreover, Ministers and their advisers soon identify those Members who will not be satisfied with a routine answer and who will press the correspondence with the utmost tenacity. Sinclair belonged to that category.

On reaching Westminster Sinclair was attracted to the Lloyd George side of the Liberal Party, already showing signs of internal strain. His maiden speech was, almost inevitably, on air matters and contained a prescient warning on Britain's vulnerability to air attack. By 1930 he was Chief Liberal Whip, an appointment which called for all his tact and self-restraint as the split in the Liberal ranks became more marked with the vicissitudes of Lloyd George and the intrigues of Sir John Simon. (A distinctly uncomfortable colleague at the best of times, Simon earned the cruel epitaph that no one took more people by the arm and called them by the wrong Christian name.) In 1931 the Liberal leaders joined the National Government and Sinclair went to the Scottish Office. The Free Trade Ministers were, however, unhappy at the Government's tariff policy, and after a summer of heart-searching discussions—many of them at Sinclair's home in Caithness—they defiantly resigned in September, 1932.

We will return to Sinclair's activities as Secretary of State, but his subsequent career also casts light on his political flair. When Sir Herbert Samuel lost his seat at the 1935 election Sinclair succeeded him as leader of the Liberal Party. The Liberals' influence in Parliament was out of all proportion to their numbers in the House, and Sinclair greatly enhanced his own standing, particularly with his trenchant attitude to the foreign policy followed by the Baldwin and Chamberlain administrations. He had a formidable ally in Churchill, but the mustering of Liberal criticism, at times more effective than that of the official Opposition, was Sinclair's achievement. Lord Cecil's view was that 'Sir Archibald Sinclair was the only Liberal leader of recent times who has infused vigour and reality into his party'.[1]

Sinclair refused office under Chamberlain, but he joined the Government as soon as Churchill went to Downing Street, becoming Secretary of State for Air. He held this post throughout the war. As Air Minister he was not automatically a member of the War Cabinet, but many of his friends thought that his best work was done in these years, fighting behind the scenes for the requirements of his service. He was an ardent supporter of the bomber offensive, but though he was generous in his tributes to senior Air Officers and others, he claimed no personal credit for the logistic and administrative support which he organised. In this he did himself less than justice. He made few speeches in the House, but the mercurial Beaverbrook described him as the best Air Minister 'in our experience'. It is significant that in the welter of post-war memoirs, diaries, and revelations, which frequently make it astonishing that we were ever able to celebrate VE Day, Sinclair's is one of the few reputations that has not suffered.

At the 1945 General Election he lost by a handful of votes to a rogue Independent candidate (Gandar Dower), and after another narrow defeat at the next election he did not stand again. In 1952 he was elevated to the Lords as Viscount Thurso, but ill-health prevented him from leading his Party in the Upper House, as had been intended. He recovered sufficiently to attend the House for several years till a further deterioration took him out of public life.

As Secretary of State for Scotland Sinclair was subject to the constraint of being a member of an uneasy coalition, and in any event his time at Dover House—August, 1931, to September, 1932—was not ripe for the exploitation of major Scottish issues. While Westminster, and the country, were bemused by the tottering pound, massive unemployment, the growth of the German menace, and the war in the Far East, it was not to be expected that Scottish affairs would often reach the headlines. For example, Scottish Members could find nothing more exciting to discuss in the House than the Treasury's traditional parsimony towards the Scottish Record Office. Depressing statistics were quoted to prove that Register House was littered with piles of uncatalogued, unindexed papers, and following a critical speech by John Buchan (later Lord Tweedsmuir) Sinclair was at his most emollient.[2]

In March, 1932, Sinclair moved the second reading of the Hire Purchase (Scotland) Bill, designed to prevent the use of imprisonment to enforce hire-purchase contracts, a desirable but scarcely dramatic piece of legislation.[3] A sense of urgency appears to be lacking in these debates, and Sinclair had no difficulty in explaining that he had not yet come to a decision about the report on the reorganisation of the Court of Session which had been gathering dust in the Scottish Office registry for the last five years.

The temper of the times among Scottish M.P.s is most clearly evident in the proceedings on the Town and Country Planning Bill, 1932, a Great Britain measure to be applied to Scotland by a 'Scottish application clause'. This is a useful, and at times essential, device, but Scottish lawyers have never liked it, and when the clause is tortuous and complicated the result is an ill-fitting puzzle. On this occasion Sinclair blandly admitted that the Clause, and the eight pages of the Schedule, which applied the Bill to Scotland would indeed be troublesome for the wretches who had to construe it. But under Clause 52, he went on, the Clerk of the Parliaments was directed to certify a copy of the Act as it applied to Scotland as if it were a separate Act. When it was so certified it could be cited as the Town and Country Planning (Scotland) Act, 1932. The House was thus getting two Acts for the price of a single debate. Sinclair concluded that

> this will clearly make matters much easier for the Scottish local authorities and I think will no doubt constitute a useful precedent for other legislation.[4]

Honourable Members nodded approvingly, but despite the skill with which Sinclair advocated the use of the fretsaw, today's Scottish Law Commission would take a very different view.

It must not, however, be supposed that the House's indulgent attitude reflected an absence of activity by the staff of the Scottish Office. The working of an alert mind was immediately apparent in Sinclair's discussions with officials, and the initiative was often his. In the thirties the Scottish Departments—apart from the Education Department and the small headquarters of the Scottish Office proper— were wholly located in Edinburgh, and the papers show the Secretary of State communicating quaintly with his advisers by letter, or even by telegram. In September, 1932, at a time when his own political future was already in the balance, he was urging Jeffrey in the Department of Health to consider whether there were any means open to him to persuade local authorities to help people who wanted to buy houses with a mortgage from a building society—a problem which has continued to trouble many of his successors.

On a more light-hearted note, he was horrified to find that the draft Bill dealing with salmon fishing proposed to make it a criminal offence to foul-hook a salmon unless the fish was returned to the water. This, Sinclair saw, was the height of folly. He minuted

> The day I made my record catch on Loch Beg I hooked a fish on the dropper, he slipped off, and I foul-hooked him on the tail fly—and I would not have thrown him back even if there had been a policeman standing on the bank.[5]

All anglers would agree.

There was a recurring complaint that Scottish Ministers, who had for the most part attended schools in England, tended to be indifferent to the separate Scottish educational system, but Sinclair could not be criticised on this score, as an exchange of minutes with Noel Skelton, his Parliamentary Under-Secretary of State, shows. Sinclair had asked him to make a point of examining the Education estimates, and Skelton replied at once, agreeing that

we should have a very careful look into Education administration—
not because I have any reason to think it faulty, but because I don't
believe that any of your immediate predecessors, or of mine, have ever
devoted much attention to it, and certainly in my time in the House
no Scottish member ever seems to have taken much interest.[6]

Shortly afterwards, in August, 1932, when the Cabinet had approved
an English education Bill, Sinclair contemplated changing the basis on
which the sum allocated to Scottish education was determined—the
Goschen formula of 11/80ths of the corresponding English figure. This
would have been a radical reform at the time, because the Scottish
Education Department had for years acquiesced in accepting Goschen
as the most convenient yardstick. Sinclair thought he might do better
by getting a grant based on need, and not linked to England. Peck, the
head of the Department, was alarmed to be asked by the Secretary of
State whether he could really confirm that 'the preservation of the
11/80ths grant is the permanent consideration in Scottish educational
finance', and could not be disturbed. Sinclair left office before this
interesting argument could be resolved, and many education estimates
were to be passed before the Goschen formula was abandoned.

Sir David Milne, who was Sinclair's private secretary at the Scottish
Office, recalled that he had an unusual gift which greatly impressed
his advisers. When Sinclair had to consider a submission he would not
only read all the papers with exemplary care. He would also ask
officials to develop their views and cross-examine them on the details.
So much one might expect. But Sinclair went further. He was able to
convince them that for the time being the question under discussion
was the one thing that mattered; that their views were important to
him; and that together they would remain in conclave until they
found a solution which they all recognised was the right one. It was a
delicate exercise in leadership. Besides, Milne added, he had style.

During the summer of 1932 Sinclair and his Liberal colleagues were
becoming more and more uncomfortable at the Government's protectionist policy. For some months they had remained in office only
with an agreement to disagree, but the decision reached at Ottawa,
which appeared to give other countries an unjustifiable advantage on
tariffs was too much for Sinclair to swallow. His own approach can be
seen in the notes on agricultural policy which he had drafted earlier.

To establish a quota for wheat is to encourage the British farmer to
kick against the pricks of economic circumstances instead of following

the more difficult, but ultimately more profitable lines for which British conditions are particularly suitable. . . .

The internal purchasing power of the pound is to be maintained. Yet the quota must to some extent put up the price of the chief food of the people. Wheat prices are going up and stocks that were in existence when the £ slipped off the gold standard are being exhausted. If a quota is given in these circumstances the inevitable rise in price will be attributed to the quota.[7]

The Liberals' resignation, when it came, was attacked for imperilling the unity of the National Government—a fiction which it was going to be difficult to sustain. But it is hard to see what else they could have done. This was a resignation on principle, not for personal or party advantage, and most contemporary political figures were prepared to regard it as such. One of these was Brendan Bracken, who wrote to Sinclair on 29th September, 1932.

It would be an insult to condole with you upon leaving the administration. You should be warmly congratulated. If it is good to be a Secretary of State, it is something greater and better to have surrendered place and power for the sake of principle. In view of Samuel's speech about food taxes, mortal damage would have been done to what are left of our old political traditions if he and his colleagues had any part in implementing the Ottawa bargain.[8]

Churchill also wrote. He had some misgivings about the course which Sinclair had taken. While fully appreciating his motives, Churchill wondered whether Sinclair might, still without damage to his conscience, have been prudent to wait till he saw what emerged from the forthcoming World Economic Conference. He went on

However, as you know, I have nothing but contempt for MacDonald personally and politically, and what I write to you is only on account of my abiding interest in your career.

Well anyhow you will be the Liberal leader in Scotland, and there is nothing like having an official dunghill of one's own to crow from, however small and redolent it may be.[9]

The Liberals in this period were, alone of the main parties, committed to Scottish Home Rule in the form of a domestic parliament for purely Scottish affairs. The Duke of Montrose, one of the more moderate nationalist leaders, approached Sinclair complaining that the Liberals only espoused the nationalist cause at election time. Sinclair refuted this allegation. Montrose also proposed that their parties should form a pact not to oppose each other at elections in future. Sinclair replied impeccably that the selection of candidates was a matter for the constituency organisations; and that he saw no reason why the Duke or his friends should not advance their cause from the Liberal platform. After a lengthy correspondence, punctuated by the Duke's ineradicable self-esteem, His Grace was eventually persuaded to accept Sinclair's argument, but little came of it. Sinclair was an intensely patriotic Scot, but nationalism was not one of his main preoccupations, either at the Scottish Office or later.

In the long gallery of former Ministers, preserved in Dover House, there are portraits of others who made more of a mark as Secretary of State than Sinclair. But, as it turned out, the opportunity was not his. In some respects he was the *alter ego* of Walter Elliot, whose chance came later. Sinclair was the only Secretary of State with roots in the far North, Elliot was a Borderer; they differed radically on protection; Sinclair resigned on principle but Elliot continued to serve under Chamberlain; Churchill's affection for Sinclair was matched by his coolness towards Elliot; Sinclair was a master of what was politically desirable while Elliot was much concerned with abstract theory. In a cordial exchange of letters at the time of Sinclair's resignation Elliot wrote to him

> I know the queer double feeling that comes over one on going out—so well—the physical relief at the lifting of the almost intolerable burden of work and the hankering that always remains for a hand on the tiller.[10]

It is neither nostalgic, nor a romantic fancy, to regret that Sinclair did not have longer at the Scottish Office. In a few months he had demonstrated what could be achieved by personal example. Given longer, he would have provided strong supporting evidence for the underlying theme in this book that the personal contribution of Scottish Ministers is often underrated. Milne was not the only one at the Scottish Office to applaud his style, his elegance, his pursuit of excellence, or to be sad at his departure.

Notes

1 *The Times*, 17th June, 1970.
2 *Hansard*, 28th June, 1932. Vol. 267, col. 1735.
3 *Hansard*, 4th March, 1932. Vol. 262, col. 1419.
4 *Hansard*, 2nd February, 1932. Vol. 261, col. 94.
5 *The Thurso Papers*, Churchill College, Cambridge.
6 *Ibid.*
7 *Ibid.*
8 *Ibid.*
9 *Ibid.*
10 *Ibid.*

CHAPTER VI

The Public-spirited Publisher

The parliamentary lobby was not surprised when Sir Godfrey Collins was appointed to fill the vacancy at the Scottish Office. But Collins was astonished. He spoke later of his 'utter amazement' when Ramsay MacDonald, the Prime Minister, telephoned to invite him to join the National Government. Collins had entered the House in 1910 primarily because he was attracted by the Liberal policies and social reforms which Asquith and Lloyd George were then carrying through Parliament. He was a strong supporter of Asquith, to whom he remained loyal through all the intrigues of the twenties. Asquith in turn had a great regard for him—high praise from that shrewd judge of character. Collins was cautious, something of a Whig by temperament, and it was natural for him to take the Simonites' side when the split with the Samuel faction came in 1931. But he had no part in the discussions which led to the Samuelites' resignation from the Cabinet, and remained on cordial terms with his former colleagues.

The first publisher to become a Cabinet Minister, Collins had three separate, but interlinked, careers in publishing, as an M.P. and finally as Secretary of State.

Collins was born in 1875 and it was intended that he should have a naval career. Trained in H.M.S. *Britannia*, he served as a midshipman, but ill-health forced his retirement and he joined the family publishing firm. It was typical of his keenness to find out how things worked that he at once applied himself to acquiring practical experience as a compositor and machine-minder. Later, when the firm adopted the latest type of German rotary printing presses Collins went to Leipzig to master their intricacies. This was the machinery that produced Collins Illustrated Pocket Classics, one of the greatest successes in publishing. We are not directly concerned with the history of the House of Collins, but Godfrey Collins was one of the mainsprings in what was, and still is, essentially a Scottish family business. Let it suffice that, in addition to the host of technical books and works of reference that regularly appear under their imprint, the House has one of the largest lists of original works in modern publishing. Much of its development, especially the 'tidal waves' of new fiction in the twenties and early thirties, ranging from Walter de la Mare to Michael Arlen and Agatha Christie, was inspired by Godfrey Collins.

Collins's publishing interests overlap with his activities as an M.P. in a revealing incident at the 1924 'Zinovieff letter' election. As David Keir tells it, Arlen's best-seller *The Green Hat* had appeared shortly beforehand. On the morning of the election, when his political future was at stake, his election agent told Collins that he would be glad to hear that the Sixth Ward was polling strongly. The only reply he got was an ecstatic murmur. 'Think of it! Seventy thousand copies! Never known it before!'[1] (Sales of *The Green Hat* eventually exceeded half a million.) Later in his career he said that he would never admit whether the publication of his first Classic or his elevation to the Cabinet had given him more pleasure. Before leaving the House of Collins it is significant that Godfrey Collins showed the same interest in education there as he did later as Secretary of State. In the 1920s he launched a new schoolbook policy, discarding many venerable Victorian texts and replacing them with a series commissioned from outstanding scholars.

As a constituency Member Collins's performance was remarkable. He was M.P. for Greenock from 1910 till his death in 1936, winning nine elections in all. No other Scottish Member had such a long, uninterrupted record. Four times in the 1920s he was strongly opposed by the Communists (whose candidate Geddes once received over 10,000 votes) but he survived with a comfortable majority. In 1935 his prospects were not highly regarded. 'We shall miss Sir Godfrey Collins from the House', wrote the Sunday press. 'There seems very little doubt that he will be defeated.' Collins was returned with the highest poll he ever achieved. Strangely for one who had few pretensions to the art of public speaking, he was more at home on the hustings than in the House. He was not a 'promiser' in his election addresses, repeating that his 'views and policy were not to be put up for auction', but he had a ready way with hecklers. On one occasion in the Greenock Town Hall disaffected elements drowned both the notes of the organ and the stentorian tones of Ernest Brown, the Minister of Labour, who had arrived to speak on the Collins platform. Collins was not dismayed. Armed with a bell, and fortified by his family, he tramped the back courts and greens to address his audience through the open windows of their tenements.[2] A local wag, in a dreadful but forgivable pun, shouted 'You're tolling us!' The electoral record is not to be lightly dismissed. In the vagaries of the Liberal Party it was something of a feat to retain a difficult constituency for a quarter of a century.

The new Member for Greenock started his political career as Parliamentary Private Secretary to J. B. Seeley (Lord Mottistone), the Secretary of State for War, from 1912 to 1914. He was a member of the War Supplies Committee and the experience he acquired led to his appointment in 1915 to the staff of the Quartermaster General. For the next two years he served in Egypt, Gallipoli, and Mesopotamia and was awarded the C.M.G. He joined the post-war Coalition Government as a Junior Lord of the Treasury and Scottish Liberal Whip, but an injury to his knee caused his resignation in 1920. He was always a strong advocate of public economy and in 1917 he played a leading part in the setting up of the Select Committee on Public Expenditure. He was Chief Liberal Whip in 1924, but resigned when Asquith gave up the Liberal leadership. In the 1931 crisis he followed Simon, and a year later he became Secretary of State.

His early political work is of less immediate relevance to us than the commercial expertise he had gained as a publisher. In present-day conditions there is a continuing debate between those who claim that the job of the M.P. should be full-time and those who adhere to the traditional view that the Member can better discharge his obligations to Parliament if he has other, outside interests. Ministers on appointment are, of course, required to abjure their commercial or financial commitments. It is, however, of interest that in our half-century Collins was the only Secretary of State to come to the office with a successful record in the direction of a large, prosperous business behind him.

He also brought two other qualities which were not necessarily likely to lead to popularity, either with the public or with his advisers. The first was his insistence on stringency in public expenditure. He had already been instrumental in persuading Parliament to examine alleged Exchequer extravagances. In 1928 he had attracted the notice of the *Punch* cartoonist for his speech in favour of reducing income tax to half a crown by abolishing Imperial Preference, the Empire Marketing Board, and securing other economies including the discontinuance of the sugar-beet subsidy.[3] (The last was not only a matter of principle: there was also a constituency interest in safeguarding his local cane refinery. The eventual shutting down of the Scottish sugar-beet factory at Cupar, which proved completely uneconomic, gave Gordon

Campbell many headaches in the seventies.) In the House he was reckoned to be an expert on financial matters, but despite the vigilance with which he examined Departmental estimates—a Pepysian thoroughness, as David Keir called it—he was seldom attacked for official parsimony.

Collins had an old-fashioned, Victorian belief in the virtues of hard work. He expected his subordinates to show the same sense of commitment as he did. 'If tired of work,' he once told a member of his staff at the House of Collins, 'refresh yourself with work of a different kind.'[4] One might have supposed that this austere, ascetic, almost Puritan attitude was not guaranteed to inspire affection among those whose job it was to submit minutes or take directions from him. But the reverse seems to have been the case. His advisers at the Scottish Office, and they included the most distinguished of Scottish civil servants Sir David Milne and Sir Charles Cunningham at the beginning of their careers, have said how much they esteemed the application of common-sense. His technique in official discussions was that which he had learned in the boardroom, a steady prodding towards the rational decision. His comments were crisp, often laconic, and David Milne would return to his desk wondering if he had really got it right. Collins's family have confirmed that he greatly disliked being surrounded with mountains of paper: his invariable habit was to write his decision on whatever was sent to him and return it to the sender. The Scottish Office, for their part, respected his prodigious industry, and though he was impatient of those who advanced obstacles to what he thought were worthy proposals, they were fully aware that he provided a very desirable ballast to the office.

Collins was concerned with over thirty Bills affecting Scotland while he was Secretary of State, but he had no great relish for parliamentary debate, and like many other modest Ministers he dreaded his appearances at the Despatch Box. His speeches suffered from being too statistical. For one who always kept his eyes on the main objective he was surprisingly apt to immerse himself in details as he developed his case in the House. And he lacked the light touch, or the concealed barb that might make his opponents wary of attacking him. When Anstruther-Gray (Lord Kilmany), not the most notorious of wits, asked whether the Secretary of State would undertake a scientific enquiry into the existence of the Loch Ness monster, Collins replied cautiously that there was no reason to suspect the presence of any baleful monster in Loch Ness, and that any researches in the interests of science were properly a matter for private enterprise aided by the zeal of the press. The hand of the official drafter is apparent in that reply, but even in response to a supplementary query suggesting that the R.A.F.'s photographic services might be enlisted, Collins was not to be drawn. He would, he said, like to have more evidence before he called on the Air Force.[5] Third leaders in the next day's press chided him for his solemnity. Towards the end of his career Collins revealed that the only speech he had made which gave him any satisfaction was the one on the Housing (Scotland) Bill of 1935.

This was the most important Scottish measure passed during Collins's administration. On Second Reading, Collins said that since the war 183,000 houses had been built with state assistance, but not nearly enough had been done to provide accommodation for the low wage-earners. The objective was now to build 'decent low-rented houses for the less well-off in sufficient numbers to abolish overcrowding and, in addition, destroy the slums'.[6] It was claimed that the Bill (which for the first time laid down a standard of overcrowding) gave local authorities greater powers and finance than ever before to deal with the problem. In uncharacteristic euphoria Collins hoped that within five years there would be no more slums in Scotland. It did not prove to be as easy as that, but Collins's Bill, on which he made many concessions to secure its passage, went as far as contemporary thinking allowed.

Sinclair, during his short stay at the Scottish Office, had been sceptical whether the Scottish Education Department was fully alive to the needs of the time. Collins shared his view. He had a professional interest in school textbooks, and in his public appearances throughout Scotland he went out of his way to urge greater co-operation between schools and the community. He tried to foster closer contact between education and industry, and in the curriculum he stressed that academic training should not be at the expense of judgment and character. It is not clear that much came of this. Tom Johnston was later disappointed at the results of his exhortations on the same theme. The teaching profession is not the least reactionary of institutions, and there are evident limits on what even the most energetic Minister can accomplish. Collins, however, had one small success. On learning that children spent too large a part of their holidays worrying about their future, he greatly reduced the time taken to publish the results of the school-leaving examinations. All who have sweated in anxiety to find out if their deficiencies have been spotted will salute this humane decision.

Collins made a long, complicated speech on the Education (Scotland) Bill in February, 1936. The Bill's main purpose was to raise the school leaving age to fifteen from 1939. It was attacked by Labour leaders for the exemptions allowed for those who obtained 'beneficial employment', and by the Liberals for not proposing immediate action—not exactly easy to defend since the matter had first been mooted in 1915. The point is now academic, but Collins's argument was closely reasoned and showed his meticulous attention to detail. He justified the interval on three grounds. Balanced and suitably arranged courses of instruction, including practical training, must be prepared; new building and extensions would be needed; and lastly if the age limit were raised before 1939 some of the new schools, equipment, and staff would become superfluous because of the fall in the birth rate.[7] Judged by today's acrimonious education debates, the proceedings had an other-wordly air. (Because of the incidence of the War, the school leaving age was not raised till April, 1947.)

Many useful domestic proposals emerged from the Scottish Office in Collins's time. He introduced an acceptable scheme for the creation of smallholdings. The procedure for examining Scottish private Bills was made less inconvenient. More important was the Herring Industry Bill of 1935, which set up the Herring Industry Board and met with more approval than is normal for that highly individualistic industry.[8] Collins could also take some pride in bringing forward the Illegal Trawling (Scotland) Bill which was much to the liking of the inshore fishermen. None of these measures were in themselves particularly spectacular. In the circumstances that had led to the National Government they might even be thought irrelevant. But Collins had assessed his market. Within the powers that the Secretary of State possessed, this was a period of modest advance and consolidation. It was also largely due to Collins that the Economic Development Committee was set up under Sir James Lithgow to consider ways of improving economic conditions.[9]

On arrival at Dover House Collins had found waiting for him a long memorandum on nationalism, which the staff had been busy preparing during the Parliamentary Recess. Analysing the policies of the three main parties and the nationalists with cool objectivity, it conceded that there was a growing demand for some form of reorganisation to meet complaints that Scotland had not sufficient opportunities for guiding her destinies and retaining her nationhood. The memorandum (13th September, 1932) doubted, however, whether Scotland could by herself maintain social and other benefits 'at their present level, at any rate for the present'. Ranging into the political field, the paper discussed the possibility that the same person could be a member of both Imperial and Scottish Parliaments, concluding that

> There is no likelihood of the withdrawal of Scottish business reducing the length of Westminster sittings and it is hardly credible that Scottish loquacity could exhaust itself in Edinburgh in less than three or four months a year.

The memorandum quotes Sir A. MacEwen, who put the difference between the Dominions and Scotland in a nutshell when he said that the former were like married daughters but Scotland was united to England in wedlock.[10]

The papers now in the Scottish Record Office show that this official appreciation was distilled from the various representations that had been received. Not all were in favour of Home Rule. The Scottish Committee of the Federation of British Industries was adamant that any movement that even tended to cause an adverse interest between the two countries 'would be disastrous to the industries and employment of Scotland'. The letter goes on to assert that no case for the setting up of a separate Parliament has been, 'or can be', established.

By now the Scottish Unionists had decided that it would be prudent to offer their own alternative, and Sir Robert Horne, their Chairman, came to tell Collins what they had in mind. According to Collins's note (28th October, 1932) Horne said the Unionists wanted a Scottish Office to be built in Edinburgh with room for all the departments and a residence for the Secretary of State.[11] Collins was sympathetic and said so in the House, but 'paramount financial considerations' meant that Horne's proposal was not realised till 1939. Meanwhile Collins accepted the need for decentralisation and in 1935 he transferred a substantial part of the administrative work of the Scottish Office from London to Edinburgh, thereby paving the way for the move to St Andrew's House. Horne's proposals extended to the creation of another Under-Secretary of State, but the Government did not agree to this until 1941.

On one of Horne's other suggestions, the publication of a Financial Return of Revenue and Expenditure between Scotland and England, Collins acted with exemplary speed. On 1st November, 1932, he wrote to Chamberlain, the Chancellor of the Exchequer

> I think you are aware that in recent months the agitation in certain quarters for a measure of Home Rule for Scotland has assumed considerable proportions. . . .
>
> My opinion is that the ranks of the supporters of the movement at the present time are greatly swelled by the prevalence of a belief that Scotland is not obtaining a fair return for her contribution to the national revenue and I am convinced that if it could be shown that this belief is unfounded a large body of moderate opinion would break away from the movement.

Collins went on to urge the 'very earliest' production of a return on the lines he suggested.[12] Chamberlain replied on 9th November. He agreed that something must be done and said that he was arranging for the collection of information forthwith. Two returns were, in time, published—the second in 1935—and while their basis was challenged they afforded no satisfaction to the Nationalists. It is clear that Collins, for his part, had no time for Home Rule. As he told the House, 'So far as the Government are concerned Home Rule for Scotland is an academic question, and I have not asked my colleagues to consider it'.

Horne's final point was, in Collins's words, for

> The King's Speech at the opening of Parliament to contain a paragraph about Scotland. (If this was not done he indicated Scottish Unionist members might place an amendment on the Order Paper regretting no reference.)[13]

Collins duly secured a Scottish entry in the King's Speech the following month. The reference, to amending private legislation procedure and reorganising the Court of Session, was brief, but since then it has been the invariable practice to ensure that Scotland is featured in the Speech. The significance of the Gracious Speech from the Throne needs a word in passing. Although it is processed by Cabinet Committees, and approved by the full Cabinet, it is not a definitive document. Items in it may be dropped as the session proceeds, and later happenings may require legislation that was not foreseen at the time. But it gives a fair summary of the Government's intentions: Ministers are keen to get a place in it for their own Bills: and there is a great deal of jockeying for position. Parliamentary time is limited and two major Bills together with a package of short or non-controversial ones are about as much as Scottish Members can manage. Bills on unpopular or contentious matters (e.g. licensing or divorce) will only find a place early in the life of a Parliament. This necessitates much furious preparation by Ministers and their advisers. When the outcome of a General Election is thought likely to be in doubt officials spend the weeks of the election campaign assembling schemes that can be got ready for legislation and may be enacted by the incoming government. In effect, they prepare suggestions for both a Red Queen's and a White Queen's Speech and then wait for the results on polling day. But the entrenched Scottish entries date from Collins.

Collins was not a partisan politician. He said that the old meanings of party had gone with the 1914 War: that the division was no longer between Capital and Labour or Free Trade and Protection, but between Evolution and Revolution.[14] With this basic philosophy he was happy in the National Government and frequently said how proud he was to serve. His work on housing and education has an honourable place in the history of the Scottish Office. His innovations took the form of making the machine operate with the maximum efficiency. This meant delegation and good public relations. As a publisher he knew the value of publicity. He started a system of regular press conferences and appointed the first Press Officer at the Scottish Office. This was noteworthy since a recurring theme in this book relates to the Office's inept attempts at communication. He was patient and understanding with the deputations that came to see him and turned no deserving supplicant away without a sympathetic answer. He visited more parts of Scotland to see conditions at first hand than any previous Minister, and he did not spare himself.

NOTES

1 David Keir, *The House of Collins*. London, 1952.
2 *Ibid*.
3 *Punch*, 15th January, 1928.
4 *The House of Collins*.
5 *Hansard*, 12th December, 1933. Vol. 284, col. 178.
6 *Hansard*, 21st February, 1935. Vol. 298, col. 551.
7 *Hansard*, 18th February, 1936. Vol. 308, col. 1663.
8 *Hansard*, 4th February, 1935. Vol. 297, col. 821.
9 *Hansard*, 1st April, 1936. Vol. 310, col. 2000.
10 Scottish Office Papers HH I/791 in the Scottish Record Office.
11 *Ibid*.
12 *Ibid*.
13 *Ibid*.
14 *Daily Telegraph*, 14th October, 1936.

CHAPTER VII

Hamlet without the Gloom

James Bridie, the most distinguished Scottish playwright, died on 29th January, 1951. It so happened that on that evening the Government were facing a delicate division, with the possibility of defeat in the House, and M.P.s were confined to the Palace of Westminster. I was in the Secretary of State's room going over official papers with Hector McNeil when Walter Elliot burst through the door. He had been asked by the B.B.C. to broadcast an appreciation of his old friend after the nine o'clock news, but the Whips would not allow him a pairing, and he felt that if this became known it would be resented in Scotland. McNeil's reaction was immediate. He told Elliot he was paired with him.

Later, after he had spoken in unrepentant terms to William Whiteley, the Government Chief Whip, McNeil reminisced over the coterie of eminent students who had been contemporaries of Elliot and Bridie at Glasgow University just before the First War—John Boyd Orr, Hector Hetherington, James Maxton, and others. Of Elliot he said he was a big man, as great as any of them, but 'he was a loser'. This was not meant to be an unkind judgment, because McNeil had maintained a respectful relationship with Elliot ever since he had been beaten by him, after a disputed recount, at Kelvingrove in the 1935 General Election. But was it just?

There is no easy clue to Elliot's many-sided character. He had a striking physical presence. Tall, craggy, gawky, with an enormous head and huge spatulate hands, he stumped the corridors of Westminster as though he was marching over his Border acres. He was not much given to pleasantries, but anyone who met him would recognise, at the first glint through his spectacles, the presence of a powerful intellect. Elliot was the only Secretary of State who was once confidently tipped by the political soothsayers as a future Prime Minister, and though with hindsight it is possible to identify events that told against him, there remains an outstanding query why he did not arrive at Downing Street. Sir Colin Coote, his close friend and biographer, suggests that the failing that prevented him from reaching the topmost top was his unpunctuality, which reflected a strong element of indecision. 'Unpunctual, unpartisan, indecisive, a real political Hamlet without the gloom.'[1] Sir Colin also says that Elliot 'could argue so brilliantly on both sides that a conflict in his mind too often ended in a draw'.[2] There is no gainsaying this, but Elliot would not have seen it as a defect in himself. In his own essay on the Scottish political heritage he asserted that it was one 'wherein intellect, speech and, above all, argument are the passports to the highest eminence in the land'.[3] It would be pleasant to agree, but the successful politician must have something of the ostrich in him: he must on occasion bury his head in the sand and let the enemy pass by, before emerging to gain his objective. This Elliot could not do. He had to destroy his opponent's arguments piece by piece. And despite his coruscations the House, or his Ministerial colleagues, sometimes became irritated or bored.

There are further peculiarities to be observed in writing about Elliot in a Scottish Office context. He was, regrettably, one of the last Scotsmen prominent in public life who spoke rich, unmistakable Scots. This is not a matter of accent or intonation, although Elliot's utterances were always underlined by a Border lilt and burr. Nor does it depend on a wide, erudite vocabulary. It is more the sinewy way in which the whole dialectic is assembled and presented. The result is at once recognisable as Scottish. Two other dissimilar egoists, Lord Reith and Sir Thomas Innes of Learney, were likewise skilled in the art of speaking Scots, but their successors are hard to find.

Another strange aspect of Elliot's public *persona* is that he always appeared as a West of Scotland, in fact a Glasgow, man. His family had lived in the Borders for more than two centuries, and his home was always there, but when he took part in debate he gave the impression that he spoke from a deep knowledge and understanding of the problems of Clydeside. He had, of course, a long association with his constituency of Kelvingrove—he refused offers of safe English billets when he was defeated there—but his declared regional interest is exceptional among Scottish Office Ministers. Over the half-century with which we are concerned in this study there has been a continuing inclination to disregard, or at least to underrate, the importance of Glasgow and the West of Scotland in the general Scottish ambit. Genuflections are made from time to time, but the criticism of indifference to Glasgow's interests remains on the charge sheet. Ministerial appearances throughout the year in the second city are usually pretty sparse, and although a 'Glasgow application' paragraph or two is prudently inserted in White Papers the complaint is not met. Judged by population, contribution to the gross national product, or any other convenient criterion, the ratio of Ministerial and official time assigned to Highland, as opposed to West of Scotland, issues would be hard to justify.

Now comes the paradox, and Elliot sprouts paradoxes. Elliot had, as we have seen, an abiding constituency affiliation which extended to the rest of the contiguous area. He thought of himself as a homespun Scot. But meeting him one never got the impression that he regarded his time at the Scottish Office as anything more significant than an interlude in a long political anabasis. He did not refer to it as the pinnacle of his career, and for one who had set his sights on higher things this is understandable. There is also the oddity that he lingered on the political stage for many years after he left his last Ministerial appointment. Other ex-Ministers have stayed in the House, but they have usually sought the plenitude of retirement to the back benches, making only sporadic interventions. This was not so with Elliot.

Those who have been Secretary of State have been known to approach the Scottish Office for, perfectly permissible, preferential treatment in minor matters, or for references to information which they could use in debate. Elliot did not do this. When he spoke it was as the Opposition spokesman, or as the Member for Kelvingrove, not as a former Secretary of State who could say how much better it could be done. To his credit also is his demeanour in the House during the post-war years. Opposition Members who spoke after him would, in the normal cut and thrust of Party politics, profess sympathy for him for not being in office as he deserved and suggest that this must affect his real feelings. Elliot took these remarks in silence and with dignity.

He was educated at Glasgow Academy and University, obtaining First Class Honours in Science in 1910 and qualifying as a Doctor three years later. (His subsequent academic attainments included a DSc degree in 1922 and Fellowship of the Royal Society in 1935.) Inevitably for one of his forensic leanings he was President of the University Union. During the First War he was Regimental Medical Officer with the Royal Scots Greys, taking a more active part in hostilities than is prescribed for the R.A.M.C. He was wounded and won two Military Crosses. Like James Stuart, a later Secretary of State, his mind was indelibly marked by the War. It is no platitude to say that the real protagonists for peace in the thirties were those who had experienced the holocaust of 1914–18, and this may have affected his judgment in the appeasement years.

We come now to the story that in 1918, when he received a telegram from Lanark asking him to stand for Parliament, he replied 'Yes. Which side?' Sir Colin Coote has confirmed that this is apocryphal, and the implication of cynical opportunism is not supported. Jo Grimond, writing after Elliot's death, might say that he should never have been in the Tory party or abandoned the mildly Fabian interests he had shown at the University,[4] but there is no reason to question the sincerity of his Conservative beliefs. In 1927 he wrote *Toryism and the Twentieth Century*.[5] Cootes, admittedly biased in his favour, sums it up as follows.

> In short the principle of Toryism was biological, the principle of Radicalism was reason—and life could not all be explained by that. Translated into political practice, this meant that the Tories might have at least occasional regard for the producer instead of eternally cosseting the consumer.[6]

Although the argument is set out with Elliot's customary verve it did not have any great effect on contemporary politics. But it is refreshing to find a future Scottish Secretary rehearsing his political doctrine in a monograph. Research has not unearthed a similar instance.

In 1920, early in his parliamentary career, Elliot reacted vigorously against a Scottish Home Rule Bill, denouncing it for parochialism. This is consistent with the article he wrote for *A Scotsman's Heritage* in 1932, when he did not agree that

> the political soul of Scotland, which is undoubtedly disembodied today, can find its proper incarnation in a synthetic Parliament at Edinburgh. The government of Scotland is another thing: good government is necessary for all communities and the technique of good government may be improved or injured by centralisation or by decentralisation according to circumstances.[7]

Present-day pro- and anti-devolutionists might with advantage be required to submit a treatise on this theme before indulging in public lucubrations. Elliot had no sympathy for the Nationalist movement, and repeatedly proclaimed that the mere mechanical multiplication of Parliaments might not solve any of the old problems, and might cause new ones 'inspired by the development of national hatred'.

In 1923 Elliot lost Lanark by 230 votes and received a gracious letter of condolence from Neville Chamberlain. This was the kind of gesture he did not forget and may eventually have influenced him to side with Chamberlain—in the event much against his own interests—at the time of Munich. He was absent from the House for only a few months, being returned for Kelvingrove in May, 1924. He held the seat till 1945 (at one time campaigning with the slogan 'Do not falter; vote for Walter'). To conclude his electoral career, he was Member for the Scottish Universities until 1950, when he recaptured Kelvingrove which he retained till his death in 1958.

Elliot had a lengthy Ministerial apprenticeship as Under-Secretary for Health in the Scottish Office in 1923, and, after the Labour interlude, from 1924 to 1929 (latterly as Parliamentary Under-Secretary of State). He seems to have been given a fairly free hand both by his first chief (Lord Novar), who sat in the Upper House, and by his successor Gilmour.

The twenties were grim for the country as a whole, but in Scotland the depression reached catastrophic dimensions. Memories of the wartime industrial boom only served to underline the immensity of the slump. World conditions greatly reduced the demand for heavy engineering. There was no requirement for commercial shipping, and the construction of warships was meanwhile at an end. Unemployment reached record levels. In Scotland only 25,000 houses were built in the five years between 1918 and 1923, less than a year's production after the Second World War. As a Junior Minister Elliot was, however, active in trying to stimulate the housing programme. His plans to build steel Weir houses were an imaginative attempt to meet the desperate shortage but were attacked on Party grounds. (Ironically, George Buchanan who denounced the Weir scheme was later responsible, under the Attlee government, for similar prefabricated dwellings.)

Much of Elliot's energy in this period was devoted to the Empire Marketing Board, which fostered many far-seeing experiments in agriculture. He had long been associated with John (later Lord) Boyd Orr in research on nutritional problems at the Rowett Research Institute in Aberdeen, and now attempts were made to apply science, in the Boyd Orr sense, to practical agriculture. He was also one of the first to see the possibilities of the documentary film and did his best to encourage John Grierson when his work was still at the pioneer stage. In the House Elliot was concerned to assist the Secretary of State in the lengthy debates on the Local Government Bill and played his part to the full. But time and public support were running out for the Government, and later in 1929 Elliot found himself in Opposition.

He was soon back in office, this time as Financial Secretary to the Treasury. This was a prestige job, reserved for those who are expected to go further up the ladder, and does not normally afford many opportunities to shine in debate, but Philip Snowden, the Chancellor of the Exchequer, suffered from such crippling physical disability that Elliot had more scope than usual. When he was promoted to full Ministerial status in 1932 as Minister of Agriculture, Chamberlain, by now Chancellor, wrote to him in felicitous terms saying that he had been 'undefeatable in the House', and had always kept his end up.

Elliot was probably most at home in the Ministry of Agriculture. He was exceptionally well qualified for the office. He came from farming stock: from his connection with the family auctioneer's business at Lanark he knew the practical side of marketing; he had a deep personal interest in nutrition; and, more immediately to the point, he saw how British agriculture had to be protected in prevailing world conditions. Livestock prices had reached a new low point, and deputations laid siege to the Ministry. Elliot's reaction was quick. Along with Walter Runciman, the President of the Board of Trade, he was successful—if highly controversial—in persuading the main exporting countries to restrict their supplies to us. There were many enlightened experiments in the nutritional field that need not concern us, although Scottish farmers also benefited.

His speech on the Agricultural Marketing Bill in 1933 was significant. The Marketing Act passed by the Labour Government in 1931 had laid the ground for marketing schemes for individual agricultural products. Elliot proceeded to demonstrate that there was now an unanswerable case for marketing boards. Prices were half what they had been three years previously, and the whole industry was at risk. Stabilisation to meet conditions of oversupply was essential, and the principles that Elliot adduced are still followed. One M.P., however, was not convinced. Aneurin Bevan, at the beginning of his parliamentary career, excused his innocent participation in an agricultural debate by saying that he had endured many ignorant speeches on coalmining, saw in Elliot an adversary worth his mettle, and inveighed against the Bill's proposals as

> commercial brigandage using the language of modern science to conceal their political brigandage.[8]

In 1936 Elliot moved to the Scottish Office on the death of Collins. His own prospects seemed fair, but the time was not propitious. The clouds reached their darkest two years later, but the omens had been there for long enough. There is no need to recapitulate the impact, and the effect, of the Spanish civil war, the League of Nations' impotence over Abyssinia, or the war in the Far East. The reoccupation of the Rhineland in March, 1936, led with dreadful inevitability to the Austrian *Anschluss* in March, 1938, and the Munich débâcle in September of the same year.

So far as the Cabinet was concerned, these were the years of the frightened rabbit, and Ministers were preoccupied with the Hitler menace, almost to the exclusion of everything else. The resolution passed by Oxford undergraduates refusing to fight for King and Country was widely interpreted, at home and abroad, as indicative of the national mood. It was the same in Scotland. At the Rectorial Election at Glasgow University in October, 1937, the winner was the candidate of the Peace Pledge Union, and Elliot, who had spoken on Churchill's platform, saw him come only third, behind the Scottish Nationalist.

The Cabinet minutes of the period show Elliot among those frantically searching for an honourable solution. His correspondence, quoted by Coote, reveals how painful was his own crisis of conscience. Twice he came near resigning—in 1936 and after Munich. Resignation at either time might have guaranteed him office after the War. Certainly Eden's departure marked him down as Churchill's Crown Prince. But a gesture by Elliot would not have influenced the march of events. Duff Cooper did resign, and though he made one of the most memorable speeches of all time it was his oratory, not his purpose, that was applauded. Meanwhile Government business had to be transacted, and Elliot remained for two years at the Scottish Office.

Despite the unhappy climate there were achievements to record. Elliot continued to take a keen interest in the progress of agriculture. He secured a minimum price for oats—never a favoured commodity in price negotiations. He also saw that Scottish farm workers were at a disadvantage compared with those in the South by not having a statutory minimum wage, and he set up an Agriculture Wages Board for Scotland. He was less fortunate in his intervention into Highland affairs. He failed to secure the passage of the Caledonian Power Bill, designed to provide electricity for a carbide factory. Though local unemployment was staggeringly high, and though carbide was urgently required for defence purposes, an unholy combination of vested interests blocked the Bill.

In housing Elliot was, according to Scrymgeour-Wedderburn the Parliamentary Under-Secretary, 'always on fire to get things done'. The bad condition of Scottish housing in the inter-war years was equalled only by the lack, or at least the ineffectiveness, of remedial measures. Collins's high hopes had not been fulfilled, and in Glasgow, always the blackest spot, the Corporation were building scarcely 2000 houses a year. Under Elliot the housing programme was stepped up and reached a record Scottish total of 26,000 in 1938. His personal contribution was to provide a new instrument. The Scottish Housing Association for Special Areas, wholly financed by the Treasury, was registered under the Companies Act on 8th November, 1937.[9] Its successor, now the Scottish Special Housing Association, has proved extremely useful in supplementing the housing stock. When local authorities are reluctant to build on the scale, or on the sites, required, Ministers can call in the S.S.H.A.

Elliot had wanted to go further. On 18th December, 1937, he wrote to Sir John Simon at the Treasury with radical proposals for improving conditions, particularly housing conditions, in Scotland. His ideas ranged from exploring alternative methods of construction to the creation of a National Housing Board.[10] Simon's response (letters of 10th February and 31st March, 1938) was distinctly unsympathetic.[11]

The Scottish Office was not directly charged with powers to combat unemployment, but Elliot was influential in the passing of the 1937 Act which provided incentives for industries in 'special', renamed 'development', areas. From this Act stemmed the first of the Scottish industrial estates at Hillington, for long the model for emulation. He was also concerned with the promotion of the Empire Exhibition which King George VI opened in Glasgow in May, 1938. Elliot retained a mischievous recollection of it. The Earl of Elgin, as Chairman of the Exhibition, was looking around for eminent figures to be introduced to the Monarch, and asked Lord Rosebery if he wanted to be presented. Rosebery was not amused. 'Presented? By you?' he snorted. 'He calls me Harry!'

The reorganisation of the Scottish Office was in the air. It had become increasingly clear that the structure and relationship of the Scottish Departments were unsatisfactory. Elliot wanted to see a more logical approach and in November, 1936 he appointed a strong committee under Sir John Gilmour to carry out a full enquiry. The Gilmour Committee reported in September, 1937 and although the processing of its recommendations took an unconscionable time, there is no doubt that the decision to accept the Gilmour pattern owed much to Elliot. Formal acceptance, however, had to wait for his successor John Colville, as discussed in the next chapter.

In 1938 Elliot moved to the Ministry of Health, another task for which he had excellent credentials. (He was only the second doctor—Addison was the first—to take charge of the Ministry.) His organisation of the wartime evacuation scheme and the emergency hospital arrangements in England does not come within our purview. When Churchill formed his Cabinet in 1940 no room was found for Elliot. He loyally accepted what were for him minor jobs as D.A.A.G. Western Command and as Director of Public Relations at the War Office. He was Chairman of the Public Accounts Committee in 1942, but though he was asked to be High Commissioner in South Africa (which he declined) he was not again to be a Minister.

He was a member of the Shadow Cabinet during the lifetime of the Attlee Government, but with the return of the Conservatives in 1951 the only two Shadow spokesmen who were not made Ministers were W. S. Morrison and Elliot. Coote says that Elliot could have been Postmaster General or Minister of Pensions, but one suspects that these offers were made in the full knowledge that they would be refused. Churchill had not forgotten Elliot's support for Chamberlain, and the tolerance he afforded to other Munich men was not extended to Elliot. There may, however, be more to it than that. Churchill is reported to have said of Elliot 'he talks too much', and there was no sympathy between them. Elliot's Private Secretary thought that the coolness started when Elliot encouraged Churchill to stand, very unsuccessfully, at the Glasgow Rectorial Election in 1937. Churchill is justly praised for his magnanimity, but it is curious that the two figures who seem to have been excluded from it were both Scots—Elliot and Lord Reith. It is easier to see why Churchill was at odds with the gaunt, ascetic Presbyterian Reith, 'this Wuthering height', than to explain why he kept Elliot at a distance. Perhaps there is something in the Scottish character, as so exemplified, that did not appeal to the organiser of victory.

Those who served under Elliot have only one criticism of his tenure at the Scottish Office. When deputations, e.g. from local authorities, are received, it is the Minister's task to agree to their request, if he can (which is seldom), or to assure them that their point will be carefully considered (which it will be), and that a reply will be sent when the Minister has come to a decision. Elliot was impatient with this formula and used to interrupt to expose the fallacies in the arguments being put forward. The deputation would then withdraw less than pleased.

If Elliot's career has been discussed at greater length than might, at first sight, be justified by his time as Secretary of State in the late thirties, that is because he does not fit easily into any preconceived pattern. Though it is forty years since he ceased to be Keeper of the Great Seal, for long afterwards he was still active in Scottish affairs as a statesman, mature in years and wisdom. His successors were aware of his presence, whether he was holding court outside St Giles' after the National Service in Coronation year, or more formally addressing the General Assembly of the Church of Scotland as Lord High Commissioner. He was, simply, there.

But he was an uncomfortable man, at times a determined enigma. There was no saying when he would take up a chance theme and develop it in his own way. In the fifties, at a dinner in Edinburgh Castle for the Burmese Prime Minister, someone remarked on the irony of the company including both Thakin U and his previous incarcerator General Sir Philip Christison. After the Highland pipers had played for their entertainment Thakin U had annoyed Elliot by commenting that the Burmese also had pipers. When Elliot rose to propose the toast he dilated on the desirability of Prime Ministers having some experience of the inside of prisons.

Writing on the Scots, Elliot said, 'A nation is known not by its defence but by its attack—its attack in science, art, philosophy, even in war'. He was the most intellectual of all those who have been Secretary of State. He was a skilled and at times a compelling debater. He showed he had a gift for organisation. His ideas were always original. If he had been given longer in office, if he had been Scotland's Minister at a time when international events did not make Scottish problems shrink into the background, if there had been time for him to develop the philosophy of attack. . . . Politics is full of ifs.

NOTES

1 Sir Colin Coote, *A Companion of Honour*. London, 1965.
2 *Ibid.*
3 *A Scotsman's Heritage*, essay by Walter Elliot. London, 1932.
4 The *Spectator*, 30th May, 1958.

5 Walter Elliot, *Toryism and the Twentieth Century*. London, 1927.
6 *A Companion of Honour.*
7 *A Scotsman's Heritage.*
8 *Hansard*, 13th March, 1933. Vol. 275, col. 1680.
9 *Hansard*, 23rd November, 1937. Vol. 329, col. 1010.
10 Scottish Office Papers HH 36/120 in the Scottish Record Office.
11 *Ibid.*

CHAPTER VIII

The Proconsul and the Card

At the time of Elliot's translation to the Ministry of Health John Colville was Financial Secretary to the Treasury. As such he was assumed to have been groomed for early elevation to senior rank, and so it proved. (Many had thought that as a rising star in the Conservative hierarchy he might have been Secretary of State before Elliot.) Colville's time at the Scottish Office, which spanned the outbreak of war, was not particularly memorable, but equity demands the observation that he is remembered for an outstandingly successful tenure in a different field—as Governor of Bombay from 1943 to 1948. There his proconsular talents, his sense of history, his gift for humane administration, found full scope. The Presidency was dominated by the Congress party, but despite their opposition to the war he won their trust and regard. The crises during his five years at Government House included the Bombay dock explosion in 1944, the Royal Indian Mutiny in 1946, and the preparations for the eventual transfer of power. In all of these he acted with justice and shrewd political sense. The evidence for this can be found in contemporary records and in the fact that on four occasions he served temporarily as Viceroy.

Colville's grandfather founded the great steel enterprise that became Colvilles Ltd, and his father John Colville of Cleland had been Liberal M.P. for North-East Lanarkshire at the end of last century. At the outbreak of the 1914 War Colville was mobilised with the 6th Battalion, The Cameronians (Scottish Rifles). He served as a captain in France and was thrice wounded. His first two attempts to enter Parliament—at Motherwell in 1922 as National Liberal candidate, and at North Midlothian in 1929 by now as an avowed Conservative—were unsuccessful. At the General Election in the same year, however, he won the Midlothian seat which he retained throughout his parliamentary career. He soon earned a reputation in the House as an eloquent Protectionist and upholder of Scottish interests. As Secretary to the Department of Overseas Trade from 1931 to 1935 he led several important missions abroad. Thereafter he had a short spell as Parliamentary Under-

Secretary of State at the Scottish Office before going to the Treasury as Financial Secretary. The Chancellor's number two has to spend long hours in the complicated, less spectacular, work of his Department and Colville had gained the confidence of his colleagues, and of officials, by his unremitting application to duty before he succeeded to the Scottish Office.

He attended his first Cabinet meeting as Secretary of State on 18th May, 1938, and although there were many weightier items on the agenda the new Minister promptly obtained authority to adopt a benevolent attitude towards a Private Member's Bill to provide for the registration and inspection of nursing homes in Scotland.[1] But throughout the summer the Government's disposition to the Hitler menace overshadowed all other questions. This was the time of the unsuccessful Runciman Mission and as the tension over Czechoslovakia grew Colville took his full share in the Cabinet discussions. His interpretation of the mood of the country is of interest. A Cabinet Minute of 30th August, 1938, records that he 'thought that the question of going to war on behalf of Czechoslovakia, or indeed the imminence of war at the present time, had not really found its way into the mind of the public'.[2]

While Parliament watched the apparently inexorable march of events in Europe there was still time for domestic legislation and Colville introduced his first Bill, designed to assist the herring industry by giving grants and loans for the building of new types of vessel and by reorganising the Herring Industry Board with increased Exchequer aid. Winding up the Second Reading debate, his Parliamentary Under-Secretary (Scrymgeour-Wedderburn) reminded the House that Colville had long taken a keen interest in the problems that beset the herring fleet. At the Department of Overseas Trade he had carried through many trading agreements with foreign countries and in them had always increased the quota of herring to be exported from this country. At the Treasury he had been frequently involved in protracted discussions with those who thought that the Exchequer bounty should be extended more generously to the industry, and there was a nice irony in his having to defend the financial benefits which he had conceded in his previous office.

In Scottish Office history, though possibly not in the minds of the lieges, the most significant measure passed in Colville's time was the Reorganisation of Offices (Scotland) Bill which gave effect to the Gilmour Committee's recommendations. Gilmour had reported on

4th September, 1937, and there was growing impatience in the House to know when legislation would be forthcoming. Eventually, on 28th July, 1938, Colville, having been squeezed off the agenda at the previous meeting, obtained Cabinet authority to announce that the Government agreed generally with the Gilmour report and intended to legislate early in the next session so that the new organisation could 'be in operation as soon as it is possible to occupy the new Government building on Calton Hill, Edinburgh'.[3]

The Cabinet approved the Bill on 9th November, 1938,[4] and the Second Reading followed in December. It is difficult not to sympathise with Colville in having to pilot the long-expected Bill through the House. There had been much too lengthy a delay while the Gilmour recommendations were being examined by Departments. Meanwhile the new office was being built—appropriately, as cynics pointed out, on the site of the old Bridewell—but where was the Bill? There was an inevitable feeling of anticlimax when Members were at last allowed to debate the proposals. Moving the Second Reading, Colville referred to the three main considerations underlying the Gilmour enquiry—the desire of many Scots to see Scottish administration brought as far as possible nearer home, the general view that the machinery had grown up in a haphazard fashion, and the opportunity offered by the construction of the new building, which Gilmour had been specifically enjoined to bear in mind. Colville went on to describe the Bill's provisions lucidly, but mundanely, and though he claimed that they would produce 'the most comprehensive reform of Government in Scotland since 1885', he did not engender much enthusiasm.[5]

In fact the reception was decidedly lukewarm. There were expert contributions from two former Secretaries of State—Gilmour who naturally supported the pattern he had devised, and Sinclair who regretted the abolition of the Fisheries Board. Sinclair summed up the feeling of the House, saying that he could not get excited about the Bill and did not think 'anyone in Scotland is going to get excited about it'. (The details of the reorganisation have been discussed in Chapter II, dealing with the development of the Office.) Tom Johnston, who had been a member of the Gilmour Committee, complained that its terms of reference had been too restrictive, and roused himself to say that 'what we desire is less bureaucracy and more democracy'. Among other Members, McLean Watson could not see that any great things would accrue. J. J. Davidson was less restrained. 'This Bill is a piece of bunkum.' Joe Westwood, winding up for the Opposition, described the new scheme as a farthing a head revolutionary measure. A more interesting intervention had been that by the Rev. James Barr, who quoted Carlyle to liken Colville to a dull public clerk, more interesting because he used the identical quotation and comparison which he had evoked to denounce Gilmour on the earlier Reorganisation Bill eleven years previously. Barr evidently believed in economy of effort. The most entertaining passages in the debate were those when George Buchanan, Campbell Stephen, George Mathers, and others tried unsuccessfully to entice Colville to explain in more detail what would be the rôle of the Permanent Under-Secretary of State in the new organisation. It is not easy, as others have since discovered, to describe the duties of the Senior Dragoman who has to operate more by instinct than by prescription. Lord Advocate Cooper observed that while the Permanent Secretary would be assigned new responsibilities he was not mentioned in the legislation. With this Members had to be satisfied and the proceedings came peacefully to a close, so peacefully that when the Bill reached Report and Third Reading there was no debate. Colville, debonair and unruffled, had done his job. He had given the Scottish Office the basic structure which still remains.

Thereafter public and parliamentary interest was focused on preparations for the emergency—to use the statutory term—and useful departmental plans for reform had to be shelved. This accounts for Colville's anodyne statement on the recommendations of the Hilleary Report on the Highlands. On 1st August, 1939, he paid a well-deserved tribute to Hilleary, but explained that he could not proceed with projects that required the creation of new machinery. There would therefore be no Highland Development Commissioner, as Hilleary had proposed, since this would need legislation and the recruitment of additional staff. All he could offer was a programme of regular conferences with the Departments and authorities concerned.[6] Scottish Members, realising that this was inescapable in the circumstances, contented themselves with complaining that the statement had been made just before the House rose for the Summer Recess, so that there was no scope for debate.

For the remainder of his time Colville was deeply involved in discussions with local authorities concerting plans for evacuation, air raid precautions, and the manifold measures required to put the nation on a war footing. This was something at which he was particularly good. Confidence and determination to get the job done, an ability to explain and inspire, coupled with a profound knowledge of the wider issues, all helped him to direct business with acceptance. His officials noted an unlimited capacity for dealing with papers, interviews, and daily staff meetings. (There were occasional diversions, such as the necessity to defend the apparently hungry inhabitants of Ross-shire for taking gannets from the island of Sula Sgeir.)

He had one oddity in his habit of work. When he had studied a sub-mission, and possibly discussed it with those responsible, so that the way seemed clear for a particular course of action, he would suddenly make it clear that he was not ready to come to a decision. 'A pause for reflection' would be the comment, or the minute in his handwriting. This was not mere vacillation. He knew what he wanted to do, and the criticism of thinking too precisely on the event is explained and answered by his sensitive, all-embracing conscience. He was deter-mined to be fair to all points of view before he gave his assent. In practice, he wanted to sleep on it. The exasperation of his advisers, once they recognised his technique, was short-lived.

Colville was not a social reformer, though he was deeply interested in local government. (He served for six years on Lanarkshire County Council.) It is doubtful whether he would have found the adminis-tration of the welfare state congenial, but with his industrial back-ground he would have been active in the post-war campaign to attract new industry to Scotland. He was a loyal member of Tom Johnston's Council of State, comprising all former Secretaries of State, and helped to lay plans for post-war reconstruction. For one who, on the surface, appeared the embodiment of Toryism he was very receptive to the views of other parties. Towards the end of his career, when he was in the Upper Chamber as Lord Clydesmuir, he introduced a visiting Indian prince to his old political adversary David Kirkwood, who had also been ennobled, saying that he had been at pains to em-phasise that the House of Lords tolerated all shades of political belief. That was right, Kirkwood replied. He had been clobbered by the police, he had been thrown out of the House of Commons, he had been in manacles, but now he was the Right Honourable Lord Kirkwood. Later Kirkwood returned to enquire if his response had been adequate. Colville assented. In that event, Kirkwood rejoined, Colville could do as much for him on another occasion.

To summarise, Colville's abilities matched the needs of the time. While the centurions were mustering the civil authorities had likewise to be mobilised. The official machine had to be adapted and kept in motion. This was a task for a Proconsul who could ensure that his lines of communication were in good working order. This was the task that Colville undertook enthusiastically, efficiently, and without incurring enmity. When Churchill broadened the basis of his Cabinet in the summer of 1940 Colville was among those who had to give way. It was in character that he immediately took up duty as a Colonel on the staff of Lowland District.

In May, 1940, Ernest Brown took Colville's place, but neither his arrival nor the business of the Scottish Office attracted much attention at the time. In the same week the Germans invaded Holland, Belgium, and Luxemburg, and for the rest of the long summer the Government and the country were entirely concerned with the B.E.F.'s rearguard action, the escape from Dunkirk, and contingency plans to resist the invasion that seemed imminent. National survival was now at risk, and the improvised mobilisation of the Local Defence Volunteers (later the Home Guard) was of more significance than the exploitation of domestic Scottish issues. The function of all Departments dealing with home affairs was simply to carry out the duties imposed by the exigencies of the War. The Scottish Office was scarcely recognisable from what it had been a few months previously. Colville had supervised the move to a wartime organisation. Government activity had been greatly extended at short notice to cover all aspects of everyday life. Much of the extra administrative work was essentially transient in nature, and the civil service had been rapidly increased by the recruitment of large numbers of temporary staff. There was no room for the studied refinement of policy.

In the context of Scottish Office history it is a pity that Ernest Brown was not in charge at a more promising time. There is no saying what the ebullient Brown might have achieved, and it would have been a matter of great interest to see what emerged from his demagogic approach. For he was a demagogue. As one reporter put it, 'He's a Card, all right. But he's a Baptist. And a teetotaller, forbye!'

Harold MacMillan once observed that when he saw M.P.s rummaging in their lockers at the start of a session he would not have been surprised to see a Member oiling a cricket bat. If the timing had been different, one of these might have been Ernest Brown. He was a keen sportsman, and rugby football, yachting, and cricket were at various times among his addictions. It was said that when he was playing in a parliamentary cricket match at Lords he called 'Come one' to his batting partner with such compelling force that he ran out a batsman who was playing at the Oval. This droll tale exemplifies his most notorious characteristic—an exceptionally loud, reverberating voice. Stentorian is, for once, not a cliché. There is another story, sufficiently hallowed by repetition to acquire a patina of veracity, which reinforces the point. Stanley Baldwin on his way through the Central Lobby asked what caused the booming noise. That, he was told, was Ernest Brown talking to a constituent. Why, enquired the Prime Minister, did he not use the telephone?

Brown's unusual oratorical gifts, coupled with his evangelical fervour, probably inspired him to seek a parliamentary career. Coming from a Baptist family from whom he learned the art of public speaking, Brown became, and remained, active in the Baptist cause. Throughout his life he officiated as a lay preacher, and Scottish Office staff who accompanied him on his journeys round Scotland learned that he was as fluent in the pulpit as at the Despatch Box. With his arresting platform manner he gravitated to the Liberal Party and was soon in demand as an exceptionally effective spokesman, particularly adept at overcoming the hazards of addressing audiences in the open air.

In the 1914 War Brown joined the Sportsman's Battalion and was commissioned in the Somerset Light Infantry, being mentioned in despatches, and winning the Military Cross and the Italian Silver Star. He stood unsuccessfully as the Liberal candidate for Salisbury in 1918 and 1922, and for Mitcham in 1923, before being elected for Rugby in November, 1923. He was defeated in the following year, but in 1927 he made a courageous sortie to win at Leith. This was very much a personal triumph for a stranger to the constituency. He persuaded large numbers of Conservative adherents—the press estimate was in excess of 3000—to vote for him, and retained the seat till the 1945 General Election.

There was lively speculation in the Lobby about how the man with the built-in loudhailer would fare in the restricted confines of the Chamber, but it was not long before his ability was recognised. In 1931 he was Parliamentary Secretary at the Ministry of Health and was also appointed Chairman of the Select Committee on Procedure. On promotion to be Secretary of the Mines Department he soon showed that he was a vigorous and active negotiator. He had by now mastered the difficult genre of aggressive defence, as was apparent in his speeches on behalf of his Department when it came under heavy criticism after the Gresford disaster. In 1935 he was appointed Minister of Labour and was largely responsible for the Agricultural Unemployment Insurance Act of 1936 which for the first time extended the insurance principle to

workers in agriculture and forestry. He did not shrink from controversy. He was often attacked for the alleged deficiencies of his policy,
and with the massive unemployment figures it could hardly be otherwise, but in 1937 he received the unusual accolade of a unanimous vote
of thanks from the Trades Union Congress for his part in reorganising
the distributive trades. By now the Ministry was deeply involved in
preparations for National Service, which was added to its title in 1939.
There is more than one view about Brown's effectiveness as Minister
of Labour. He continued to argue the rightness of what he was doing,
particularly in the allocation of manpower between industry and the
Armed Forces, but Ernest Bevin who succeeded him said he found the
Department in a state of chaos. One thing is, however, clear. Though
Brown was a great reader, and an avid book collector, the owner of an
extensive library which he kept in his improbable flat in Shaftesbury
Avenue, he was not an original thinker. His contribution was to seize
the official brief and proclaim its content, stridently but persuasively,
as though it had been distilled from his private thoughts.

This was not an art form at which his predecessors at the Scottish
Office had excelled, and one can only guess how Brown would have
countered, say, Nationalist critics in the seventies. An intriguing conjecture. As it turned out, Brown's first appearance on the Front Bench
as Secretary of State could not have come at a more difficult time. On
18th June, 1940, Churchill gave Parliament a stern warning of what
lay ahead, concluding with his 'This was their finest hour' peroration.
But the King's government had to go on, and the House immediately
moved into Committee of Supply to consider the Estimates of the
Department of Health for Scotland. In the atmosphere of painful self-
criticism and defiant resolution engendered by the Prime Minister this
might have produced a sense of bathos. Undauntedly Brown launched
into a skilful summary of the work of his Department—where he had
just arrived—referring in sequence to the emergency hospital service,
evacuation, and education problems. He commented thankfully on the
1939 reorganisation of the Scottish Office, without which wartime
administration would have been infinitely more difficult, if not impossible. George Mathers complimented him on 'compressing into a
very small compass a great deal of information'.[7] A month later the
House debated another Scottish Estimate, that of the Department of
Agriculture. Mathers pointed out that the circumstances were now
marginally different from those of 18th June when, following the
Prime Minister's statement, Members had been reluctant to enter upon

any extended discussion of purely Scottish affairs.[8] The indefatigable Brown was ready again with an exhaustive review of the government's agricultural policy.

Agriculture was one of Brown's main concerns as Secretary of State. When *The Times* came to write his obituary, the only reference to his stay at the Scottish Office was the remark that he had made a special study of hill sheep farming, and got a special subsidy for breeding ewes, his last act being 'to frame a Bill to continue the Arterial Drainage Act of 1930'.[9] Agriculture had, in fact, to be given a high priority in view of the need to increase home food production. Brown actively supported the claims of the hill farmers, whose peculiar difficulties are not always recognised by the Ministry of Agriculture, and it was with unconcealed pleasure that he announced a new subsidy to be payable 'on each breeding ewe in hill flocks, including shearling ewes or gimmers'. His Land Drainage (Scotland) Bill was presented in his last week of office.

His subsequent career can be briefly mentioned in order to complete the picture. When Malcolm MacDonald was surprisingly appointed High Commissioner in Canada in February, 1941, Brown having, according to *The Times*, proved himself 'an acceptable and energetic Secretary of State for Scotland',[10] succeeded him at the Ministry of Health. There he faced recurring bouts of abuse, particularly on the ramifications of evacuation and the housing of warworkers. In June, 1943, a group of M.P.s tabled a motion of no confidence in his administration, but his supporters easily outnumbered them. A few months later he was moved to the non-departmental job of Chancellor of the Duchy of Lancaster. He was Minister of Aircraft Production in the Caretaker government of 1945. He also became Chairman of the National Liberals and made overtures for a reconciliation with the Liberals under Sir Archibald Sinclair, but this called for more tact and self-restraint than he possessed.

None of this tells us a great deal about the man. Some further indication of his inner temperament can be found in his replies to questions in the House. On 16th October, 1940, he was asked what he had done about a resolution from the Council of the Baptist Union of Scotland, which *inter alia* deprecated the continuance of dog-racing at a time of national emergency. Brown's lifelong devotion to the Baptist movement must have made this difficult for him, but the reply was bland and pragmatic. He said he had explained to the Union that facilities for relaxation must be provided if the war effort was to be maintained, and that 'it would be unreasonable to deprive those who wish to attend race meetings of all opportunity of doing so'.[11] An orthodox return to the bowler.

There were frequent complaints about wartime drunkenness, calls for more drastic licensing laws, restrictions on the supply of alcohol, and so on. Brown was a confirmed, insistent abstainer. One one occasion, when he was on his way to pay an official visit to a canteen near St Andrew's House, he turned back at the door on hearing that a licensed bar was one of the main attractions for thirsty warworkers. But it was seldom that he allowed his personal convictions to obtrude. Asked about a representation from the Scottish Temperance Alliance he went no further than the oracular statement that 'a careful watch is being kept on the incidence of consumption'.[12]

The way in which Ministers handle deputations is often revealing. Brown's method was very individual. When the suppliants had taken their places round the table he would allow them no more than a few introductory sentences before interrupting with a loud, positive 'I know!' Thereafter the deputation would be lucky if it was allowed any further chance to develop its case. Brown rapidly explained that he knew exactly what the alleged grievance was. By so doing he demonstrated that he had done his homework, but he did not convince his audience that he recognised that they were entitled to a reasonable discussion of the merits. (This is reminiscent of Walter Elliot who could not refrain from getting the better of the argument with those who had come to depute before him.)

The most fascinating question about Brown relates not to what he did as Secretary of State, but to what he showed no interest in doing. The query can be further defined by enquiring how it came about that Brown's tenure was so unlike that of his successor Tom Johnston. Brown's technique was to assimilate all the details of schemes submitted to him, and when he was satisfied of their validity—he was no mere rubber stamp—proclaim them with such vigour that he obliterated his critics. What was feasible was his criterion. Officials who worked closest with him were often astonished at the speed with which he would absorb the most complicated submission, but there was little sign of an imaginative, long-term approach. It was invariably an *ad hoc* answer that he sought. As we will see, however, Johnston started to manipulate the mood of national unity to Scotland's advantage, and to prepare the ground for post-war reconstruction, as soon as he took up office.

There are two possible explanations for this radical difference in attitudes. The most easily identifiable one is historical. In one of the conversations Brown had with me in the fifties, when we were exchanging wartime experiences, he said that there were a few weeks in May and June, 1940, when the country completely lost its nerve. Faced with the sight of the survivors from the B.E.F. shipped back to the Channel ports without their equipment, and learning that the French had laid down their arms, there was a strong disposition among Ministers to believe that an immediate negotiated peace was the best that we could expect. It was Churchill's unassailable achievement to transform these days of despair into his own mould of resolution. Churchill did it, Brown said. Not perhaps an original thought, though Brown was emphatic that Duff Cooper's part in restoring morale was seriously underrated. But having seen the edge of the precipice the country remained numbed for far longer than anyone was prepared to admit. No one was willing to think far ahead. That meant that Ministers' job was to keep blowing the trumpet, and that, Brown reminded me, was something which he knew about. He did not lack self-confidence.

The second explanation is more personal. The only Englishman to be Secretary of State, Brown was always a somewhat exotic figure on the Scottish scene. When he took up office he was given an ironic welcome, as the representative of an alien minority, by Sir Thomas Moore, M.P. He had no roots in, or previous connection with, Scotland. He was a competent, hard-working, popular constituency Member, as his record shows, but it is very doubtful if he had any real feeling for native Scottish conditions or aspirations. Alleged inequities in the allocation of wartime factories, or in the drift south of the Scottish labour force, that enraged Johnston, were of less importance to Brown, provided they did not impede the prosecution of the war. In his customary black suit and come-to-Jesus collar, Brown was essentially a performer, an impresario. There is no reason to accuse him of cynicism, but one wonders if he had any preference among the various Departments where he served. What interested him was the opportunity to display his oratorical talents to advocate a cause, preferably a contentious cause, which he had decided was the right one.

Most governments, especially Conservative governments, include one, or maybe two Ministers who on the face of it are unlikely choices. Ernest Marples, Charles Hill, and J. R. Bevins suggest themselves as examples. Brown was an unlikely Secretary fo State. On the eve of polling day at the 1945 General Election Brown indulged in some interesting speculation with the P.R.O. at the Scottish Office. The subject was which Ministerial appointment he would be offered. Brown was not the only Minister who failed to foresee the Conservative débâcle, but he may have been the most astounded. He could not believe that the days of the trumpet were over.

An incident with the Royal Commission on Scottish Affairs in 1953 will serve as an epilogue to this chapter. Brown, who had been invited to give evidence as a former Scottish Minister, asked me as the Commission's Secretary to have breakfast with him on the morning when he was due to appear. He said he was rather out of touch with contemporary developments and wanted an assessment of current political problems, the matters that were engaging the Commission's closest attention, and the questions on which he would be pressed. For good measure he enquired about the personalities who would interrogate him. I gave him as informative a summary as time and the circumstances allowed.

It was the Commission's practice to ask witnesses whether they wished to make a statement or confine themselves to answering points made in discussion. With one exception—Sir John (Lord Redcliffe-) Maud who appeared with a cigar and a garden party waistcoat to deliver his enchanting, elegant discourse—they had all opted for the easier alternative of dealing with questions. Brown had no doubt what he would do. The windows rattled as he poured out a succinct summary of the topics in the Commission's mind, interlaced with some cautionary comments derived from his own experience. A few perfunctory queries out of politeness, and the Commission adjourned, wiser but bemused. Brown was a Card.

NOTES

1 Cab. 23/93, Public Record Office.
2 Cab. 23/94.
3 *Ibid.*
4 Cab. 23/96.
5 *Hansard*, 13th December, 1938. Vol. 342, cols. 1838-51.
6 *Hansard*, 1st August, 1939. Vol. 350, col. 2171.
7 *Hansard*, 18th June, 1940. Vol. 362, col. 77.

8 *Hansard,* 17th July, 1940. Vol. 363, col. 258.

9 *The Times,* 16th February, 1962.

10 *The Times,* 10th February, 1941.

11 *Hansard,* 16th October, 1940. Vol. 365, col. 709.

12 *Hansard,* 15th October, 1940. Vol. 365, col. 570.

CHAPTER IX

The Lion Rampant

Tom Johnston arrived in office with some refreshingly innocent prejudices. In his early years he had earned a formidable reputation in journalism as the founder of the lively, and at times notorious, weekly *Forward*, which he edited for some twenty-nine years before handing over the chair to Emrys Hughes. He later assembled a collection of searing articles, which had appeared in *Forward*, lampooning the Scottish aristocracy, and published it under the title of *Our Scots Noble Families*. This impertinent pasquinade enjoyed a wide circulation. According to Johnston over 120,000 copies were sold, and 'it rankled in many an old family bosom long after it had left the market'.[1] But eventually it became an embarrassment and led to his being excluded from membership of the Caledonian Club in London. There were credible reports that he eventually tried to buy all the extant volumes with a view to suppressing them, and certainly it is impossible to find one except in the Copyright Libraries. Since it is not now generally obtainable a few quotations may serve to give something of its flavour.

The book was an undisguised indictment of the landed classes in Scotland. 'The House of Lords is composed largely of descendants of successful pirates and rogues. . . . Today the shadow of the "Big House" blights and withers the soul of the villager; he votes, thinks, and prays (or pretends to), as factor and flunkey suggest. . . . The peasant has been ruthlessly swept aside to make room for the pheasant.'[2] After claiming that 'We have convicted some 33 of our Scots "Noble Families" of taking in the year 1874 land rents (mostly from stolen territory) amounting to over £2,602,000' he goes on to give examples of 'the additional plunder they secured by foisting themselves into sinecures by abstracting from the public funds huge remunerations for more or less imaginary services'.

The general approach is well seen in his comment on the Boyle (Earl of Glasgow) family. 'The family motto is "Dominus providebit" —the Lord will provide. So far the task has been undertaken by the working classes of the West of Scotland.'

His attitude to the Roseberys is more germane to our enquiry. He starts gently enough. 'The Primroses, the family to which the Earl of Rosebery belongs, have only sprung up in comparatively recent times; and consequently they have not had many opportunities of perpetrating land robberies or of steeping themselves in deceit, cruelty, and blood.' But the fifth Lord Rosebery had infuriated Johnston by recommending frugal habits for the workers. The family's acquisitions of land in Scotland provoked him to say that 'although he killed the Scots Small Holdings Bill, he himself has taken care to see that he has room to plant a few cabbages'. And his parting word on the 'Apostle of Thrift' is 'looking after Number One, persuasive, dexterous, words meaning little to him; a soupçon of the cynic about him; ploughing the lonely furrow'.

But Johnston had not finished with the Roseberys. 'His son and heir, Lord Dalmeny, M.P. for Midlothian—M.P. until such time as the workers there waken up politically, appears to be a bright specimen of the young nobility, if we may judge from the sporting pages of the *Glasgow Herald* of 3rd April, 1908.' Beneath the headline 'Lord Dalmeny the object of a hostile demonstration' the *Herald* reported a regrettable incident at the Vale of Aylesbury Steeplechase when Kilcullen II ridden by Dalmeny led the first time round, but allowed a horse that had fallen and been remounted to beat it. 'Lord Dalmeny thereupon met with a hostile demonstration from the occupants of the grandstand and others, and there was considerable booing.' Johnston adds 'Comment on this would be improper'. No libel writ was, however, issued.

This equine anecdote has its own piquancy. The Lord Dalmeny who features in it not only succeeded his father as the sixth Earl of Rosebery. He also succeeded Johnston as Regional Commissioner for the Scottish Region in 1941, as Secretary of State in 1945, and eventually as Chairman of the Scottish Tourist Board. Latterly Johnston admitted that the 'rather pungent and scurrilous' series of tracts in *Our Noble Families* had tended to be onesided, and in public he and Rosebery displayed an appearance of respect for each other. Rosebery would add that he expected to see Johnston following him as Senior Steward of the Jockey Club.

The aristocracy was not Johnston's only innate prejudice. He disliked the English. The Renaissance Pope Pius II after his visit to Scotland (before his elevation) recorded that the Scots liked nothing as much as hearing the English abused. He would have found that Johnston upheld the tradition. When both Churchill and Attlee offered him a seat in the Upper House in 1945 Johnston was explicit that one of his reasons for declining was that he had already had enough of London. He even thought of forming a band of kindred spirits 'who would refuse to travel south for residence' and 'who would fight it out in Scotland'. He often reminded audiences that on his later, and reluctant, journeys to the Capital he used to finger the return ticket in his pocket as a talisman guaranteeing his speedy escape.

Another prejudice of a different order was his conviction that all arguments should be supported by a flood of statistics. Long after he was out of office (when the Scottish Office had been relieved of the task of supplying the tables) he would fix his adversary with a pene-trating glance and draw out his diary. 'It might interest you to know' would be the usual prologue to a stream of incomprehensible, and often obsolete, figures relating to the number of tourists visiting Scotland or megawatts produced by the Hydro Board. It was a successful device, as he conveniently omitted any basis for comparison.

These are the warts. But they do not detract from the success of his tenure at the Scottish Office. In time it became folklore, and Arthur Turner's verdict in 1952 is still the accepted one. He said that Johnston

> secured more for his country than any recent holder of the office. He seems to have stood out strongly for Scottish interests against the pressure of his English colleagues in Cabinet meetings, and he was responsible for the inauguration of several measures which have undoubtedly been, and will continue to be very beneficial.[4]

How did he acquire this almost mythological reputation, much higher than any of those who went before him and an onerous legacy for those who came afterwards? There were some portents in his early career. Born in Kirkintilloch in 1881, after attending Lenzie Academy and Glasgow University he soon showed that he had an uncanny gift for getting things done. There was the floating of *Forward* with a paid up capital of £60. He was instrumental in setting up the Kirkintilloch Municipal Bank, the first of its kind, and protecting it against its critics. There were other innovations during his time in local govern-ment, but he was soon drawn to national politics and was elected Member for West Stirlingshire in 1922. In 1924 he was returned for Dundee, and was again elected for West Stirlingshire in 1929. From 1929 to 1931 he was Parliamentary Under-Secretary of State at the Scottish Office under William Adamson, the first Labour Secretary of

State. Adamson was not much at home in dealings with Treasury Ministers, and Johnston acting on his behalf soon made his presence felt in Whitehall. As he put it, 'There used to be a joke at the Treasury that so persistent were the demands from the Scottish Office for money that they ran to take in the cat's milk when they heard us coming'.[5] This was the time when unemployment overshadowed all other domestic issues and Johnston was a member of the Cabinet Committee under J. H. Thomas charged with producing public works projects. Characteristically, Johnston's contribution was a practical one. He wanted to build a road round Loch Lomond as a tourist attraction. But the Unemployment Committee made little progress and much to his surprise Johnston was appointed Lord Privy Seal and told to take charge of relief schemes. MacDonald's government did not last long enough for anything substantial to be done.

Johnston's reflection on these years is of interest as it reveals a theme he was to develop when he became Secretary of State. In the late twenties he came firmly to the conclusion that there were many important public issues which ought to be removed entirely from the arena of partisan political strife. Examples were unemployment, road construction, and water supplies. Throughout his career, both at the Scottish Office and later in other appointments, he was the zealous advocate of government by consent.

At the General Election in 1932 he stood for Dunbartonshire in the Labour interest but the Scottish Nationalists contested the seat and polled enough votes to secure the return of the National Government candidate. J. M. McCormick, the Scottish Nationalist leader, was later to admit that his Party was mistaken in opposing him.[6] The Labour Party was then in a state of disarray; George Lansbury was elected as leader almost on a caretaker basis. Johnston, in view of his standing as a former Lord Privy Seal and his reputation with the public, might have taken over from him if he had been in the House. In the event his energies were to be deployed on behalf of his own country.

In the spring of 1939 he was invited to become Regional Commissioner for Civil Defence in Scotland. He was a natural choice for the job, and the vigour he displayed in it made his promotion to be Secretary of State inevitable. As Regional Commissioner he had to supervise the civil defence arrangements; to persuade and convince the laggards among the local authorities; to remove difficulties and jarring edges; to keep up civilian morale: and, in short, 'to prepare for the worst and hope for the best'. To all of these tasks he brought his own down-to-earth common-sense. He was skilful in his dealings with the press, who knew that he would insert some Scottish dimension which they could develop. On one occasion, however, his publicity arrangements misfired. In a daring exploit, which in Churchill's words warmed the cockles of the British heart in the gloom of a wartime winter, H.M.S. *Cossack* had boarded the German ship *Altmark* inside Norwegian territorial waters and rescued a large number of British seamen. Churchill was anxious to forestall protests about the violation of international law and instructed Johnston to make the most of the dreadful condition of the starved prisoners when the *Cossack* landed them at Leith. Johnston mustered a full attendance of London and American pressmen, along with bands and a large welcoming crowd, at the dockside. But the *Cossack*'s crew had meanwhile re-equipped the prisoners and fed them so well that they could not have looked more cheerful. Johnston used to tell this story against himself, though he had no great sense of humour.

At the beginning of 1941 Churchill told Johnston that he wanted him to be Secretary of State in his reconstructed government. Johnston protested that he was doing a useful job as Regional Commissioner and that he 'loathed London'. Realising that to argue with the Prime Minister was like a rabbit trying to escape from a boa constrictor, Johnston managed to make two stipulations before he accepted. He said he would not take a salary while in office, and he proposed to set up a Council of State, composed of all the living ex-Secretaries for Scotland, irrespective of Party. He would expect the Prime Minister's backing whenever they were agreed on a Scottish issue. Churchill promised to look sympathetically upon anything about which Scotland was unanimous.

By the autumn of 1941 Johnston had persuaded Lord Alness, the one surviving Scottish Secretary, and Sinclair, Elliot, Colville, and Ernest Brown, all former Secretaries of State, to serve on the Council. Their function was described as being to collaborate with the Secretary of State in surveying problems of post-war reconstruction in Scotland—a far-seeing, and at the time an optimistic, remit. It was fundamental that the Council would act only when they were all agreed. In that event they would be expected to seek the agreement of their own parties, and where there was no agreement the matter would be laid aside. The Council met at intervals until 1945, and with their consent Johnston set up enquiries into such questions as hydro-electricity, the herring industry, hill sheep farming, and land settlement.

Johnston's action in seeking the advice and assistance of the Council, and in making public that he was doing so, was shrewd. He was applauded for an imaginative concept, and more important, he exploited the prevailing national spirit of co-operation for specific Scottish purposes. His claim that he had roused a new spirit of independence and hope, not least in the civil service, was euphoric, but may be pardoned. He was seldom backward in taking credit, and he could not refrain from adding that the Scots could now meet the English without any inferiority complex. (This may be thought self-revelatory.) But the fact remains that this experiment in political amity was entirely due to his initiative. It also realised an idea which Johnston had cherished since his days as a junior Minister.

It was, however, an experiment which could succeed only in the exceptional circumstances of the wartime coalition. There were perfunctory attempts to revive it. For example, in March, 1950, Hector McNeil, as Secretary of State, assured Sir Will Y. Darling in the House that he was considering this 'most carefully, but not hastily'.[7] McNeil had no intention of recalling the Council. The Royal Commission on Scottish Affairs referred wistfully to the possibility of the Council meeting again, but recognised that the Party leaders were unlikely to condone agreement in a Scottish context, even by their senior figures, to measures which might be opposed in Great Britain terms. The significance of this body is that it was, though temporary, a purely Scottish development. There was nothing like it in England. No one proposed that, say, former Home Secretaries—there were usually some at large—should unite to reach agreement on the discharge of Home Office functions. Churchill would have been surprised, possibly irritated, if anyone had suggested such a course. But Johnston had enlisted his support for the Council in Scotland.

No one could doubt Johnston's native patriotism. But despite his distaste for the English (he was criticised in Whitehall as a Little Scotlander), he was at heart no more than lukewarm towards the Nationalist movement. This was another facet of his realism. To his mind the real flame-throwers of Scottish nationalism were 'the frustrations and irritations of government and administration by a long distance bureaucracy' and he set about meeting these complaints by demanding the recognition of Scottish requirements within the existing framework. His concern was to exact what he wanted from the English, on his own terms. Although he had seconded the Rev. James Barr's pre-war Home Rule Bill he also resolved at the same time

that what he wanted was a Scottish Council of Industry and Development, which he eventually achieved. This is consistent with his declared
unease lest the Home Rule movement in the thirties should result in
the Scots getting political power without having an adequate economy
to administer. In practice, during Johnston's time at the Scottish
Office wartime exigencies submerged most nationalist activities. Their
main manifestation was the election of a Scottish Nationalist member
at a by-election, in breach of the truce between the Parties.

An assessment of what Johnston achieved at the Scottish Office is
made easier by his own description of what he hoped to bring about.
In his *Memories* he explains with engaging candour the things he was
certain he could do, even in wartime. His objectives were (*a*) the
creation of an industrial parliament to begin attracting industries
north, face up to the Whitehall Departments (his penchant for tribal
warfare appears again), and reduce emigration across the Border; (*b*)
the establishment of a public corporation to harness Highland water
power for electricity; (*c*) the teaching of citizenship in schools; (*d*)
reform of the Scottish rating system; (*e*) development of the hospitals;
(*f*) an increase in afforestation; and (*g*) a Convention of Scottish M.P.s
to meet in Edinburgh. This formidable programme provokes two
immediate comments. First, it was evidence, if any were needed, of
Johnston's remarkable confidence in his ability to manipulate the
machine. Second, it did not stem from any particular Party doctrine. It
was the product of his appreciation, over years in public life, of what
Scotland needed. We will look at his proposals *seriatim*.

The Scottish Council on Industry, later the Scottish Council
(Development and Industry), was formed in February, 1942. From the
start it drew strength from its bipartisan membership, including those
representing employers, the Scottish T.U.C., local authorities, Chambers of Commerce, and the Scottish Banks. It worked closely with the
Scottish Office. The background to Johnston's initiative is relevant.
The Board of Trade had no mandate to favour Scottish projects and
there was no machinery for making industrial contacts. The Scottish
climate was bleak; heavy industry was apparently in irreversible
decline; motor manufacturing had gone south (a source of great
resentment to Johnston); in wartime Scotland had been assigned more
storage capacity than rearmament plant; and there was a steady drift
of labour to work in the new factories in England.

In this unpromising atmosphere the Scottish Council was remarkably
skilful in stimulating new projects. Johnston's label of an 'industrial

parliament' may be flying a bit high, but between 1942 and the General Election of 1945 some 700 new enterprises or substantial extensions had been authorised in Scotland, and the Supply departments had been persuaded to commit £12m. on factories and plant. The Scottish Council rapidly became the most effective pressure group in Great Britain and its success is still envied by English regions. Whitehall Departments often complained that in one respect the Scottish industrialist had a positive advantage compared with his competitors in the South. The English firm could approach the appropriate Ministry through the local M.P. The Scottish industrialist could also enlist the aid of the Secretary of State, if necessary in Cabinet, and he in turn could cite an impressive consensus of support from the Scottish Council. The Council's activities feature later in this book, especially for their sortie into economic planning with the Toothill Report (Chapter XIV). Meanwhile two things may be said. Although they later seemed to develop a vested interest in their own advancement, as these bodies do, and to arrogate responsibilities that were not properly theirs, their beneficial effect on the Scottish economy cannot be overestimated. Nor could they have operated so successfully without the close support of, and at times near-integration with, the Scottish Office. Their joint activities in themselves provide strong justification for the existence of a 'geographical' Minister.

Johnston acted with speed to set up the North of Scotland Hydro-Electric Board. In October, 1941, with the agreement of the Council of State, Lord Cooper was commissioned to carry out an enquiry. He reported ten months later (Cmd. 6406) and the Bill to give effect to his proposals was introduced in the House of Commons in January, 1943. Johnston had cashed his credit with the Cabinet; the members of the Council of State had been active; and for the first time since 1832 a major Scottish Bill was passed without a division. Of course there were objections, from lairds, environmentalists, and others, both in the House and outside. One of the most eccentric came from a Welsh M.P., Professor W. J. Gruffydd, who painted a frightening picture.

> A deadlier method of destroying what remains of Highland life I cannot conceive. It is a method which will end for ever the life and civilisation of the Highlands, and substitute for them not even the life and civilisation of the Connemara cabin; it will be the life and civilisation of the Dublin slum.[8]

Johnston dealt with this and other criticisms in a cavalier way. Nothing could stop the impetus he had started.

When he ceased to be Secretary of State he succeeded Lord Airlie as the Board's Chairman and continued to dispose of objections to each Hydro scheme. When electricity was being nationalised under the Great Britain Act of 1947 there was alarm lest the Board should be absorbed in the new authority. This was vigorously opposed by the Scottish Office, and Johnston had a trick or two of his own. He persuaded both Shinwell (Minister of Fuel and Power) and Herbert Morrison, the architect of the nationalisation measures, to come to Scotland and commit themselves to retaining the Board's independence.

Johnston took pride in the Board's creation and operation. It was another Scottish experiment, this time in Scottish public ownership. Two misgivings may be mentioned. The Board's remit enjoined it to promote the social and economic welfare of the Highlands. This function was not pursued with any notable success. (The Hydro Board staff saw their primary task as being the generation of electricity.) Johnston could point to isolated projects—the encouragement of stone quarrying, a trout laboratory at Faskally, and experiments with the gas turbine—but their effect was limited. If the Board had been more energetic in this field, or had devised an overall strategy, the case for the later appointment of the Highlands and Islands Development Board (Chapter XVI) would have been even weaker. Johnston also refused to earmark power at preferential rates for large industrial concerns as an incentive to attract them to set up factories in the Highlands. Most responsible opinion at the time thought this was a mistake. But these are minor blemishes on a major achievement.

Johnston met with mixed fortune in the attainment of his other objectives. His efforts to introduce the teaching of citizenship in schools and to provide instruction in mechanical engineering were unavailing. This was unfortunate as few Scottish Ministers have found time to interest themselves in the school curriculum. The reform of the Scottish rating system had to wait another fifteen years before the Sorn Committee's recommendations were given effect in the Valuation and Rating (Scotland) Act, 1956. But Johnston was ahead of his Party in realising that the poor quality of much Scottish housing was partly due to landlords being saddled with owner's rates. One statistic that stuck in his mind was that between 1918 and 1939 English private builders had constructed thirty houses to every one in Scotland.

Future historians of the National Health Service may well give Johnston credit as a pioneer. He insisted that the Civil Defence Hospitals, first in the Clyde Valley and later throughout Scotland, should extend their facilities for specialist examination to civilian war workers. He secured the co-operation of both general practitioners and the voluntary hospitals. Hector McNeil was later to say that Johnston's Emergency Hospital Scheme was his greatest administrative achievement.

In 1943 the Forestry Commissioners, not then answerable to a Minister, said that if they had to be brought under direct Ministerial control they should be responsible to the Lord President. Johnston took this much amiss, and thanks to his vigorous representations control of the Commission was vested in the Minister of Agriculture jointly with the Secretary of State. He also insisted that four out of the nine Forestry Commissioners should be Scots. At the end of the war Johnston served for a time as a Commissioner and was Chairman of the Commission's Scottish national committee. Both as Secretary of State and later Johnston showed himself alive to the folly of importing timber that we could grow ourselves and to the necessity of increasing the planting programme in Scotland.

The last of his objectives on assuming office, a meeting of the Scottish M.P.s in Edinburgh, proved to be a non-event. Twenty-seven M.P.s attended but Johnston soon concluded that the meeting served no useful purpose. 'It had no teeth', and it was not repeated.

Some of his remaining activities at the Scottish Office may be briefly mentioned, as evidence of his ubiquitous energy and as showing what a determined Scottish Minister could, or could not, do. With the active assistance of the Council of State he got approval for a Bill to control the rents of furnished dwellings, which did not come within the protection of the Rent Restrictions Acts. This was opposed by the Minister of Health in England, where similar legislation came much later. At an entirely different level he set up the Scottish Ancestry Research Council which undertook to provide applicants with a Scottish pedigree in return for a modest fee. This aroused some ribald comment, but, as we have already noted, Johnston was not handicapped by a sense of humour.

There were defeats as well. He failed in a long-term battle with the Minister of Agriculture to obtain a uniform price for milk throughout Great Britain, with the result that Scottish producers continued to get less per gallon than English farmers. As early as 1943 he foresaw that the day of the Planner was about to arrive and he contrived another version of government by consent, this time at the local level. Two regional associations of local authorities were set up for the East and

West of Scotland, with Sir Frank Mears and Sir Patrick Abercrombie as consultants, to prepare outline plans. Much useful work emerged, but Johnston was particularly resentful at the eventual disbandment of these two bodies. Lastly, he confessed his disappointment at failing to get Prestwick designated as an international airport.

By any standards Johnston's record is outstanding. He left his stamp on many of the diverse functions carried out by the Scottish Office and showed how they could be exercised to the greater benefit of the Scottish economy. He was fortunate in his timing, in coming to office during the wartime coalition, and in being able to rely on Churchill's benevolence. But that does not detract from his personal contribution, which has not been equalled, and Turner's verdict, which we have noted, stands the test of time.

Under his direction the Scottish Office moved into a higher gear. It is no criticism of earlier bureaucrats to say that in Johnston's time the civil servants at St Andrew's House were conscious of a different sense of purpose. Knowing how much clout their Minister carried, they greatly enjoyed curing English Departments of any vestigial belief that they were the vassals of Whitehall, and inevitably they canvassed their proposals with much more urgency. Johnston, as is the way with great men, did not take kindly to criticism of his projects (he also had a maddening habit of asking several officers to do the same thing), but once the principles were settled he was confident in the ability of his advisers to carry his schemes to fruition. I have met none who served under him who resented the abrasion that sometimes occurred during their discussions. What civil servants dislike is an indecisive Minister, and indecision was not one of Johnston's shortcomings. He was not a niggler.

In retrospect it may seem strange that, with his cold look at anything emanating from South Britain, he had so little overt sympathy with the Nationalists. He might have become their archetypal figure, but in fact the success of his administration was an embarrassment to them. He saw a place, a better place for Scotland within the existing system. He hoped that the message he had been able to give his countrymen was that

> in co-operation and mutual aid and not in fratricidal strife can we win through to material plenty for all, and to a spiritual and cultural development and greatness for each of us.

Few marks for style, but the meaning is clear. He was not interested in theoretical argument and found more satisfaction in watching the concrete mixers at work on the latest hydro-electric dam.

One of the best Tom Johnston stories brings to life his typical contribution to the war effort. It appears in different forms in the *Memoirs* of John Winant and of Harry Hopkins. Early in the war, when the United States were still uncommitted and Joseph Kennedy, the American Ambassador, was sending despatches commenting adversely on our prospects of survival, Roosevelt sent Hopkins as his personal envoy to assess the progress of our war effort and report to him direct. Lord Halifax was about to sail to the States from Scapa Flow on board the *King George V* to be our new Ambassador to the States, and Churchill decided to invite Hopkins to accompany him to the Orkneys to see him off, the real objective being to demonstrate the strength of the British fleet. By the time the party was on its way back to Glasgow Hopkins had given no sign of what his disposition was, and Churchill was for once pessimistic. At the final dinner, Johnston, the host as Secretary of State, proposed a toast to Hopkins and said he welcomed him especially for the sake of his grandmother who had been born at Auchterarder in Perthshire. Hopkins then had to reply, and in a speech that fully matched the occasion he recalled the words his grandmother had read him from the good book.

> Whither thou goest, I will go; and where thou lodgest, I will lodge; thy people shall be my people, and thy God my God.

Churchill was in tears. No one had any doubt how Hopkins would advise his President. Years later I heard Johnston relate this historic incident during dinner in Dunvegan Castle, and I seem to remember him saying that his intervention took place while they were dining on the train as it actually passed through Auchterarder, which makes it even better. In his *Memories* he states that the dinner was in the North British Hotel, Glasgow. No matter. He had, as usual, found a distinctive Scottish element.

NOTES

1 Tom Johnston, *Memories*. London, 1952.
2 Tom Johnston, *Our Scots Noble Families*. Glasgow, 1913.
3 *Memories*.

4 Arthur Turner, *Scottish Home Rule*. Oxford, 1952.
5 *Memories.*
6 J. M. McCormick, *The Flag in the Wind*. London, 1955.
7 *Hansard*, 14th March, 1950. Vol. 472, col. 906.
8 *Hansard*, 27th May, 1943. Vol. 389, col. 1779.
9 *Memories.*

CHAPTER X

Intermission

Churchill's appointment of the Sixth Earl of Rosebery to be Secretary of State in the Caretaker government of 1945 was reckoned at the time to be a bizarre choice. But it was no more eccentric than one of Churchill's other invitations.

The Scottish judge, Lord Birnam, who—in his earlier title of Sir David King Murray—had been Solicitor General for Scotland in the National government, dined out on the story. He received a message asking if he would be available to take a call from the Prime Minister in the course of the afternoon. Dismissing the possibility of a practical joke by one of his brethren at the Scottish Bar, he said he would. Eventually the rich, unmistakable voice came on the line. 'Is that you, Sir David? Would you accept the post of Attorney General in the administration I am now forming?' Birnam was bracing himself to explain that he was not learned in English law when Churchill spoke again. 'I am very sorry. I thought I was speaking to Sir David Maxwell Fyfe.' The unworthy thought occurs that Rosebery might have been another case of mistaken identity.

However that may be, Rosebery's arrival at St Andrew's House revived memories of earlier days when the Scottish Secretary was a grandee. The closest resemblance was perhaps to Lord Pentland (1905–12), the ex-Lancer who affected a forbidding martial demeanour. Rosebery brought to the Scottish Office all the political finesse to be expected of a former officer in the Grenadier Guards and Captain of Surrey County Cricket Club. His remit was, in terms, a holding one, as officials awaited the outcome of the General Election. Kenneth Young in his biography recalls that Rosebery's parting words were 'Well. I didn't make a bad job of this, did I? Didn't have time.'[1] Later, with uncharacteristic humility, he declined to give evidence to the Royal Commission on Scottish Affairs on the grounds that he did not know what to say.

He did make his presence felt when he attended a reception at Dover House to mark the Scottish Office's return to their original home, which had been used for other purposes during the war. A busy official had affixed cards to each of the portraits that line the Secretary of State's room, identifying the artist and the subject. Suddenly the genial hum of conversation was interrupted by the noise of Rosebery pawing the ground. He pointed a shaking finger at the inscription beneath a Rigaud. It read 'A copy hangs at Dalmeny.' 'Copy?' Rosebery blustered when he was able to speak. 'Copy? I don't have copies!'

As Chairman of the Scottish Tourist Board, Rosebery later waged an unproductive battle with the British Tourist and Holidays Association which was not prepared to concede the parity, far less the hegemony, that he thought was his due. He had a peremptory way of treating Board members who dared to criticise his rulings. Anyone who questioned him would receive in reply an insolent jet of Havana fumes from Rosebery's cigar, or would hear him mutter to the Secretary in an audible *sotto voce* that he couldn't remember the fellow's name. Rosebery's insensitive arrogance did not equip him to be a post-war Secretary of State.

No question of mistaken identity arose on the appointment of Joseph Westwood to be Secretary of State in the 1945 Labour Government. He had earned his promotion by long service as an M.P., sitting for Peebles and South Midlothian from 1922, and for Stirling and Falkirk since 1935, and as a Junior Minister. He was Parliamentary Under-Secretary of State for Scotland in 1931, and again from 1940 to 1945. Westwood did not measure up to the job, but one must sympathise with a sincere, honest man, who had no personal enemies, in the hazards he faced on his elevation to the Cabinet. Not all these difficulties were of his own making.

Westwood's tenure exemplifies cruelly, but vividly, the difference between what is expected of a Junior Minister and what a Secretary of State has to do. If he has sufficient tolerance from his colleagues, and respect from Government supporters on the back benches—as Westwood had—a Parliamentary Under-Secretary can survive in the routine business of taking adjournment debates, seeking Parliamentary approval for statutory regulations, and deputising for his Minister. He will receive the less important deputations. He may establish a good working concord with officials, although what he gets to do in the office will depend on the extent to which his Minister delegates responsibility. Between these tasks and the duties that fall on the Secretary of State there is an immense gap. There are many things that the Secretary of State cannot delegate, ranging from Cabinet business to senior appointments, the overall direction of the policy of the office, and his activities as Scotland's Minister. This calls for capacity that Westwood did not possess.

A former Secretary for Scotland, Robert Munro (Lord Alness), in his memoirs recalled that the Scottish Minister had not only to administer a limited series of statutes and keep in touch with all the proceedings of Government which might affect Scotland. He had also 'to attend Cabinets, to think of Upper Silesia as well as, let us say, Auchtermuchty'.[2] As becomes apparent later in this book, the more successful Secretaries of State have been those who were prepared to extend their influence by the contributions they made to Cabinet discussions on wider topics. It was notorious that Westwood, in his attendance at Cabinet, would speak only on narrowly defined Scottish questions.

This was not Westwood's only disability. The new Labour Government were intent on proceeding with their programme of nationalisation and social reform, for which they had a clear mandate. There was no time to spare for the delicate susceptibilities of the Scots, and Attlee was intolerant of any regional variations that might impede progress. There was the further difficulty that Westwood was in the Cabinet because that was where the Secretary of State had to be, not because of personal merit. In sum, Westwood's chances of securing acceptable treatment for Scotland, or of obtaining recognition that the Nationalists were once more gaining strength, were pretty poor.

Westwood appears to have been conscious of his own shortcomings. So much is evident from two of his speeches in the House. In June, 1946, he referred nostalgically to his years as Tom Johnston's Parliamentary Under-Secretary, asserting that they 'were able to do more for Scotland than any other two have ever done'. Then he continued, defiantly, to say

> I claim that I will set up a good record, and I will leave it to the people of Scotland to determine whether or not I have been successful when I leave office.[3]

That sounds suspiciously like whistling to keep his courage up, but there is something pathetic in the last speech he made in the Chamber.

> If I had remained longer in office, I would have had proposals ready for increasing the number of senior Ministers for Scotland. . . . I will

conclude by saying again that one man cannot be made the Pooh-Bah of Scotland and effectively carry through its administration.[4]

A miner by origin, Westwood served in the pits for nearly twenty years. He left school when he was thirteen, and as a Minister he took a keen interest in education, being emphatic that others should not be denied the opportunities he had missed. The raising of the school leaving age under the Education (Scotland) Act of 1945 was a source of much satisfaction to him. But housing was his main concern as Secretary of State, and on this he staked his reputation. The Government were committed to a strenuous campaign to build both temporary and permanent houses. As an incentive, the Housing (Financial Provisions) (Scotland) Bill of 1946 practically doubled the Exchequer subsidy on houses built by local authorities, and paid it retrospectively on houses completed after March, 1944. But the difficulties were great. There was not enough trained technical staff, and nearly all the materials required, timber, steel, slates and electrical components, were in short supply. In June, 1947, Westwood appointed a Committee to review the rising costs of house building, but as the *Economist* noted, it was hard to see what they could do except record facts. There was little scope for dramatic proposals. The building labour force, the price and supply of materials to sites, were all fixed and could not easily be altered.[5] In April, 1947, Westwood had to admit that there was no hope of reaching his target of 24,000 houses in 1947. In the first five months of the year only 7500 houses had been completed, and there was now a shortage of bricks and cement.

None of this was Westwood's fault, although he was criticised for not securing better co-ordination between supply Departments. The Department of Health's attempts to stimulate the building industry towards quicker progress can be most charitably described as amateur. But Westwood was inept at defending himself. He was also unlucky in the Opposition spokesman who faced him across the Despatch Box. J. S. C. Reid (later a Lord of Appeal) was a master of the most destructive oratory. Earlier Reid had engaged in some sport—there is no other word for it—over Westwood's statement in August, 1945, that his target was 20,000 permanent houses in his first year of office. Reid made great play of the fact that in July, 1945, the previous Government had left 3800 houses under construction, but a year later only half of them had been completed. Westwood's reply that he had meant houses 'built or building' lacked credibility.[6]

One of Westwood's handicaps was that the Government's main legislative proposals were first debated in English terms, with the corresponding Scottish Bills coming later. The National Health (Scotland) and the Town and Country Planning (Scotland) Bills are examples. But since the House had already approved the principles involved it was extremely difficult for the Secretary of State to demonstrate that he had any room for manœuvre, and Westwood was not very good at it. On the Second Reading of the Town and Country Planning Bill, Reid was again at his most mischievous.

> More than nine-tenths of his (Westwood's) speech was nothing but an uninspiring précis of the detailed provisions of the Bill. I should have thought that anyone who had taken the trouble to read the White Paper would have gained little or nothing from his speech, whereas anyone who had not taken that trouble would have found his speech unintelligible.[7]

Scottish Office civil servants who sat in the Official Box on Mr Speaker's right were dismayed to see their Secretary of State so frequently at a loss. But however eloquent the brief it is the Minister who has to speak from the floor of the House.

Officials were also finding that the climate had changed in their relationship with Whitehall Departments. The Ministries were now less inclined to entertain proposals based on distinctive Scottish conditions. It is no exaggeration to say that some English Departments had resented Tom Johnston's achievements. They considered that Johnston had enjoyed too easy a run, and as they realised that Westwood did not have the Prime Minister's ear, they were less willing to agree to anything if there was the remotest likelihood that it would give Scotland the advantage. The Treasury may not have been overtly obstructive, but there was a period of excessive vigilance.

Officials were, however, keen to rally to Westwood's support, from loyalty to their profession, from devotion to the Scottish cause which it was their job to protect, and because they liked the man. Internal discussions were amicable, but those who took part were often alarmed that the Secretary of State underrated the opposition he was likely to encounter. This rallying round could give rise to some embarrassment. For example, the Secretary of State had to decide whether a particular site should be allocated for school or hospital building, and received a joint deputation from the conflicting authorities. After they had submitted their arguments the two sides waited for Westwood's arbitration. There was an uncomfortable pause. An officer from the Scottish Education Department, attempting to fill the breach, reminded the Minister that he felt strongly that more educational facilities were needed in the area. Westwood assented. This was too much for a self-confident junior official from the Department of Health. 'You will remember, Secretary of State', he exclaimed, 'that you feel equally strongly that we need another hospital.' The meeting broke up in confusion. When he heard about this undignified fracas the Permanent Under-Secretary's post-mortem was prolonged, and as far as the officials were concerned, punitive.

Political commentators would not be stretched to point to cases where parliamentary seniority has proved an inadequate qualification for high office. But this can seldom be said of Secretaries of State for Scotland, and it is unfortunate for Westwood that he suffers in comparison with the others who have been Keeper of the Great Seal. His officials must take their share of the criticism which he met, but there is no doubt that they received little direction from above. Westwood was dogged by ill-health throughout his tenure, and the Cabinet circumstances were not favourable to him. It is the writer's melancholy task to conclude that Westwood proves in a negative way the proposition that the efficiency and the acceptance with which a Department carries out its duties depends primarily on the Minister in charge.

Westwood was greatly pleased that one of the first New Towns would be built in Fife. He wanted to preserve his own name in its title, but he was not allowed this harmless vanity, and Glenrothes was preferred as the designation. It is best to regard Westwood's time as an intermission.

NOTES

1 K. Young, *Harry, Lord Rosebery*. London, 1974.
2 Robert Munro (Lord Alness), *Looking Back: Fugitive Writings and Sayings*. Edinburgh, 1930.
3 *Hansard*, 7th June, 1946. Vol. 423, col. 2350.
4 *Hansard*, 28th April, 1948. Vol. 450, col. 415.
5 The *Economist*, 14th June, 1947.
6 *Hansard*, 10th October, 1946. Vol. 427, col. 386.
7 *Hansard*, 24th February, 1947. Vol. 433, col. 1727.

CHAPTER XI

Head above Water

No Ministerial appointment to the Scottish Office had been so widely forecast as that of Arthur Woodburn in 1947. Westwood's experience had been singularly unhappy, and Attlee later recalled in the course of a television interview how summarily he had dismissed him. Attlee saw this as an example of the Prime Minister having of necessity to be a good butcher, but the impression left was somewhat callous. Anyhow, Woodburn was the obvious successor.

His early career had been spent in minor administrative jobs in the engineering and ironfounding industry. Later he had been concerned with the Labour Colleges, both as Secretary and as Lecturer. He was Secretary of the Scottish Labour Party from 1932 till he entered Parliament in 1939 as Member for Clackmannan and East Stirling, a seat he held till his retirement in 1970. He wrote three books on economic and financial topics, and one of them, *An Outline of Finance*,[1] met with some success. It is a thoughtful work, though it does not pretend to any profound academic expertise, and attempts to relate Socialist theory to the world market. He was Tom Johnston's Parliamentary Private Secretary from 1941 to 1945, and when the Attlee government was returned he became Parliamentary Secretary at the Ministry of Supply.

As Secretary of State, Woodburn started with a great deal of goodwill, both in the House and from the press. Some of this was soon dissipated by a thoughtless *bêtise*. At a time when the motoring public were particularly annoyed by government restrictions Woodburn saw fit to denounce motorists as 'the most selfish section of the community'. It is one of the pitfalls awaiting Ministers that they cannot foresee when an unguarded remark will be held against them indefinitely. Shawcross's 'We are the masters now', Nye Bevan's 'Tory vermin', Heath's 'at a stroke of the pen' are the most notorious examples. Woodburn's comment did not receive anything like the same currency, but he was to regret it.

This was the more unfortunate since it was out of character. A warm, generous, avuncular figure, he was personally popular both with Scottish Members and with the staff at the Scottish Office. One instance makes the point. The Scottish Standing Committee had adjourned just before considering a complicated amendment to the Bill before them. In the interval before the next session the Opposition, as they were entitled to do, made a small but significant change which entirely altered the sense of their amendment. When discussion was resumed neither Woodburn nor the draftsman noticed the alteration on the Order Paper. Woodburn spoke to the official brief, originally apposite but now irrelevant. Tom Scollan, a worthy Labour backbencher, was quickly on his feet to say that he expected to hear nonsense from the Opposition, but this was going too far. Walter Elliot, seeing Woodburn's discomfiture, intervened with polite sarcasm. If Mr Scollan could not understand the Secretary of State, how could those who lacked the Honourable Member's undoubted intellectual capacity be expected to follow the government argument? Others joined in the hunt and a red-faced Woodburn had to confess his error. Thereafter his officials were full of apology, but Woodburn would have none of it. The Opposition were making fun of him, he said, and it was his own fault.

Despite the warmth of his initial welcome, Woodburn was unfortunate in the timing of his arrival at the Scottish Office. Party politics had by now been resumed with some acrimony, and Woodburn, though blessed with that most useful parliamentary asset a deep sonorous voice, was not an agile debater. More important was the disposition of the Prime Minister. As Westwood had found, Attlee was not inclined to give much time to Scottish problems, and the influence of the Scottish Office was waning from the peak reached under Tom Johnston. Whitehall Departments realised that things had changed, and Woodburn's administration still suffered something of a backlash. Moreover, the great nationalisation and social measures were in the hands of Whitehall Ministries and only the National Health Service came within the Secretary of State's ambit. Inevitably cries of 'remote control' began to monopolise headlines in the Scottish press. Without attempting any verdict on the merits, a government committed to high state expenditure, and therefore high taxation, and depending on centralised arrangements to carry out its policy, was bound to afford targets to the Nationalists. If dissident criticism was to be countered, a strong, authoritative Scottish Minister was needed.

Employment, as such, did not come within the Secretary of State's jurisdiction, and his statutory powers over industry were at best only marginal. During Woodburn's time the unemployment figures, always the most obvious barometer, showed Scotland still lagging behind. In 1948, for example, the percentage of insured persons unemployed in Scotland was more than twice the English figure, though both percentages, 2·7 and 1, would now be regarded as highly acceptable. But the differential provided more ammunition for the critics.

Housing remained the main parliamentary battlefield. Scottish housing conditions after the war were so bad that it needed a massive operation by local authorities to make any inroads on slum clearance and the building of new dwellings. Progress quickened as local authorities gained experience, and as materials became more plentiful. The government had provided generous subsidies and continued to monitor local plans, but Woodburn took a very rigid line as regards private building. Few licences were given, and at one time there were no licences at all for houses built for sale. (There was more flexibility in England.) In this Woodburn was much influenced by John (later Lord) Wheatley, a Lord Advocate of strong left wing convictions and impeccable Socialist ancestry. The outcome was not entirely beneficial. Building firms vied with each other for local authority contracts, but combined to represent that they could do far more to increase the country's housing stock but for the Secretary of State's doctrinaire approach. More unfortunately, the pattern of industrial immobility, under which the council tenant would not move to another area lest he lose his privileged tenancy, became more rigid.

Instances of indecision, of a lack of firm purpose in the Scottish Office during this period are not hard to find. Two will suffice. Shop premises, unlike houses, were not protected by the Rent Restrictions Acts, and towards the end of 1946 there were complaints of landlords serving 'buy or quit' notices on their tenants when their leases expired. Westwood had set up a committee of enquiry under Sheriff (Sir) T. M. Taylor to consider whether shop tenants should be given protection. Woodburn received its report (Cmd. 7285) in November, 1947. It said that less than 1 per cent of the shops in Scotland were affected, and that there were not more than fifty cases of hardship. Not surprisingly, it found no case for protective legislation, and no action was taken. Then there were renewed complaints that landlords, seeing the report as a green light, had increased their evictions. Woodburn reappointed the committee, this time under Sheriff (Lord) Guthrie. The Guthrie

Committee in its report (Cmd. 7603) recalled that the Secretary of State had meanwhile beaten the pistol by invoking the wartime Defence Regulation 51 and the Supplies and Services Acts to requisition premises under notices to quit, in order to safeguard the tenants. These powers were used legally but dubiously to take over not only shops, but billiard saloons, pawnbrokers' establishments, and buildings used by religious orders. But despite an appeal to local authorities to submit cases in their areas only 191 notices of requisition were served. This might still be thought an insignificant number, but the Guthrie committee recommended that the tenant should have the right to apply for a year's renewal at a time, if hardship could be adduced. Legislation was promptly enacted, and there were allegations that the Scottish Office had panicked.

The strange happenings on the Public Registers and Records (Scotland) Bill showed further signs of vacillation. The Bill proposed *inter alia* that, following an investigation by the Organisation and Methods Division of the Treasury, the procedure for registering deeds when property was conveyed should be brought up to date. The legal profession did not like this intrusion on their remunerative preserve and made their voice heard. As a result, proceedings on the Bill were suspended to allow a hastily appointed committee under Lord Macmillan to examine the matter further. Macmillan, who was already on record rhapsodising over the existing system,[2] knew what he had to do. He compressed the hearing of evidence into a week and was already thumbing through the draft report while the Lord President of the Court of Session was appearing before him. His report ruled firmly against any change. His views were accepted and Woodburn bowed to the solicitors' indignation. The offending clauses were withdrawn.

Dissatisfaction with Whitehall's treatment of legitimate Scottish demands began to get more space in the press, and the implication was that the Scottish Office was impotent to intervene. It was no use referring to the orthodox doctrine which the Treasury had embodied in a circular to Whitehall Departments in June, 1946. No exception could be taken to its statement that

> The status, organisation and staffing of Scottish Regional Offices requires to be considered with the greatest possible care, and with particular regard to the effect on Scottish opinion and the adequate representation in Whitehall of the Scottish point of view.

The great Fowler might not have approved the wording, but the intention was sound. Departments were enjoined to give their Scottish representatives sufficient authority 'to enable Scottish business to be settled on the spot, with the minimum of reference to London', and to ensure that 'in the settlement of large matters of principle, Scottish aspects are fully considered'. Forward the loyal men. The Secretary of State's status as 'Scotland's Minister' was formally commended, and there was a reminder that he would 'naturally interest himself in the commerce, industry, manpower, and general economic development of Scotland'. This memorandum was an internal document, not intended for general consumption. When it came to the notice of the Royal Commission on Scottish Affairs in 1954, they endorsed its principles without reservation—they could scarcely have done otherwise—but added tartly that 'in view of the evidence we have received, however, we doubt whether Departments have in all cases gone as far as they might have done in putting them into effect'.

Some changes in the official disposition towards industry were, however, effected during the Woodburn régime. Through the Distribution of Industry Panel the Scottish Office were consulted on the siting of factories, the scheduling of development areas, and the allocation of grants to industry. The Office also had a seat on the Scottish Board for Industry (appointed by the Treasury) which gave general advice on the industrial climate. But the body which in time made the most public impact was the Advisory Panel on the Highlands and Islands. The Highland Panel, as it was known, included M.P.s, local councillors, and nominees of the Secretary of State. For most of its life it had a vigorous and far-seeing Chairman in Lord Cameron. First appointed in 1947, it produced a programme of Highland development (Cmd. 7976) in 1950, and for the next fifteen years, until it was superseded by the emasculated Highlands and Islands Consultative Council in 1966, it acted as a lively pressure group to keep Highland problems on the back of the national conscience.

But looking at these and other contemporary fringe bodies, they seem very like a substitute for action. Governments notoriously react to demands for something to be done by conjuring up advisory machinery, and this was an epidemic disease at the end of the 1940s. The regular mobilisation of committees presents a peculiar problem for the Head Recruiting Sergeant in St Andrew's House. When a committee is set up in England a similar body has to be appointed in Scotland. But with a tenth of the population this has its own hazards, resulting in the same people being recalled too often to the colours, or in the dilution of membership. Duplication of effort is another by-product. Woodburn even contemplated a separate Scottish Medical Research Council, before he accepted wiser advise.

Woodburn and his advisers were not insensitive to stirrings of discontent which transcended Party political boundaries. Some of the press comment could be discounted as being inspired by anti-government doctrine, but the Scottish Labour Party had now passed two resolutions (in 1945 and 1947) calling for an enquiry into the government's treatment of Scottish matters. Woodburn's White Paper on Scottish Affairs (Cmd. 7308) published in 1948 solemnly took note of the Scottish people's widespread desire to deal with affairs of purely Scottish concern. It had two positive proposals and one very negative conclusion. We will consider them in turn. (There was also an undertaking, discharged with ever-diminishing enthusiasm until it was finally abandoned, to present an Annual Review to Parliament.)

The White Paper proposed the appointment of a Scottish Economic Conference, which would include detachments from every unit in the stage army. Departments, nationalised industries, local authorities, and other important interests were all to be represented. Only the doorman at the Caledonian Hotel was not invited, because, it was said, he was too busy. This was the ultimate in talking shops. Elaborate plans were made to service the Conference, but it had no mandate, no authority, and it lacked the political muscle to achieve anything, either in practical terms or in appeasing nationalist sentiment. The members spent too much time thanking each other for their informative speeches, and there was little sign of sinewy, effective debate. The Conference met seven times between 1948 and 1950. Hector McNeil, newly arrived at the Scottish Office, attended one—the last—meeting and decided that this ill-starred body should be allowed a peaceful demise.

Much more important was the proposal in the White Paper to extend the powers of the Scottish Grand Committee. As this is the first time the Committee has featured in our study, a brief description of its genesis is in order. The appointment of the first Scottish Secretary in 1885 seems to have prompted the Scottish M.P.s to act more as a body. Lord Advocate Balfour, for example, said in the House that

> It has been the custom for the Scotch Members, in conference with the Government, to come to an understanding on Scotch questions; and effect has invariably been given, not only by the Government, but by the House, to any understanding thus arrived at by the Scotch Members.[3]

A sanguine view, but this voluntary agreement was sometimes productive, e.g. on the Crofters Bill of 1886 when substantial amendments
by the Scottish M.P.s were accepted. Its limitations were, however,
exposed during proceedings on the Local Government Bill three years
later. Amendments by Scottish Members were thrown out by the
English majority. This was largely because the Conservatives controlled the House although the Scots were predominantly Liberal.
When the Liberals returned to power in 1892 they devised a modest
scheme to assuage Scottish resentment and the Scottish Grand Committee was set up on 27th April, 1894. It comprised all the Scottish
Members, together with fifteen other M.P.s to reflect the balance
between the parties in the House. The Committee was to take the
Committee stage of non-controversial Scottish Bills, but all other
stages were reserved for the House as a whole.

The Committee was dropped two years later by the Conservatives
who had never liked it. In 1907 it was revived by the Liberals, and
remained in being, with its original powers, till the 1948 extension.
(There was a short interval in 1922 when, although the Conservatives
were in power, there were so many Scottish Labour Members that the
addition of fifteen Conservatives would not have been enough to
restore the balance.)

The White Paper proposed that the Scottish Grand Committee
should take the second reading (as well as the committee stage) of
Scottish Bills and should also consider Scottish Estimates. Put like that,
this was an appreciable enlargement of the Committee's scope. But
the Scots were not to get quite as free a hand as might be supposed.
The types of Bill that were to come under the new procedure would be
those of a technical nature applying only to Scotland 'which though
debatable, are not controversial in a Party sense'; Scottish Bills similar
to English legislation already introduced; and, in a vague concession
to the critics, 'certain Bills of purely Scottish interest for which time
cannot immediately be found under existing arrangements'.

The amendments made in the Standing Orders of the House to give
effect to the White Paper provided that the Committee should consist
of the Scottish M.P.s plus between ten and fifteen other Members to
preserve the Party balance. There were, however, some restrictions.
The Speaker must first certify that the Bill relates exclusively to
Scotland. (If the Exchequer is involved this is not as simple as it sounds.)
Thereafter the Bill is automatically referred to the Scottish Grand
Committee, unless ten Members object. The Committee then consider

the Bill 'in relation to its principle' and report accordingly. It is thereafter read a second time without further debate. To complete the pavane the Bill goes back to the Scottish Committee for the committee stage—unless six Members object—and the remaining report and third reading stages follow the normal procedure.

Two points may be noted. First, Parliament reserved the right not to allow any particular Bill to be sent to the Scottish Committee for what is in effect second reading, although it is very rare for the veto to be exercised (e.g. the Licensing (Scotland) Bill, 1961). Second, although Scottish M.P.s were for all practical purposes in control up to the end of the committee stage the Government could use its overall majority later to reverse amendments passed by the Scottish Committee.

Despite these restrictions the White Paper innovations were an ingenious devolutionary experiment. (Tom Johnston had made similar proposals in a note attached to the Gilmour Report in 1937: Walter Elliot was also interested; but it was Woodburn who had them carried out.) Once made, the concessions could not in decency be withdrawn, and they have since been further extended. The present position is that the Scottish Grand Committee can take the consideration of principle and report stages, so that a Scottish Bill can proceed entirely, apart from formal second and third readings, without intervention by the House as a whole. There are now two other Scottish Standing Committees which can undertake the detailed examination at the committee stage. The first was set up in 1957, and a second was added in 1962. Since 1971 they have both had a minimum of sixteen Members. To show how these arrangements have worked in practice, from 1958 to 1970 86·4 per cent of Government Bills certified as Scottish went to the Grand Committee, and 81 per cent were committed to a Scottish Standing Committee.[4] Woodburn's proposals have borne fruit.

Debates in the Scottish Committees are well attended. They have to be, since divisions may be called and it is not so easy to scramble into the Committee room to vote in time as it is to file into the Lobby when the Bell sounds in the Chamber. The attendance contrasts with that in the House itself where the number present at any one time during a Scottish Bill seldom runs into double figures. Apparently it has always been so. As long ago as 1894 Sir G. O. Trevelyan, the Scottish Secretary, observed that

> Nothing is more striking—it is one of the best-known phenomena of Parliamentary life—the indifference which English Members show to the details of Scotch Debates.[5]

It has also been the practice for the House as a whole to debate Scottish affairs for two days annually. In some years these debates have not been held and in others the dates have coincided with other engagements (the Derby, Ascot, the Royal Garden Party) which have priority with English M.P.s. But spare a thought for the English Members who are added to the Scottish Committees. If they intervene in the debate they are chided for speaking on matters about which they have no local knowledge. If they remain silent, attending to their correspondence or their manicure, they are taunted as lobby fodder. New Members taking their seats after a by-election have been startled to hear cries of 'Send him to the Scottish Grand Committee!', a fate which they do not always relish.

To come back to the 1948 White Paper, it was further proposed that the Scottish Grand Committee should sit on six days a year to consider the Estimates of the Scottish Departments. The votes to be discussed are chosen by the Opposition and in theory this should be the time to put the work of the Departments under the microscope. Certainly voluminous briefing is required to arm Ministers against all the barbs that may be fired at them, but the Clerk to the Committee has been known to observe that the one thing not discussed is the Estimates. These days, however (together with the two annual 'matter days' chosen by the Government), allow room to review the whole range of the Scottish Office's activities, and their introduction went some way to dispel the criticism that there was not enough time for the ventilation of Scottish issues.

The White Paper ended with one profoundly negative conclusion. It came down firmly against any general enquiry into Scottish affairs. The Scottish Labour Party was not alone in calling for this, but despite the contemporary tendency to set up committees on all conceivable subjects Woodburn was not in favour. It was to be only a few years before the Catto and Balfour enquiries took their place in the long line that stretches from Camperdown to Kilbrandon, but not yet. The reasons adduced were remarkably ingenuous.

> The matters of opinion into which it is suggested a Committee should enquire also cover a wide field and are, of course, acutely controversial. . . . The possibilities of disagreement are therefore obvious.

James Bridie's comment on the White Paper was

> I don't think I can say anything pertinent about Mr Woodburn's White Paper except that it gives me a pain in the neck.[6]

But this is hardly fair. The White Paper was Woodburn's main contribution while in office, and the increase in the powers of the Grand Committee was much more important than his opponents would admit. It is worth remembering that the White Paper did not have an easy passage in the Cabinet. Woodburn had to resist the Chief Whip's request that the enlarged remit to the Grand Committee should lead to the surrender of one of the Scottish Supply days in the House. There were also fears that the Welsh would want similar treatment and Woodburn was sternly instructed 'to avoid any statement that might encourage Welsh demand'.[7]

It was fashionable at the time to regard Woodburn simply as the obedient servant of his Party, but he was more than that, and few would agree with J. M. MacCormick's jibe that he was incapable of looking at anything except through the narrow eyes of Party bias.[8] He was intensely proud to be Secretary of State and tried unceasingly to find a Scottish aspect in all Government business that came before him. On the other hand, he was convinced that his rôle was to speak only on Scottish affairs and this restricted his influence in Cabinet. This was a time when the Socialist (nationalised, centralised) solution was not necessarily the answer that would be most acceptable as the answer for Scotland, and Woodburn was aware of the conflict. He tried to find a compromise by setting up advisory bodies which would appear to safeguard Scottish interests, but in this he was only partly successful. The truth is that the Attlee government were so engrossed with their great social programme that they ignored national or other aspirations that did not conform. The temper began to change after the 1950 General Election which drastically reduced the Government's majority, but for the time being Woodburn was bound to appear something of a lonely figure in the inner councils. He epitomised the dilemma of trying to find a Scottish solution and at the same time subscribe to Party (U.K.) policy, and he lacked the political agility to conceal that this dilemma existed. He just kept his head above water.

Woodburn was returned with a good majority at the 1950 Election and expected to stay at St Andrew's House. But Attlee thought otherwise, probably influenced by an unwise attack that Woodburn had recently made on the Nationalists (see the following chapter), and said he wanted him to move to the Ministry of Fuel and Power. Woodburn declined and did not get office again. His Ministerial colleagues at the Scottish Office felt he had been badly treated, and it was common knowledge that his Parliamentary Private Secretary, James (later Lord)

Hoy, indignantly refused to accept promotion elsewhere in the Government. It was another fourteen years before Hoy's loyal gesture was forgiven and he was given a junior Ministerial appointment.

NOTES

1 Arthur Woodburn, *An Outline of Finance*. London, 1928.
2 *A Scotsman's Heritage*, essay by Lord Macmillan. London, 1932.
3 *Hansard*, 3rd August, 1886. 3rd series, vol. 308, col. 972.
4 *The Scottish Grand Committee*, essay by G. E. Edwards, *Parliamentary Affairs*, XXV, 1972.
5 *Hansard*, 2nd April, 1894. Vol. 22, col. 1121.
6 *Scottish Opinion*, March, 1948.
7 Cab. 128/10, Public Record Office.
8 J. M. MacCormick, *The Flag in the Wind*. London, 1955.

CHAPTER XII

A Wider Horizon

Hector McNeil, 42 years old, was the youngest Minister ever to be appointed to take charge of the Scottish Office when he succeeded Arthur Woodburn at the end of February, 1950. McNeil was born at Garelochhead, Dunbartonshire, the son of a journeyman shipwright. His father's family came from Barra, and his mother's from Islay. He was proud of his Highland lineage. During the Summer Recess the Secretary of State traditionally visits some of the remote islands on board a Fishery Cruiser, which for the time becomes the Scottish Office Yacht, and McNeil was clear that his first voyage should be to his ancestral territory. He attended schools and the University in Glasgow. At first he studied for the Ministry, but after a visit to Canada and the U.S.A. as a member of the British Universities' debating team he gave up the idea of taking holy orders and decided that his future lay in journalism and politics.

Starting as a freelance, he joined the staff of the *Scottish Daily Express* and eventually became leader-writer. Throughout his subsequent career he maintained a close friendship with Beaverbrook. Few of Beaverbrook's former employees stayed on cordial terms with the mischievous newspaper proprietor, and McNeil was often criticised for this association. He defended it on the ground that while the *Express* would not support a Labour Government, it could still cause a great deal of harm, and alone of his Cabinet colleagues he could on occasion act as an emollient. Besides, he was stimulated by Beaverbrook's wit and apocalyptic vision.

During his time with the *Express* McNeil took an active part in local politics, serving on Glasgow Town Council between 1933 and 1938, latterly as river bailie. But his eyes were already on the wider horizon. He had stood unsuccessfully as the Labour candidate for Galloway in 1929 and 1931, and at the General Election in 1935 he failed by only 149 votes to unseat Walter Elliot at Kelvingrove. In February, 1936, he took part in a much publicised by-election in Ross and Cromarty where the other candidates included Malcolm MacDonald (National

Government) and Randolph Churchill. McNeil doubled the Labour vote and said privately that he might have done better but for the death, while the campaign was at its height, of King George V. MacDonald immediately announced that he would not continue electioneering while his Sovereign lay in State. The other candidates were hamstrung, and MacDonald was returned. Finally, in the wartime electoral truce between the parties McNeil was returned unopposed for the burgh of Greenock, a seat he represented till his death.

His rise in Parliament was rapid and impressive. After a spell as Parliamentary Private Secretary to Philip Noel-Baker at War Transport he was appointed Parliamentary Under-Secretary of State at the Foreign Office, a post much to his liking. His successful tenure was recognised by his elevation to the Privy Council in 1946, when he was promoted to be Minister of State for Foreign Affairs. He remained at the Foreign Office till Parliament was dissolved in February, 1950.

McNeil's background has been itemised in some detail because, as will appear, various elements derived from it were to have an appreciable influence on the way he carried out the duties of Secretary of State. Meanwhile it may be noted that he was the first professional politician, in the sense that for him politics was a career and a way of earning a living, to direct the Scottish Office. He saw politics as a business to be carried on in a business-like way. His approach was essentially pragmatic.

Two distinct circumstances occasioned his arrival at the Scottish Office. The first relates to the structure of the Cabinet at the time. Prime Minister Attlee was careful to preserve a balance of power in his great triumvirate of Cripps, Bevin, and Morrison, and this delicate equilibrium extended to their protégés. It was well known that Bevin pressed for McNeil's advancement. This he did to fortify his own position in the Cabinet, from affection for his colleague, and as a reward for the way in which McNeil had undertaken much of the burden of office when his own health was impaired. He was also aware that McNeil had done well, perhaps too well, in his absence, particularly at the United Nations assembly. McNeil had earned great acclaim as the official government spokesman when the cold war was taking the form of a bitter propaganda struggle between the U.S.S.R. and the Western powers. As a result, McNeil came to St Andrew's House better known abroad than at home.

He was often tipped as the next Foreign Secretary, but he had no illusions. He did not conceal that he hoped for the Foreign Office eventually, but this was not the time. He was still too junior in the Party. He continued to give his loyal support to Bevin, and thereafter to Herbert Morrison who succeeded him—although it soon became apparent that Morrison was a disastrous choice. (It is of interest that none of Bevin's other young men, Christopher Mayhew, Aidan Crawley, and Ernest Davies, made their expected mark as Ministers.)

The second reason leading to McNeil's appointment as Secretary of State was more intimately domestic. The rise of Scottish Nationalism was beginning to cause concern. Arthur Woodburn had unwittingly provided grist to the Nationalist mill while speaking in a Devolution debate in the last months of the previous Parliament. He attempted to make something of a statement by Mr (now Lord) John Cameron, K.C., who had earlier flirted with the Nationalists. Cameron's typically pungent assertion was that

> Scottish Nationalism, with its pinchbeck heroics, its political pos-
> turings, and its sham sentiment is just a will-o'-the-wisp. . . . There is,
> I think, no doubt that Scottish Nationalism in its present form is a
> charlatan movement. It prefers political quackery to conservative
> effort. It is disruptive and destructive.[1]

Woodburn, however, continued in hysterical vein, attributing to the Nationalists the view that

> the only way Scotland would get justice would be if somebody threw
> a bomb on Downing Street.[2]

This was not well received, and McNeil's appointment was widely seen as a remit to defuse the Nationalists. Neil McCallum writing in the *New Statesman* described McNeil's arrival as 'an intelligent matching of the man and the moment'. and went on:

> To some extent the Scottish question is now resolved into two strong
> personalities Mr McNeil and Mr MacCormick (the Nationalist
> leader).[3]

Public appetite was further whetted by their very similar background. They had been at the same school and university. Professor Turner, writing two years later, commented that

> These two epigoni of Mr Johnston (Westwood and Woodburn)
> caused great dissatisfaction even among moderate Scots, and this was
> not allayed until the appointment of Mr Hector McNeil.[4]

It was, however, McNeil's preoccupation with foreign affairs that first made its impact on the Scottish Office. He was very critical of the way in which previous Scottish Ministers had confined themselves to speaking only on Scottish issues in Cabinet, and had made no contribution to discussion of matters outside their immediate responsibility. In his view this led the Cabinet to regard the Scottish Secretary as no more than a regional spokesman and, frequently, a source of irritation. McNeil saw it differently. His advisers were encouraged to provide briefs on all topics on the Cabinet agenda where they had any expertise —or even theoretical wisdom—to offer. Foreign Office telegrams from Embassies overseas are circulated to Ministers in the Cabinet. An official in the Scottish Office was given the fascinating task of summarising these despatches to provide a speaking note. McNeil was probably right in this. The immediate benefit accrued to his standing in Cabinet, but there was an incidental gain in the improved reputation of the Office. McNeil's approach also had a good effect on his officials and prompted them to look beyond what Sir Alexander Gray once described as the confines of Regulation 2 (a) (iii) sub-paragraph (b).

McNeil had taken part in the Paris peace conference in 1946 and the negotiations leading up to the Brussels treaty in 1948. He retained a keen interest in the International Refugee Organisation, and now he seized every opportunity to carry the Scottish Office flag overseas. In July, 1950, he accompanied the Highland Provosts to St Valéry for the unveiling of the Memorial to the 51st Highland Division and the 2nd French Cavalry Division. On the same trip he paid a carefully heralded visit to the cemetery at Dieppe where many of the Canadian soldiers killed in the Dieppe raid are buried. This was especially opportune as Canadian opinion was greatly incensed at recent revelations about the conduct of the operation. He insisted on leading the British delegation to a meeting of U.N.E.S.C.O.—hitherto the preserve of the Minister of Education—in Paris, and the Scottish Education Department had to address their minds to questions they had previously ignored. McNeil's own contribution was to exhort U.N.E.S.C.O. to behave more like Whitehall and less like Chelsea. The official head of the delegation, Sir John (now Lord Redcliffe-)Maud, returned convinced that the Scottish Office's views on educational policy would have to be given more weight.

Still in Paris, there was an odd incident when he was leaving the Ritz Hôtel. He later told me the background. While he was still at the Foreign Office, McNeil and his wife were asked to dinner by Lady Cunard. The McNeils were unaware that the intention was that they should meet the Duke and Duchess of Windsor. (It was known that the Duke was very keen to be an Ambassador.) By the end of the evening the Windsors had not appeared, and McNeil took leave of his hostess. On the way out they met the Windsors arriving, and the Duchess pressed him to stay. McNeil firmly but politely explained that it was late and they had a baby to look after. The McNeils left. Now, years later, he had met the Windsors again at the door of the Ritz. The Duchess was insistent that he should join them for a drink, but McNeil demurred, saying that he was already late for his next engagement, as was the case. Sharp as a scalpel came the reply, 'Another baby to feed?' McNeil, the most classless of politicians but prone to irreverence, laughed all the way down the Champs-Élysées.

A more spectacular event was McNeil's attempt to bring the General Assembly of the United Nations to Edinburgh. It became known that the United Nations, while the ebony matchbox that was to be their permanent home in New York was being completed, were prepared to meet in Europe. McNeil, through his contacts in the United States, was quick to urge the attractions of Edinburgh, and in July, 1950, he persuaded Col. Virgin, the director of the U.N. conference department, to come to Edinburgh on a reconnaissance. He offered to vacate St Andrew's House for the U.N. secretariat and proposed that the Assembly should meet in the Usher Hall. Virgin, though impressed, observed that the South Americans had the decisive vote of the conference committee, and he doubted whether they would find the facilities for nocturnal entertainment adequate. So it proved.

McNeil's foreign connection was not to everyone's taste. A projected visit to Canada to address Scottish organisations there had to be cancelled, ostensibly because a three-line whip required his presence in the House, but in his view because a recent visit to Ottawa by the Commonwealth Secretary had been noticeably unsuccessful and jealousy was evident. Scottish M.P.s complained that he spent more time with his friend Lew Douglas, the influential American Ambassador, Averill Harriman, and other leading figures from the States, than with his fellow-countrymen. This criticism was wide of the mark, particularly at a time when our special relationship with the States was under intermittent attack from the Left. More unwisely, he made foreign affairs the main feature of many of his public utterances—notably when he delivered the annual State of the Nation speech at the City Chambers in Edinburgh. The worthy burgesses waiting for a dissertation on the housing programme were disappointed. Speak up for your country, Mr McNeil, the *Scottish Daily Express* urged. The implication was that he was not doing his job as Secretary of State. But was he not?

The Scottish public were inevitably going to judge him by his treatment of the Nationalist issue. This was by no means the most important problem facing the Scottish Office, but it was the one that lent itself most easily to exposition in the media. The continuing effect of the Nationalist mystique on the conduct of the Scottish Office is discussed in detail in Chapter XIX, but meanwhile McNeil's defusing activities were, at least temporarily, successful. *The Scotsman* was mildly favourable to the Nationalists' cause, but this was no more than consistent with its critical attitude to everything that emerged from St Andrew's House. The *Glasgow Herald* was solidly anti-Nationalist, and only the *Bulletin* was unreservedly on the other side—due to a fervent editor J. M. Reid, whose rabid opinions eventually led to trouble with his employers. From the start, McNeil was not going to repeat the mistakes of his predecessors. On 10th March, 1950, in what he described as his maiden speech on devolution, he said

> Anyone of sensitivity who hopes to be regarded as responsible will not push, or attempt to push, this movement aside off hand. I certainly will not.[5]

Two months later the Scottish Nationalists, who now claimed 1·25 million signatures to their new Scottish Covenant, were demanding to be met. *The Times*, whose same edition carried a strong leader arguing against the creation of a separate Scottish Parliament, observed:

> Mr McNeil has shown himself readier than Mr Woodburn his predecessor to go into the whole question of devolution, and he would no doubt be willing to hear what the leaders of the home rule movement have to say at some convenient time.[6]

In July McNeil played an undisguised straight bat. He told the House.

> I met on 17th June a deputation (from the Scottish Covenant Commissioners) which submitted to me their case for the setting up of a Scottish Parliament for domestic affairs. I undertook to bring their submissions to the attention of my colleagues. This I have done.[7]

In the meantime he had appointed a Committee under the Chairmanship of Lord Catto, a former Governor of the Bank of England, and comprising bankers, economists, an ex-civil servant, and a trade union official, to report on the facts of the financial and economic relations between Scotland and England. Signatures were still being appended to the Covenant, but the original impetus seemed to have been lost, and it was clear that the Catto Committee would take months to report. McNeil met MacCormick, whom he regarded as an agreeable romantic, in private, but nothing of substance emerged from their discussion. An uneasy stalemate had been reached.

On Christmas morning, 1950, a small party of extreme Nationalists stole the Stone of Scone from Westminster Abbey. Dr Don, the Scottish Dean of Westminster, overreacted in a violently emotional broadcast. For the rest, some were disposed to be amused at what might be thought a misguided escapade, but the great majority were incensed at the affront to tradition and the element of sacrilege involved. The *Spectator*'s comment of 29th December was typical.

> And it is true that, if the supporters of Scottish Nationalism can find no better way of drawing attention to themselves, hooliganism will serve.[8]

If McNeil kept a dignified silence and refused to be drawn in public, he was still active behind the scenes. He sniffed about with a journalist's nose. In a strange partnership with a reporter Andrew Ewart, and William Kerr, later Chief Constable of Dunbartonshire, he early identified the culprits, but he said nothing. He did, however, astound Mr John Rollo, a prominent Nationalist who was thought to be implicated. Rollo approached him after a meeting of the Highland Panel saying they had not previously met. 'I know you', McNeil replied. 'You are in the stone mason's business.' A bizarre episode was a meeting with John Gordon of the *Sunday Express*. Gordon said he knew the whereabouts of the Stone and offered to return it in exchange for exclusive rights and an undertaking that there would be no prosecution. Otherwise the Stone would be thrown into the North Sea, and the Secretary of State would be responsible. McNeil replied coldly that Gordon had mistaken his man.

The recovery of the Stone was an anticlimax. On 11th April, 1951, it was left in Arbroath Abbey with letters addressed to the King and the General Assembly of the Church of Scotland asserting loyalty to the Crown and expressing the hope that the Stone would be kept in Scotland. On 19th April the Attorney General told the House that he had studied the police reports, which included statements from three of the four responsible. While deploring the vandalism of the theft he had decided that no criminal proceedings would be taken. The Stone—in chains for security—was back in its original place at Westminster. *The Times* thundered:

> The removal of the Stone had 'exposed the history of their proud country to the ridicule of comedians and taproom jokers. . . . The most ancient and most honourable part of the Scottish regalia' had been treated 'like a sack of coals'.[9]

In observing that nationalism was once again under a cloud *The Times* concluded with a pregnant sentence. 'The politicians will feel once more that they can bide their time.'

The Nationalists were now in some apparent discomfiture. Early in 1951 the *New Statesman* was already reporting that

> The Covenant movement, after a year of very successful agitation, has stalled.[10]

In October, Neil McCallum writing again in the same periodical described McNeil as 'a most diplomatic Secretary' and remarked

> Ever since the affair of the Coronation Stone the question of Home Rule has diminished in the press from a great interrogative to a small query. The return of the Stone marked a quick disappearance of the Covenant movement from the news columns.[11]

Subsequent events have shown that the Nationalist movement was not to be so easily dismissed, but in the 1951 context McNeil had done his job well. In retrospect his task was fortuitously easy. There were plenty of other questions to engage public attention—rationing and scarcity at home, the Schumann plan and Korea abroad—and he had bought time by appointing the Catto Committee. In one respect, however, his influence was unfortunate. *The Times* was right. 'Biding his time' was his policy towards the Nationalists. He adopted, and encouraged his officials to adopt, a *laissez-faire* attitude. The Nationalists were to be treated seriously in public, but he did not believe that their claims, whether for separation or more arguably for increased devolution, should affect Scottish Office policy. In this he was moved, not by adherence to Socialist centralisation, but by his own vision of Scotland against the wider horizon. He equated nationalism with parish-pumping, which he abhorred. His successors were to reap an unwelcome harvest.

McNeil's early experience, both at University and in the cauldron of the United Nations, had made him a formidable debater but, perhaps for this very reason, he was not seriously tested in the House. He was adept at winding up debates on Great Britain matters where he shared the responsibility with an English Minister. This is a hazard which Scottish Ministers try to avoid, knowing that they stand to be caught out on details by English M.P.s. McNeil's dialectic skill was equal to the challenge. In the Chamber he had a delicate relationship with Churchill. After he had followed the Leader of the Opposition to conclude a Housing debate he received a graceful note of congratulation. When he resisted the Conservative call for a Royal Commission instead of the Catto Committee, Churchill replied:

> Part of my anxiety in this matter is due to my desire that the reputation which he (McNeil) acquired in a subordinate position at the Foreign Office shall not be squandered now that he is the head of a Department.[12]

Other interventions were less successful. In a fisheries debate when other business prevented him from reading his brief he said he would tempt the Opposition to their feet to consume the time available. This he did. Mr Speaker took note and summoned McNeil for a stern reproof.

McNeil was a keen angler and took personal charge of the Salmon and Freshwater Fisheries (Protection) (Scotland) Bill which prescribed severe penalties for organised gang poaching, although showing a 'tenderness for the traditional poacher'. Against strong vocal criticism from his own party he insisted on doubling the close time for commercial netting, in order to improve salmon stocks. This may seem a trivial point, but it is highly exceptional for a Minister to devise and carry out his own amendment. Ministers' predilections on details of this kind seldom reach the Statute Book. Lord Dunglass (later Lord Home) complimented him that the debate had been 'a happy Parliamentary occasion'.[13]

McNeil had strong views on the structure of the Scottish Office. These extended beyond reorganising his Private Secretariat. He was impatient at the limited scope of most of the functions exercised by the four Scottish Departments—agriculture, education, health and housing, and law and order. To his mind they were irrelevant to the real economic problems affecting the country. To this extent he was inconsistent, because he was not an advocate of increased devolution to the Scottish Office.

He did, however, take a keen personal interest in the work of the

Department of Agriculture. This was somewhat unusual since questions of principle requiring the attention of the Secretary of State were in the main centred on the Annual Price Review where the Agriculture Ministers negotiated jointly with the farmers' leaders on a U.K. basis. But McNeil had his own ideas, particularly on the problems affecting the hill farmers. One episode is revealing.

McNeil visited the Great Glen Cattle Ranch at Inverlochy, near Fort William. Starting with a few thousand acres of heather and scrubland, Mr Hobbs, the owner, had undertaken an extensive programme of reclamation and was now rearing, and wintering, cattle on the hills. He increased his herd to over a thousand head, and was able to sell four hundred calves a year at Stirling Market. This, from land recently non-productive, caught McNeil's imagination. He wanted to set up a Beef Board, an entirely new form of nationalised enterprise, to breed and market cattle. He saw this as a simple logical scheme which would go some way to revive agriculture on the hills. But there were technical considerations against it. Hobbs's breeding stock was not proved, and there were arguments that his was a special situation. By the time McNeil's proposals had been processed and agreed with the Ministry of Agriculture and the Treasury they were severely etiolated. The Hill Lands Commission which was eventually appointed was an advisory, not an executive, body, and little action followed its report (Cmd. 9759). Hobbs's minority reservation showed how great was the departure from McNeil's original concept. McNeil confessed ruefully that there were evident limitations on what a Minister could do.

More success attended his efforts in the health field. The National Health Service was still in its infancy, and the medical profession retained a latent suspicion about the Government's intentions. But some of McNeil's closest friends came from the profession and he took great pains to gain the doctors' confidence. Tuberculosis was still one of the most distressing problems and the waiting lists for hospital treatment ran into thousands. McNeil took an inspired initiative in arranging that accommodation in Swiss sanatoria should be made available through the Health Service. The scheme was announced in April, 1951, and by July he could tell Parliament that the first patients were already in Switzerland.

> The first group left on 15th June—normally persons requiring at least six months' sanatorium care, but unlikely to need any major surgical operation.[14]

Numerically, this had little effect on the waiting lists, but it afforded a glimmer of hope to those with no chance of admission to a hospital in this country. McNeil was entitled to the satisfaction he felt when he visited Scottish patients at Crans and Montana.

Despite his limited statutory powers he made strenuous attempts to bring new industry to Scotland. The scope for government action was much more restricted than it later became, and consisted primarily of steering firms to chosen areas by granting, or refusing, industrial development certificates. The Scottish Council (Development and Industry), however, under the inspired leadership of Lord Bilsland, were carrying out a vigorous campaign to attract industrial investment, particularly from abroad. McNeil and his officials afforded them whole-hearted co-operation, and the tally of new enterprises mounted. One instance shows how far he was prepared to go in the Scottish interest.

It became known that the giant American company International Business Machines intended to set up manufacturing capacity in Great Britain, but had not selected a location. McNeil had met the head of I.B.M.—the venerable tycoon Tom Watson—in New York, and persuaded him to come to Scotland to inspect possible sites. On a Saturday an impressive cortège consisting of McNeil, Watson, and their staff drove to Greenock, but none of the sites on offer found favour. Then Watson indicated a couple of fields, saying that this was the kind of area he wanted. McNeil did not know who owned the land, but immediately proposed a bargain. He would provide an option on the site within a week if I.B.M., for their part, would undertake to accept it. Watson, though sceptical whether this could be done, agreed. McNeil and his officials then roused a startled Town Clerk and identified the owner as a Dowager living in Sussex. McNeil took off in a chartered plane and before the weekend was over he had his option. In the face of strenuous opposition from Sir Hartley Shawcross who, as President of the Board of Trade, was canvassing a site in St Helens, McNeil prevailed. An industrial development certificate was granted and I.B.M. moved to Greenock. An unorthodox, but imaginative sortie. Morale in the Scottish Office rose.

McNeil went out of office on the fall of the Labour Government at the October, 1951, General Election. He did not play a prominent rôle in Opposition, and became Chairman of the British company producing the Encyclopaedia Britannica. While travelling to the United States on business he suffered a haemorrhage and died in New York on 11th October, 1955.

McNeil inclined to the right of his Party, but he did not see politics in terms of right or left labels. He had a clear perception of the U.K.'s place in world affairs, but he had not evolved a political philosophy of his own to govern his attitude to domestic matters. As a result, his zeal for reform found expression in a series of *ad hoc* solutions. He was, however, involved in one major Cabinet schism. Along with Hilary Marquand, the English Minister of Health, he was responsible for the introduction of charges in the national health service. When Nye Bevan attacked the decision in the country McNeil and Marquand represented to the Prime Minister against this breach of Cabinet solidarity, and Bevan's resignation followed.

McNeil's period at the Scottish Office was brief, a bare nineteen months, but eventful. His success in containing the Nationalists was skilful in the parliamentary and public relations sense, but sowed the seeds of future trouble. Otherwise, he was an exceptionally constructive, creative Minister. He encouraged the Scottish Office to take a positive line, and the Office knew they could count on his formidable support in conflicts with other Departments. He exemplified the possibilities of, and the limitations on, a personal Ministerial approach He left his staff in no doubt that they would be judged by what they achieved in improving the conditions and economic prospects of the lieges. He had little appetite for routine legislation, leaving that to his Parliamentary Secretaries, and he saw the administration of statutory, regulatory, functions as a chore. He did much to turn the office into a modern, businesslike organisation. He brought Tom Johnston's concept of 'Scotland's Minister' up to date.

It is impossible to leave McNeil without one speculation. No Secretary of State for Scotland has been promoted to higher office, though some must have been runners. McNeil was a close friend of Hugh Gaitskell, and their political doctrine was very similar. If he had survived, could the mantle as Leader of the Party have fallen on him? He was senior as a Minister to those who contested the succession.

Notes

1 *Hansard*, 16th November, 1949. Vol. 469, col. 2095.
2 *Ibid.*
3 *New Statesman*, 25th March, 1950.

4 Arthur Turner, *Scottish Home Rule*. Oxford, 1952.
5 *Hansard*, 10th March, 1950. Vol. 472, col. 635.
6 *The Times*, 2nd May, 1950.
7 *Hansard*, 4th July, 1950. Vol. 477, col. 218.
8 The *Spectator*, 29th December, 1950.
9 *The Times*, 12th April, 1951.
10 *New Statesman*, 20th January, 1951.
11 *New Statesman*, 20th October, 1951.
12 *Hansard*, 25th May, 1950. Vol. 475, col. 2275.
13 *Hansard*, 13th December, 1950. Vol. 482, col. 1180.
14 *Hansard*, 24th July, 1951. Vol. 491, col. 191.

CHAPTER XIII

The Patrician

When James Stuart was told by Churchill that he was to be Secretary of State for Scotland in the new Conservative Government he immediately asked for Lord Home as his Minister of State. Churchill, who could not resist the innocent pun 'Home, sweet home', agreed. Lord Home recalls his own arrival to join Stuart.

> On the first day of my association with him in the Scottish Office, he said to me, 'I think we ought to put a notice over our connecting doors'. I said 'All right, what shall it be?' He answered 'We will not overwork.' I was not deceived.[1]

Nor were the staff of the Scottish Office, although it took them some time to find out what lay behind Stuart's languid, laconic manner.

James Stuart was a self-confessed anachronism. Traces of his Edwardian upbringing were always apparent. (He never took a taxi: he 'picked up a growler'.) But his patrician ancestry went much deeper into the past. King James V left one legitimate child, Mary, and several royal bastards, including James Stuart, Earl of Moray (the Regent Moray). Dame Edith Sitwell remarked in *The Queens and the Hive* that although Mary was queen, it was that most remarkable man James Stuart her elder half-brother who was in all but name the ruler of Scotland, and concluded 'It was his misfortune and Scotland's that he was not king'.[2] The later James Stuart, who was directly descended from the Regent, used to comment with quiet amusement that history might have brought him the crown.

Stuart was born in 1897, the third son of the 17th Earl of Moray. He was still at school at the outbreak of the First War and went straight from Eton to the trenches. Joining the Royal Scots, he was in the front line before his eighteenth birthday: he was soon made adjutant of his battalion and won two M.C.s in action. His wartime experience remained in his mind, and the chapters in his autobiography dealing with these years can be commended for their vivid evocation of the horrors of Flanders. 'As soon as a man's nerve gives way, he is liable to die quite soon.' Or the verdict of one who had survived, 'All wars last too long. They waste too much of a nation's best blood, dissipate the national wealth and resources and achieve nothing useful at the end of the agony.'[3]

In later life Stuart was proud of his connection with the Royal Scots. The lift at St Andrew's House would be delayed while he exchanged reminiscences with the attendant wearing a regimental tie. By what he thought a happy coincidence two of his closest advisers—Sir David Milne, the Permanent Under-Secretary, and at the political level Sir P. J. Blair, who ran the Scottish Unionist Party organisation, had both served in the First of Foot.

On demobilisation Stuart read, briefly, for the Scottish Bar, but this was not his *métier*, and in his own words 'the Bar certainly lost nothing of great value when I moved elsewhere'. This was to an unusual posting. He became the first Equerry on the staff of Prince Albert (King George VI). His years in the Palace he described in affectionate, respectful, but strangely distant terms. He did not feel he could remain indefinitely as a courtier (at a salary of £450, on which he had to keep a valet), and early in 1922 he accepted an offer to join the Pearson organisation and go into the oil business as a learner at the production end in America. There followed some months in the New York office of the Amerada Petroleum Company, where Stuart soon discovered that if he was not destined for the law he had less gift for accountancy. He was then sent to the oilfields proper in Oklahoma where he shared the rough and tumble of life as a 'roustabout' on the rigs. The contrast with life at Court was pretty complete, but in both these different *milieux* Stuart displayed one of his main characteristics. Beneath his indolent exterior he was determined to get on with the job in hand. He had a feeling for history and tradition, but, as the Scottish Office was later to learn, no respect for red tape, and very little for convention.

The wheel of fortune was about to turn again for Stuart and when he was home on leave in 1923 he was astonished to receive a telegram from the Moray and Nairn Unionist Association asking him to stand for the constituency at the General Election. Taking his father's advice to 'have a shot', he accepted and was returned at the hustings. But the Baldwin government was not, and Ramsay MacDonald formed the first Labour Government with the support of Asquith's Liberals. MacDonald's administration lasted less than a year and at the next election Stuart, by now deciding that he might as well continue with what he had started, retained his seat which he held until he retired in 1959.

Stuart was puzzled to find himself in Parliament. He was even more surprised at his subsequent political advancement. But others, as his Colonel in the Royal Scots did when he made him adjutant at the age of nineteen, had detected his unassuming ability to get on with all kinds of people and his latent power of command. Stuart was much concerned with the idea of leadership. There is, for example, his criticism of A. J. Balfour whose perfect logic and reasoning inclined to produce indecision 'which is fatal for a party leader'. Stuart's deduction was that

> Ordinary men can back a horse each way, but a leader cannot: he has to make a decision and lead his party, for better or worse, over a chosen course, whatever the hazards.[4]

This incidental observation, simplistic though it may seem, is near the core of Stuart's political approach. If he believed he was right he was not going to be deflected from his objective. He had no great appetite for the hurly-burly of party politics. (He was never a prominent figure in Opposition.) It is doubtful if he ever thought that the Labour Party provided a credible alternative. Though this may appear the height of Olympian disdain, to his mind power should be exercised by those who understood how to wield it responsibly, and who were prepared to subject themselves to the self-discipline required.

Stuart was appointed Scottish Whip in 1935 and Deputy Chief Whip in 1937. In 1941 when Margesson was moved to the War Office Stuart succeeded him as Churchill's Chief Whip. Since Stuart's relationship with Churchill became so intimate that the term unique is for once appropriate, it is surprising that his appointment was originally against the Prime Minister's wishes. Stuart did not claim that he had any prescriptive right to promotion and Churchill had already recalled Thomas Dugdale (Lord Crathorne) from the Middle East and earmarked him for the post. It says much for both Stuart and Dugdale—the most selfless of politicians whose career was unhappily terminated by his honourable resignation over the Crichel Down affaire—that they served amicably together in the Whips' Office, with Dugdale in the subordinate rôle.

Stuart's time as Chief Whip falls outside the scope of this book, but there can be no doubt that he was one of the most effective holders of the office. As he summed it up,

Whips can, of course, be rude to Members, but this is harmless enough
and spills no blood. Members, in turn, can be rude to Whips, which is
fair enough.

Two things, however, are clear. First, though Churchill was the most
exacting of masters, no one was closer to him than Stuart who earned
his complete trust and, eventually, his affection. In 1950, when senior
Tories began to have doubts whether Churchill, at his advanced age,
should lead the Party at the next election, Stuart was selected as the
only one who could report their misgivings—to no purpose as it
turned out—to the great man. Second, although Stuart in his autobiography deliberately played down this aspect, he had an extremely
influential, and often decisive say in Ministerial appointments. In his
book he was careful not to stoop to vulgar revelations that would
cause distress, but it is evident that few Ministers reached office if
Stuart did not approve. Iain Macleod, for example, attributed his
appointment as Minister of Health to Stuart and wrote to thank him
for it.[5] Sir John Colville, Churchill's Private Secretary, noted in his
diary that 'James stands up against the Beaver-Brendan schemes and
wields too much influence over appointments for their liking'.[6]

The only two major figures for whom he did not share Churchill's
admiration were Eden and Beaverbrook. His dealings with Eden were
always uneasy, and when Eden became Prime Minister, Stuart, as he
confessed, disagreed with him 'in the most vigorous terms'. Stuart's
summing up of Suez was 'I did not object to our going IN: what I did
object to was our coming OUT.'[7] He regarded Beaverbrook, 'this
Press Baron', as a political adventurer, and was pleased to learn that he
was on Beaverbrook's 'black list', and was to be attacked whenever
opportunity offered, or could be manufactured. In this, as in almost
everything else, he was in complete contrast with his predecessor at the
Scottish Office, Hector McNeil, though both enjoyed the friendship of
Beaverbrook's mysterious acolyte Brendan Bracken.

Stuart had many friends on both sides of the House. He was even
consulted by Nye Bevan, who sought his advice on what line he should
take to counter Gaitskell's bid for the leadership of the Labour Party.
Among Scottish M.P.s, Tom Johnston always looked on him with
respect. 'There's steel in that man', he would say. Stuart seems to have
been particularly attracted by the Red Clydesiders. Like others, he was
susceptible to the charm of James Maxton, and John McGovern was
his standing 'pair'. His tolerance of the Opposition did not, however,
extend to the Liberal Party.

> I do not think I have ever suffered or enjoyed the friendship of a Liberal. I regard this as fortunate for they form a race apart, sitting on the fence and incapable of deciding whether to jump down on one side or the other. It must be a great worry to them and I thank God I was not constructed that way, even though I may be less intelligent than, say, Lady Violet Bonham-Carter.[8]

When the Conservatives were returned to power in 1951 Stuart did not want, or expect, the Scottish Office. He always maintained that he was not driven by ambition, and, referring again to Churchill, 'neither of us had any illusions that I was a political genius'. Summoned to Chartwell immediately after the General Election, Stuart was warned by Harry Crookshank what lay ahead, and he was ready with thanks for the compliment and his regrets that he was not qualified to be Secretary of State. He persisted with his demurring, but Churchill prevailed. It is not unusual for Ministers to say that office has been wished on them, but in Stuart's case there is no reason to doubt his sincerity. He cited a meeting with George Buchanan, a Clydesider and a former junior Scottish Minister, as confirming his reluctance. Buchanan's forthright assertion was:

> 'I never thought ye were such a bloody fool, Jimmy.' 'I'm sorry, Geordie,' I said, 'but what have I done wrong?' 'Och,' he said, 'to take on that job at the Scottish Office. Ye'll never make a bloody thing out o' that.'[9]

We will examine what he did, in his own way and in his own time.

Stuart had no experience of running a major Government Department. (The Whips' Office had a minute staff, controlled by Sir Charles Harris, the indefatigable Figaro of Westminster.) It soon became evident, however, that he was fully seized of the virtues of delegation. He was assisted by a strong Ministerial team, and he made no secret that the choice was his. Lord Home, the first to hold the new post of Minister of State, was his second-in-command. Lord Home's subsequent career in senior appointments, and eventually in the most senior, needs no additional encomium in this book. It was intended that the Minister of State, having lighter parliamentary duties as a Member of the House of Lords, should work mainly in Scotland where he would be readily available to consult local authorities and other representative bodies. The theory was that a resident Minister would be an antidote to the disease of remote control from Whitehall. Lord Home proceeded to put this theory into effect with very considerable acceptance. He also made the Highlands his special care, and he pointed with some pride to his part in the framing and passing of the Act which set up the Crofters Commission. There were high hopes, only partly fulfilled, that the new body would be effective in restoring the crofting communities.

The complement of Parliamentary Under-Secretaries of State was increased from two to three. Commander T. D. Galbraith (later Lord Strathclyde), whose quarterdeck vocabulary was on occasion a salutary purgative for costive deputations, was put in charge of the housing programme. Galbraith had moved the resolution naming 300,000 houses a year as the Great Britain target at the Party Conference that preceded the 1951 Election. This figure was reached in 1953, the Scottish total being of the order of 40,000, or 14·5 per cent of that for England and Wales. William McNair Snadden, a successful farmer, brought his own expertise to the oversight of the Department of Agriculture. Stuart gave him a free rein, but one of his interventions illustrates how he saw the broader picture. In the course of an Annual Price Review the Agriculture Ministers were addressed at quite extraordinary length by Sir James Turner (later Lord Netherthorpe) on behalf of the Farmers' Unions. Stuart did not care for being harangued in this manner and entertained some doubts about the whole machinery for fixing the level of agricultural support. He told Sir Norman Brook (later Lord Normanbrook) privately that he was not happy at settling such a vast annual subvention to the industry without some more effective way of ensuring that the consumer's voice was heard. Stuart was looking a long way ahead, but the time was not ripe for a change.

James Henderson Stewart, an experienced Parliamentarian, was the third Under-Secretary of State and took charge of Education and the diverse work of the Home Department. To complete the team, Stuart appointed Jack Nixon Browne (later Lord Craigton) as his Parliamentary Private Secretary, and this merits a special mention. There is some confusion about the rôle of the P.P.S. He is unpaid: he is not a member of the Government: he is not supposed to speak in the House on matters where his Minister is involved: nor is he expected to criticise general Government policy. In return for this vow of silence he gets what is popularly seen as a toehold on the Ministerial ladder, and can learn at first hand how the official machine works. He has some mechanical duties—arranging his master's 'pairings', and conveying notes between his Minister, if he is speaking from the Front Bench, and the official box on the Speaker's right, where the civil servants are hastily scribbling briefs. This requires some agility. More important, he keeps the Minister informed of the temper of the House, and reports any undercurrents that are likely to come to the surface. All this is common form.

There are areas where the P.P.S.'s functions are less clearly defined. He has no right of access to Cabinet papers or other classified material, though the Minister may, naturally, consult him on their content. Here the possibility of conflict arises. A tactless P.P.S. may arrogate to himself rights that are not his, and demand to be consulted by officials, see papers, etc. Very few P.P.S.'s do this, but when they do there are red faces all round.

Nixon Browne took his duties very seriously. He spent his first few months sitting unobtrusively in the Private Office, emphasising that he was a learner and wanted to be of help. Officials realised that his interpretation of the feeling among M.P.s, and the mind of the Secretary of State, was invaluable, and he played a vital part in the running of the office. He succeeded Galbraith as Under-Secretary of State (in which capacity he piloted an extensive collection of Bills through the Scottish Grand Committee) and later as Minister of State. His own contribution at each stage was a very personal one. He emphasised that he was a layman and he told officials that before he could approve their proposals, or submit them to the Secretary of State, they would have to convince him that they were comprehensible and could be justified in lay terms. It was, he said, his job to ask innocent questions. After many lengthy sessions with the Home Department Nixon Browne could claim that he was the only Minister who could negotiate the labyrinth of the equalisation grant formula for grants to local authorities. As a result of his probing, Scottish Office policy might be attacked, quite properly, by the Opposition, but it had at least some relation to common-sense. Stuart relied heavily on Nixon Browne to act as devil's advocate when White Papers were being drafted, or Bills hammered into shape. He chose his man well.

The Scottish Office received early warning of Stuart's standing with his colleagues. A decision had to be taken on the granting of liquor licences in the developing New Towns in both Scotland and England. It had been intended that public houses there should be run by the State Management Districts organisation. This body was set up during the First War to control the sale of liquor in designated areas (the North-West of England and round the Moray Firth) where drunkenness had become a social problem, e.g. among munition workers. The S.M.D. still existed, under the jurisdiction of the Home Secretary and the Secretary of State, and ran a number of hotels and public houses. There were respectable arguments on both sides whether the State should have the monopoly of selling liquor in the New Towns. But Stuart thought the S.M.D. philosophy was illogical in a free society, and during a weekend in his constituency he paid a visit incognito to the S.M.D. premises at Conon Bridge, Evanton, and Invergordon. He returned convinced that State pubs were not the answer.

Stuart and his advisers then met the Home Secretary, Sir David Maxwell Fyfe (later Lord Kilmuir) and his staff at the Home Office. Maxwell Fyfe made an eloquent speech in favour of the S.M.D. solution, using all his familiar gestures—the waving of his glasses, the break in his voice, the carefully-timed pause—but to no effect. Stuart said that he was more reluctant to legislate on liquor than on any other subject except divorce, knowing that whatever he did he would be criticised by half the electorate. But a Conservative Government was meant to stand for free enterprise and he did not favour any extension of State ownership. Seeing that he would not prevail against Stuart, Maxwell Fyfe assented. He did not, however, bear any resentment for the crisp way in which he had been defeated. In his *Memoirs* he recalls that 'Old Lord Finlay had said a quarter of a century before: "Beware of men like James Stuart who talk slowly and think quickly." ' He adds that Stuart was 'one of the most consistently underrated men I have known in political life'.[10]

S.M.D. did not move into the New Towns and a few years later their premises were sold to private companies. (Hector McNeil, who was not faced with the New Town complication, took a different line towards the S.M.D. set-up. He wanted to transform one of their inns into a model hotel, furnished with the best Scottish Products, as a shop window for the tourist industry. A constructive proposal, but there were insuperable accounting difficulties.)

It would be foolish to exaggerate the importance of the S.M.D. issue, although Stuart saw it as a question of principle. The significant point is that he had demonstrated, quietly but firmly, that Ministerial disputes would be resolved as he wished. There was a further instance soon afterwards regarding a technicality of legal process on both sides of the Border. Again the precise subject does not matter. The Scottish Office felt that the Whitehall scheme would be inimical to Scotland and submitted a counter-memorandum. Stuart agreed with his officials on the substance, but said he did not want a paper circulated. He would attend to the matter personally. The record of the subsequent meeting showed a monotonous unanimity among the other Ministers that the offending proposal should be dropped. There was no reference to the Scottish objections, but Stuart had done his groundwork to good effect.

It might be thought that the Scottish Office would now have taken one or two things to heart. The Secretary of State had the ear of the Prime Minister. He was probably number three in the batting order after Churchill and Eden, a ranking not reached by any Scottish Minister before or since. So much was well known. Just as important in the everyday run of government business, the Office had a Minister capable of exercising the most decisive influence over his Cabinet colleagues. Put another way, if the officials' case was good it was unlikely to founder because of obstruction in Whitehall.

One might accordingly have envisaged the five years of Stuart's tenure as being marked by a spectacular series of measures for the benefit of Scotland. But, by and large, this did not happen, and one can offer only a tentative explanation why the opportunity was not grasped. Officials will bring forward projects, or plans for legislation, based on Committee reports or wisdom garnered from exhaustive consultation. But these will deal mainly with tidying-up, or non-contentious, matters. They will not be in advance of public opinion, and the usual complaint is that the proposals come far too late, but the preference for an orthodox—descending sometimes to an undisguised *laissez-faire*—attitude, is the result of requiring the civil service to adopt a moderate view, to provide ballast, to restrain the enthusiasm of new governments and their more extreme supporters. This does not lead to an adventurous approach. The more imaginative bureaucrats, the bobby-dazzlers as Sir John Maud called them, may become impatient, but the machine is designed to operate in low gear. In any event the prime responsibility for initiating policy rests with Ministers, and Stuart was not an innovator. The Conservative Party, he said, was not notorious for its anxiety to legislate. He was much more concerned to make the existing arrangements work. If he could make them work more efficiently and acceptably, so much the better.

There is also a contemporary explanation. Politicians must, if they are to survive, be sensitive to the temper of the times. When the Attlee government went out of office in 1951 after passing an un-paralleled series of major Acts to bring public utilities and resources into State ownership, the country was becoming weary with a surfeit of legislation. There were still relics of wartime austerity to be removed, but this was not the season for a further programme of reform. There were few attempts to put the clock back (the Steel Bill was an exception), and in general Parliament was content to debate minor matters at extraordinary length. Stuart's appreciation coincided with the national mood.

This appreciation extended to the Nationalist movement. The Conservative's nostrum for the Nationalists was the appointment of two more Scottish Ministers, already in post, and of a Royal Commission. The Prime Minister announced the setting up of the Commission in Parliament on 24th July, 1952, but left the ensuing debate to Stuart. The Opposition were in something of a quandary. While in office they had refused to allow a similar enquiry. How were they to react? Arthur Woodburn welcomed the Commission, adding that their remit was 'at least on a practical basis'. But John Wheatley was keen to draw attention to the restricted terms of reference. He enquired innocently whether the Commission were being excluded from considering legislative devolution. Stuart made clear that there was to be no meddling with home rule, or a separate Scottish Parliament.

> The Royal Commission can ask for evidence, or receive evidence, from any quarter, but the question whether there should be Parliamentary or political devolution is, I think, a matter for Parliament itself.[11]

The Times agreed that the restriction, which would 'cause disappointment', was wise, since this was a matter of 'great historical and constitutional moment, on which the British Government must make up its own mind'.[12] Scottish opinion, on the whole, was prepared to wait and see.

As Commissions go, the Scottish one had a strong membership. The Chairman, the Earl of Balfour (nephew of A. J. Balfour), had practical experience of working in a nationalised industry. The members included Sir John Spencer Muirhead, founder and first President of the Law Society of Scotland, as Vice-Chairman; two prominent industrialists in Sir Hugh Chance and Sir Murray Stephen, the shipbuilder; Sir Thomas Gardiner, a former Permanent Secretary; and Claude Guillebaud the distinguished economist. The Commission heard evidence in public in the stately ambience of the Signet Library. The three Nationalist parties came with their supporters, and John

MacCormick earned respect for the moderate, reasoned way he presented his case. Dr Lamont of the Scottish National Congress was less impressive, attacking Sir Murray Stephen for building oil tankers to carry imports at the expense of the Scottish shale industry. Stephen was stung to reply that his yard had not built a vessel of this kind. Three ex-Secretaries of State gave evidence, along with the surviving Scottish Secretary, Lord Alness. The Permanent Secretaries from all the major Departments in Whitehall were given a searching examination about their attitude to Scottish requirements, and Sir Edward Bridges came North to relate the message from the Treasury tablets.

The Commission visited the Highlands and Islands and took evidence in Northern Ireland. With hindsight it is possible to be thankful that they concluded that the Northern Irish system 'however well adapted to conditions there, would not further the special needs and interests of Scotland'.

The Commission found that discontent had been 'aggravated by needless English thoughtlessness and undue Scottish susceptibilities'. They identified the causes as 'increased intervention by government in everyday life; economic difficulties; and lack of knowledge of the extent to which devolution of Scottish affairs has already taken place'. They defined the principles to be followed as including the necessity for settling Scottish business in Scotland; the recognition by United Kingdom and Great Britain Ministers of Scotland's national status; the need for consultation when policy was being formed as well as executed; and, conversely, 'a recognition of the community of interests between Scotland and other parts of the United Kingdom'. All good, statesmanlike stuff.

The Commission endorsed the recent report of the Catto Committee (Cmd. 8609), particularly their negative conclusion that it was impossible to identify Scotland's imports from, exports to, and balance of payments with other countries, including the rest of the United Kingdom. Another conclusion, unpalatable to the Nationalists, was that Exchequer expenditure on domestic services in Scotland was larger than on corresponding services in England and Wales, and that in some fields, e.g. housing, agriculture, and fisheries, Scotland had been given special treatment. Housing, health, and unemployment were matters of deep and justified concern, but the Commission found no reluctance to recognise their seriousness or lethargy in taking measures to meet them.

On Ministerial responsibility the Commission said baldly that 'the office of Secretary of State has been an invaluable asset to Scotland', and they were opposed to any diminution or division of his powers. They recommended that he should take over responsibility for roads in Scotland and two minor matters. (These transfers were eventually effected.) They thought that his right to speak as 'Scotland's Minister' should be fully recognised and that no attempt should be made to define or limit it.

The Departmental arrangements, both in the Scottish Office and in other Ministries, came under examination. It is noteworthy that while other Commissions and Committees—Priestley and Fulton—have scrutinised the civil service, these bodies were mainly interested in remuneration or structure. The Balfour Commission were primarily concerned with the end product, i.e. efficiency and acceptance. They gave the Scottish Office a clean bill and their criticism of other Departments was mainly related to general attitudes and nomenclature. There were some strictures on the offensive Whitehall habit of referring to Scotland as a 'region'.

In one respect the Commission exceeded their remit. They considered in detail the arrangements for dealing with Scottish legislation. They pointed out that the Scottish Committee's power to take the Second Reading (in effect) and committee stages of Scottish Bills was 'a measure of practical devolution which Scotland alone enjoys'. They could not see how the machinery could be altered to provide for further devolution, or how the responsibility for legislation could be 'placed more surely on the Scottish Members of Parliament'. They also decided that the practical disadvantages of the Scottish Grand Committee sitting in Edinburgh outweighed the arguments in favour of that course.

The Commission's Report (July, 1954) received a less than rapturous welcome, and there was a general feeling that it was printed in whitewash. Cynics will say that governments do not appoint Royal Commissions, or select the members, unless they have a fair idea of what the outcome will be. Certainly if the Moderator of the General Assembly was invited to deliver a sermon, his congregation would be surprised to hear a homily in favour of sin. But Commissions can embarrass governments—the Pilkington and Donovan enquiries are cases in point—and the Balfour Commission's Report is not to be lightly disregarded. If it appeared something of an anticlimax this was because the mood of the country had been changing in the years since the Commission was first promised in the Conservative Election Manifesto. Throughout this period there was a reaction against the Nationalists, and there were traces of nostalgia for the recent past in MacCormick's evidence.

One learned commentator described the Commission's approach as 'romantic', but not enough attention was paid to one of their observations—the criticism about failure in communication. This was, and obstinately remains, a problem for Scottish Ministers. During his tenure Stuart received at best a lukewarm reception in the press. He admitted that he had 'always tended—wrongly or unwisely perhaps— to keep the press at arm's length'.[13] He was not an inspiring public speaker, and his interventions from the Front Bench were diffident, almost reluctant. In a debate on industry and employment Arthur Woodburn suggested that it would assist the House if Stuart would outline 'his comprehensive policy for Scotland'. The *Spectator* commented that this 'was a good deal too much for Mr Stuart'.[14] His amiable speech gathered together some ill-assorted items, a peat-burning power station in Caithness, new shipbuilding orders, etc., but neither the form nor the content was impressive, and he lacked the oratorical gift to convince his listeners that he had anything resembling a comprehensive plan. Stuart once told the writer how much he disliked speaking from Despatch Box. 'I know they don't want to hear me', he said. He even told the House that he didn't think anyone was listening. A strange sign of humility in a man of such unswerving courage. To complete the picture, in private or in after-dinner speeches he was invariably fluent, witty, and amusing.

One episode, trivial in itself, reveals how Stuart looked intuitively at the wide perspective. In April, 1955, the Director of the Scottish National Gallery reported that the Gallery had a chance to acquire an important Velásquez painting if they could find the purchase price before a fixed date. Otherwise the masterpiece would go to the United States. The sum was far in excess of the Trustees' funds, and a special grant would be needed. The Scottish Office drafted a suitable letter to the Chancellor. Stuart signed it, and since it was Budget week, not the best time to rely on Treasury generosity, he said he would speak to the Chancellor as well. But, he added, he was not too happy. The painting, however admirable, was not by a native artist. It had already been in this country for a long time. Shouldn't we let the Americans have it for a spell? Despite his historical appreciation, Stuart persuaded the Chancellor to authorise a grant, and the 'Old

Woman cooking eggs' is one of the chief glories in the Gallery at the foot of the Mound.

Stuart found himself in an unfamiliar rôle when the Russian leaders Bulganin and Krushchev visited Scotland in the summer of 1956. There are plenty of outrageous anecdotes about how Stuart, first down the gangway at Turnhouse, turned to nod his head and release the rulers of the Supreme Soviet tumbling down to join him: how the cortège, driven at breakneck speed for security reasons, overshot the welcoming committee at Queensferry to be pursued by a perspiring Provost on foot: or how the Russian party began to get out of hand when Stuart, bored with a whole day's pleasantries through an interpreter, withdrew for a couple of hours' rest. Many of the best stories are in his autobiography. One that is not concerns the final dinner in the Banqueting Hall at Edinburgh Castle. When the pudding stage was reached Stuart observed that he would eat his first so that his guest could see that it was not poisoned. The interpreter was seen to be sweating.

But this is a digression. Stuart continued his equable course till his resignation in January, 1957. Despite his distaste for legislation some notable Bills had been passed during his time at the office. The historic anomaly of owner's rates was abolished, and the Scottish share of the Exchequer grant to local authorities greatly increased. The Secretary of State's responsibility for electricity in Scotland was made complete with the transfer to his jurisdiction of the South of Scotland Board. Progress was made with the encouragement of light industries, and without direct responsibility the hand of 'Scotland's Minister' was apparent in some of these developments. But Stuart's régime should not be evalued by statutory enactments passed or the publication of White Papers. His real achievements lay in the influence he brought to bear on his Ministerial colleagues. This was most apparent in the decision to go ahead with the Forth Road Bridge. There were at the time responsible economic arguments against incurring the enormous (in contemporary terms) expenditure involved. The pursewardens at the Treasury had allies in other Ministers, but Stuart persevered, confident that events would support his judgment.

The Scottish Office worked at least as smoothly under Stuart as under any other Minister who has held office during the half-century since the first Secretary of State was appointed. In his five years Whitehall Departments, taking their cue from their masters, were wary of engaging the Scottish Office in arguments that might eventually go to Ministers. As a result there were few frustrations and the Office came in for less criticism than usual. If one is conscious of disappointment it is only because Stuart must be judged by the highest standards, and with his record, reputation, and personal aura the opportunities seemed exceptionally favourable. The staff realised that he lacked the entrepreneurial enthusiasm of McNeil and concentrated on more orthodox activities. The moral to be drawn from his period in office is that a 'geographical' Minister can be expected to function most acceptably when government intervention is not increasing and economic conditions, if not showing any dramatic improvement, are not visibly deteriorating. In these circumstances a suppliant Department, as the Scottish Office is, will find it easier to obtain satisfaction for its justifiable demands. This Stuart achieved, but his successors did not have his highly individual technique and had to search for other expedients.

When Stuart resigned as Secretary of State he thought for a time that he might become Leader of the House, free of the heavy burden of Departmental responsibility, but R. A. Butler insisted on combining this post with that of Home Secretary, and Stuart did not press his claim. He was appointed a Companion of Honour and went to the Lords as Viscount Stuart of Findhorn. His career might be summarised in the terms that Machiavelli used to describe the founder of the Medici dynasty.

> He never sought the honours of government, yet enjoyed them all. When holding high office he was courteous to all. Not a man of great eloquence, but of an extraordinary prudence.[15]

NOTES

1 James Stuart, *Within the Fringe*. London, 1967.
2 Dame Edith Sitwell, *The Queens and the Hive*. London, 1962.
3 *Within the Fringe*.
4 *Ibid.*
5 Nigel Fisher, *Iain Macleod*. London, 1973.
6 Sir John Colville. *Footprints in Time*. London, 1976.
7 *Within the Fringe*
8 *Ibid.*
9 *Ibid.*

10 Viscount Kilmuir, *Political Adventure*. London, 1964.
11 *Hansard*, 24th July, 1952. Vol. 504, col. 770.
12 *The Times*, 25th July, 1952.
13 *Within the Fringe*.
14 The *Spectator*, 17th July, 1953.
15 G. F. Young, *The Medici*. London, 1910.

CHAPTER XIV

A Jolly Nice Chap

'In public Mr Maclay may not be the most assertive of Ministers, but his success in delivering the goods suggests tireless work behind the scenes.'[1] A leader in the *Scotsman*, not notoriously favourable to the Scottish Office, in January, 1960, included this perceptive remark. By then Jack Maclay had been at St Andrew's House for three years, and his reputation was growing. He was not, however, a peremptory, aggressive figure. He declined to blow his own horn, and as a result he got less credit for some of his achievements as Secretary of State than he deserved. This in turn provokes some comments on the dissemination of information by government Departments and on the rôle of the Public Relations Officer (in Scotland, the Director of the Scottish Information Office).

The P.R.O. has an uphill task, and he has to face two main hazards. The first is that many or, to be accurate, most senior civil servants are ingenuous about public relations. Often they are actively hostile to them. This does not imply furtiveness, or a sinister wish to suppress information. On the contrary, they will maintain that once a government decision has been announced, if there is to be any further exposition the legitimate channel is either through parliamentary questions addressed to the Minister, or, if public funds are involved, in appearances before the Public Accounts Committee. It follows that, on this reckoning, the P.R.O.'s activities are an unwelcome intrusion on the higher thought. Successful government publicity campaigns, of which that on the eradication of tuberculosis is the outstanding example, arise not from the desire of officials to obtain public approval for their own pet schemes, but from the determination of the P.R.O. to make the best of the material at his disposal. In the Scottish Office the P.R.O. attends the regular meetings of Heads of Departments, and if he learns of a major issue he will obtain authority to organise appropriate publicity, but the comparison with what would be found at the Board meeting of a large-scale commercial concern is instructive.

There is another inhibition on the work of the P.R.O. His job is to promote the Government's case, as illustrated by his Department. But he must take care not to be the instrument of Party doctrine. He can, for example, draw attention to the Secretary of State's increase in subsidies for hill farmers: he must not appear to endorse the personal benevolence of a Conservative, or Labour, Minister. The line is not easy to draw, and most good P.R.O.s are extremely sensitive about this aspect, which is fundamental to the impartiality of the civil service. In practice, the P.R.O. will circulate a handout; he may, off the record, fill in some of the background; but if the handout has been well done there is little for him to add. The press are then left to speculate on the Minister's own contribution.

For much of the post-war period the Scottish Office had an outstanding Director of Information in W. M. Ballantine, who enjoyed the confidence of Ministers of both Parties and the affection of the Scottish press. But the difficulties mentioned, and a gradual deterioration in the Government's standing throughout the country, led to Maclay's achievements being underrated. When he had a good story to tell he did not always get his due acclaim, and when—on one conspicuous occasion, as we will see—the news was bad, his reputation suffered.

This failure in communication, an endemic problem at the Scottish Office, was particularly unfortunate in Maclay's case because it did not reflect a failure to seize the initiative or any lack of understanding with his officials. Maclay was the easiest man to talk to. He had a ready grasp of the most complicated submissions, and his advisers leaving a meeting with him would say that he would have made a good Permanent Secretary. Maclay might not take this as a compliment, but it was so intended.

Coming from a family with a distinguished record in public life, in philanthropic work, and in Church affairs, Maclay had been in Parliament since 1940 when he was elected for Montrose Burghs. The seat was abolished in 1950, and he was then returned at West Renfrewshire, a seat he held till he retired in 1964, moving to the Upper House as Viscount Muirshiel. His successful leadership of the British Merchant Shipping Mission to Washington in 1944 was recognised by the award of the C.M.G., and he had a short spell as Parliamentary Secretary at the Ministry of Production in 1945. He was Minister of Transport and Civil Aviation in Churchill's 1951 Government, but had to resign because of ill-health. Happily recovered, he returned to office as Minister of State for Colonial Affairs in October, 1956, and he was the

obvious successor to James Stuart at the beginning of 1957. Maclay
was a National Liberal. He was for ten years President of the Party's
National Council, and he was always conscious of the vestigial Liberal
tradition. Though no one could impugn his loyalty to the Conservative
administration, he would at times say, rather disarmingly, 'I'll have to
find out what the Tories think'.

In the House, the Opposition never quite got the measure of him.
His sincerity was not in doubt, but his palpably reasonable approach
masked an inner determination. He was not readily put out of his
stride, and in April, 1960, the *Scotsman* reported that 'he had been
showing recently signs of a new fire and fury which have astonished
the Commons'. One of Maclay's recurring themes, which reappeared
in a debate on industry and employment in July, 1960, was to attack
those who, in his view, denigrated Scottish prospects. He had his full
share of Housing debates, and it must be said that a perusal of *Hansard*
confirms that this subject invariably brings out the worst in both sides.
Of course it is a vital, human problem, but the arguments adduced are
seldom new, and nearly always repetitive. The Labour Party react with
furious indignation at anything that will increase rents, while the
Conservatives make little progress in convincing their opponents of
the equity of their allegedly more flexible proposals. So it continues.
In November, 1961, Maclay was attempting to assuage Opposition
anger by pointing out that nearly one third of the Scottish population
now lived in post-war houses. 'Really, it is not right to pretend that
this is a very poor achievement',[2] he exclaimed indignantly as he
pounded the Despatch Box.

Maclay's five years at the Scottish Office (longer than any of his
predecessors) saw a marked change in the Government's attitude to
regional development, and it is with this that we are principally concerned in the rest of this chapter. The negative control exercised by the
refusal of industrial development certificates in congested areas, and
the modest incentives dating originally from the Special Areas Acts of
1934 and 1937, and modified by post-war legislation, to persuade
firms to move to depressed districts were no longer considered adequate. A combination of factors brought about this change in policy.
The affluence of the fifties had largely by-passed the underprivileged
areas. Those parts of the country which had previously depended on
the traditional heavy industries—coal, shipbuilding, and steel—called
for a redistribution of government money to assist them: economists
pointed to the adverse effect of 'overheating' in the South-East on the

national economy: and at the same time there were unmistakable signs of a decline in the Government's popularity. Remedies had to be found, and an early legislative measure was the Local Employment Act which offered grants to those who provided and occupied undertakings in defined depressed areas. The administration of these grants was firmly in the hands of the Board of Trade, but the influence of the Scottish Office could be seen in the list of eligible areas in Scotland.

There were also large individual projects which proved susceptible to government steering in their choice of location. The first of these was the Ravenscraig strip-mill. The Government won few favourable comments from economists for their decision to divide the strip-mill between Lanarkshire and Wales. It was essentially a political decision, taking account of political realities, the unemployment in the areas affected, and the need to stimulate development there. Ravenscraig was not, however, selected without a strenuous conflict between Departments and, later, their responsible Ministers. In this and other cases where the claims of competing locations were publicly canvassed in the House and elsewhere it is possible to evaluate Maclay's success. On Ravenscraig he won against the odds.

More was to follow. At the 1959 General Election the Government, against the trend, lost five seats in Scotland. It is not cynical to suppose that this had some bearing on the successful attempts to persuade the motor industry to develop North of the Border. In January, 1960, B.M.C. announced plans to invest £9m. on a factory at Bathgate, with eventual employment for 5600 workers. Scottish reaction was explicit. The *Scotsman* said that no one would derive more satisfaction than Maclay 'who has fought valiantly in this instance, as in the tug-of-war over the steel mill, to see that Scotland's interests are properly recognised'.[3] It was a fair appreciation. In the following month there were reports that Rootes were also coming to Scotland, and on 1st October they announced that they would build a plant at Linwood with an employment potential of 3500–4500.

Ravenscraig, Bathgate, and Linwood were the most significant enterprises to be committed to Scotland in Maclay's time. A few relevant comments may be made. It was in order for the Opposition to argue, as Tom Fraser did in the House, that the decision by the motor industry to come to Scotland had been taken by the firms themselves. But the Government had provided massive incentives, and since the Board of Trade and the Treasury had no mandate to give Scotland preferential treatment, the outcome was largely due to

Maclay's political muscle. Admittedly more might have been done. In March, 1960, he told the Scottish Branch of the National Union of Manufacturers that he had hoped for more in the car shareout, (only commercial vehicles were to be built at Bathgate). But those who had memories of the Albion works were satisfied that motors would again be constructed in Scotland. There were further consequences to the Bathgate and Linwood decisions. Intractable difficulties with the local authorities in these areas influenced the later decisions to re-examine the planning structure of the Scottish Departments and to embark on the reform of local government.

Maclay was personally involved in two unusual experiments in regional planning—the Fraser scheme for the expansion of the tourist industry in the Highlands, and on a much wider front the Toothill report on the Scottish economy. Both were highly original exercises, and both had considerable impact. Hugh (later Lord) Fraser, the store magnate, was selected as a 'new man' to make the most of the tourist potential. (The Prime Minister's conception of new man usually turned out to be Sir Percy (later Lord) Mills, but Maclay did not think that Mills would look right in the land of the mountain and the flood, and Fraser was persuaded to accept the remit, although he claimed no planning expertise.)

The Fraser plan, presented in the autumn of 1959, had many incidental features that need not concern us. It was generally well received, and obtained the approval of the House, on a motion by Ian Mac-Arthur, on 12th March, 1960.[4] I have written elsewhere of the lasting benefits that flowed from Fraser's work.

> They are worth recording since their existence is now more or less taken for granted. First, he aroused an enormous interest in the possibilities of making far more of tourism in the Highlands. As a result of his efforts this interest extended far beyond Great Britain. It might be said nowadays that this was bound to come anyway, but Fraser was the first to identify and publicise in an expert way the potential that existed for future development. He was not deterred when he sometimes went too far ahead of public opinion. . . .
>
> Secondly, by arousing this interest and by such exploits as the formation of the Highland Tourist Development Company, he gave the industry a much-needed self-confidence. If hôteliers from now on found it easier to get financial facilities this was indirectly due to his demonstration that tourism could be made a good financial risk.[5]

The Highland Tourist Development Company was floated as a

normal commercial company to provide loans for hôteliers who wished to expand. With Maclay's encouragement, Fraser underwrote it and the public were asked to buy shares. Those who took a stake would know that they were helping the development of the tourist trade 'and thus the prosperity of Scotland as a whole'. This was at a time when the banks and the finance houses were not keen to lend money for investment in the industry. The next Labour Government were to provide loans and grants on a large scale that led to a great increase in hotel accommodation, but Scotland had shown what was required.

Another proposal that emerged from the Fraser exercise was to levy a *kurtax*, or *taxe de séjour*, on the continental model, to find funds for tourist amenities. Maclay liked the idea, but he was irritated that it was launched without adequate preparation. In this he was right, as the subsequent failure of the Bill to give it effect showed. (This unhappy event is described in the next chapter.) The genesis of the proposal is, however, of interest. Members of Parliament were sufficiently intrigued by the Fraser plan to form a voluntary committee to visit the Highlands and see for themselves what the prospects were. The Committee (Messrs Stodart, MacLean, and Clark Hutchison (Conservative) and Steele, McInnes, and Bennet (Labour)) came out in support of the *kurtax*, and reported accordingly to their respective Whips. When Michael Noble, as Secretary of State, introduced the Bill to enact the levy, they loyally spoke in favour. An unusual constitutional attempt at government by consent.

The Fraser plan was also to produce the Aviemore Tourist Centre, although it was not opened till after his death. Fraser had always emphasised that 'We must produce something in bricks and mortar without delay; otherwise we shall be lost in a cloud of Scotch mist'.[6] A lot of nonsense has been talked about Aviemore. It was carried out as a private, commercial undertaking, not as a government enterprise. The State's contribution was a grant under the Local Employment Act, which would have been available to anyone who satisfied the statutory conditions, and some expenditure on basic services which again would have been provided for any large scale development. The Government naturally hoped that Aviemore would succeed, both for the facilities it offered and as an example to existing hôteliers to modernise their own establishments, but that was the extent of the official involvement.

Aviemore has been a success, as the number of visitors shows, though it has not developed quite on the lines that Fraser had in mind for his pleasant place of all festivity. But the pioneering spirit manifested in Maclay's time seems to have been lost. There have been no similar schemes. The Aviemore story also shows how diffident the Government can be when faced with a novel, imaginative proposal. Aviemore was largely based on the French resort at Courchevel in High Savoy. There the French Government, who had similar problems of unemployment and depopulation in the area, provided the whole infrastructure, roads, drainage, electricity, etc., as one operation and left private entrepreneurs to build hotels and amenities on the serviced sites. The Scottish approach from the start was very different, and Aviemore had to depend on the Local Employment Act—which was not originally intended for hotel purposes. The verdict on the whole episode is that it was an amateur scheme, relying on the Secretary of State's initiative in choosing Fraser; it was a pioneer scheme; and pioneers usually have to be expended.

The Scottish Council (Development and Industry) set up their enquiry into the Scottish economy under the Chairmanship of Mr (later Sir) J. N. Toothill in February, 1960. This was primarily a Scottish Council operation—the report probably marked the high point in the Council's influence—but the decision to go ahead with it was taken with Maclay's active approval, and the Scottish Office provided assessors and a joint secretary.

The Report, published in November, 1961, was a far-reaching one. The *Economist* described it as the most raptly interesting document to appear from Scotland since the days of Adam Smith. The Report identified as the main question not why Scottish unemployment remained much higher than in England, but why Scottish industrial production had increased by only 13 per cent between 1953 and 1960, compared with the rest of Britain's 30 per cent.

Its diagnosis was that Scottish industry was too committed historically to 'quality specialised articles', i.e. ships, bridges, bespoke clothing, 'craftsman's goods', which did not need expert selling organisations. In the post-war years, however, 'large quantity standard' industries had taken the lead, and once new industries of this type were established in the South vast economies were to be obtained by concentrating further growth in the same places. In short, Scotland was at a disadvantage from not having this second phase development, and from not integrating production, advertising, and marketing. The complaint that Scottish industry was seriously handicapped by transport charges was not supported, but further criticisms were that the apprenticeship system was out of date; that the Local Employment Act subsidised moves only to depressed, decaying areas; and that low local authority housing rents hampered mobility.

Much of this went far beyond the ambit of the Scottish Office, but two of the principal recommendations were particularly germane to St Andrew's House. The main proposal was that future investment should be concentrated on growth industries and should take place in new industrial centres and complexes to breed new industries. New Towns and overspill reception areas—very much a Scottish Office responsibility—were cited as examples. The Report also emphasised that Local Employment Act incentives, less rigidly linked to unemployment, should be made available there.

The second proposal was that there should be a new Department in the Scottish Office which would bring together the industrial and planning functions of the Scottish Departments, the new organisation to be supported by an economic unit. Incidentally, Toothill endorsed the view of the Balfour Commission that further devolution from Great Britain Departments to the Scottish Office would have more disadvantages than merits.[7]

The growth area policy was to be modified by the next Government, but there is no underrating the significance of the Toothill Report. Influenced by its general philosophy, regional economic planning was henceforth to be a major commitment in the Scottish Office. Maclay did not stay in office till the full effect of the Report had permeated government thinking, but there were some immediate developments. An outline plan for an additional New Town at Livingston was announced. In March, 1962, his Parliamentary Under-Secretary (Brooman White) told the House that a steering committee had been set up to co-ordinate action within the Scottish Departments and gave a general acceptance of the Toothill recommendations as a basis for the future.[8] In April Maclay announced an important reorganisation. Planning and housing from the Department of Health, and roads, local government, and electricity from the Home Department would now be administered by a new Scottish Development Department. The Health service and the remaining duties of the Home Department would be assigned to a Scottish Home and Health Department. The former Health and Home Departments would be abolished. The Scottish Council welcomed these changes as being in line with Toothill, and the *Scotsman*, in one of its less happy phrases, said that 'the name

Scottish Development Department has at least a purposive ring about it'. (To bring the story up to date, Maclay had earlier transferred two other functions from the Home Department—fisheries to the Department of Agriculture, and child care to the Education Department.) The Scottish Office had a new look, and a more logical pattern.

Nor could Maclay be accused of indecision in other fields. On the Second Reading of the Sea Fish Industry Bill he announced an immediate ban on drift netting of salmon to conserve stocks. At the same time he said he was appointing a committee to examine all aspects of salmon fishing.[9] Governments have been known to temporise by resorting to committees of enquiry. Maclay acted differently, and though there were mutterings of Jeddart justice, he was justified on this occasion. Both this committee (under Lord Hunter) and another appointed (under Mr C. H. Mackenzie) to review the arrangements for generating and distributing electricity were later to produce reports that showed there was a need for a full investigation, but made recommendations that gave his successors headaches.

Maclay's last days were clouded by his decision to undertake the responsibility for an unpalatable statement on pit closures. The plans had been approved by the Cabinet, and on 11th July, 1962, he announced that 8000 miners in Scotland would lose their jobs. (It was alleged, and not denied, that further closures under review would make another 16,000 workers in the industry redundant.) To counter this enormous redundancy the Government's main proposal was to take over five new sites for advance factories.[10] The parliamentary outcry can be imagined, and the Press Gallery reported that 'at times during the exchanges Mr Maclay was to be admired for boldly facing a mass of hostile faces and voices with an aggressive pride in his policies'. The Secretary of State was not the Minister in charge of the coal industry, but loyally accepting the doctrine of Cabinet solidarity, and placing a generous interpretation on his rôle as protector of the general wellbeing of the Scottish economy, he chose to take the fire from the Opposition front bench. But it was either a quixotic gesture or an error in political judgment. The remedial measures he could announce seemed inadequate, and he incurred the bitter hostility of the unions. The *Scotsman* observed wryly 'If there had been better news the Minister of Power would probably have been chosen to spread it'.

A few days later he was out of office. In Macmillan's sudden, drastic reorganisation of his Cabinet seven senior Ministers were replaced. Some were, quite evidently, sacked, and there was much resentment in the Scottish Office that Maclay was left to make clear in a personal statement that he had earlier told the Prime Minister that he wished to retire at a convenient time.

While he was Secretary of State Maclay was fully aware that the winds of change which the Prime Minister had evoked in his memorable speech in South Africa were also blowing on the domestic scene. He was alert to the need for a better planning machine and for the Scottish Office to involve itself more actively in regional planning. His close co-operation with the bipartisan Scottish Council indicated a willingness to make use of advice from other than official sources. (When he sent his Minister of State, Lord Craigton, to Sweden to explore the possibilities of increasing trade there, the Scottish Council formed part of the team.) One of the difficulties facing the Scottish Secretary is that he is part of the United Kingdom government, a member of the United Kingdom Cabinet, and it is their policies he has to apply in the Scottish context. Maclay showed that this need not prevent experiment to take account of Scottish conditions. An essentially discreet Minister, he was courteous, patient even in adversity. Toothill's parting comment was that he was a 'Jolly nice chap'. A familiar, colloquial phrase, it suggests a lightweight. But Maclay was no lightweight, and there are many less admirable political epitaphs.

NOTES

1 The *Scotsman*, 22nd January, 1960.
2 *Hansard*, 7th November, 1961. Vol. 648, col. 744.
3 The *Scotsman*, 22nd January, 1960.
4 *Hansard*, 11th March, 1960. Vol. 619, col. 855.
5 George Pottinger, *The Winning Counter*. London, 1971.
6 *Ibid.*
7 Committee of Inquiry into the Scottish Economy, Edinburgh, 1961.
8 *Hansard*, 7th March, 1962. Vol. 655, col. 368.
9 *Hansard*, 15th November, 1961. Vol. 649, cols. 213, 313.
10 *Hansard*, 11th July, 1962. Vol. 662, cols. 1347, 1350.

CHAPTER XV

Cock Robin

Michael Noble's over-bland air sometimes provoked the comment that he regarded his political duties as an extension of his social obligations. This was misleading because no one could question the energy he brought to the office of Secretary of State. His appointment came as a surprise, since he had not been tipped as the most likely candidate. Lord John Hope (now Glendevon), the Minister of Works, was the favourite in the ante-post betting, but he had been described, perhaps unfairly, as averse to any great physical or mental exertion, and instead of being promoted he disappeared in Macmillan's July bloodbath. So Noble, the Chairman of the Scottish Unionist Party, filled the vacancy caused by Maclay's departure. After wartime service with the R.A.F., he had been M.P. for Argyllshire since June, 1958. He was for a short time Maclay's Parliamentary Private Secretary; he had served in the Whips' Office, from November, 1961, as Scottish Whip; but he had no Ministerial experience.

In retrospect it appears that during his two years at St Andrew's House the Scottish Office somehow lost the place, particularly in the sense that public opinion, and responsible organisations, increasingly turned to Whitehall Ministers for the remedies they sought. It was as if the Scots began to realise that the Secretary of State was not doing what they thought he was, namely running the Scottish economy, although to be fair he had not claimed to do so, and as we have already seen his statutory powers were limited. In the event the Scottish Office found itself in the unusual rôle of spectator as indignant cohorts took their way South to lay their representations before Great Britain Departments. The doctrine of a benevolent, semi-omniscient Scotland's Minister was impaired, and it is doubtful whether the mythology, best exemplified by Tom Johnston and maintained in different ways by McNeil, Stuart, and Maclay, has been—or can be—completely restored. This is a subjective judgment, and it would not be right to attribute the seeming change in the public attitude to the Scottish Office to a lack of dedication on Noble's part.

The reasons lie deeper than the personal performance of the Secretary of State. First, there was the steady decline in the Government's hold over the country. The whole period of Noble's tenure (1962-4) can be seen as a run-up to the General Election which ended thirteen years of Conservative rule. Ministers at the fag end of a failing administration have a hard time of it, and they were not helped by the weakening in the authority of the Prime Minister. This was accelerated by the banishment of senior Ministers in the July, 1962, reshuffle—not so much for its alarming extent as for its suddenness. Parliamentary journalists had no time to indulge in their favourite game of speculating on who was going where. They were caught unawares and they did not readily forgive Macmillan. Sir Alec Douglas Home on arrival at Downing Street made a heroic attempt to revive Conservative fortunes, but the omens were easily read.

There was also a formidable collection of immediate domestic problems to engage the Secretary of State. Unemployment in Scotland remained twice the Great Britain average. Under Maclay there had been some spectacular projects—Ravenscraig, B.M.C. at Bathgate, and Rootes at Linwood—but the series could not be continued indefinitely. Noble also inherited the aftermath of the Toothill Report, and the absence of an immediate, explicit, response to it soured the relationship with the Scottish Council. Beeching's axe was about to fall on the railway system, and long before his report was published there were rumours that its effect on Scotland would be severe. (The original recommendations would have left no railway services north of Inverness, and very little north of Perth, with wholescale inter-mediate cuts.) The Mackenzie report on the future of the Hydro Board was pending and pressure groups were active in anticipation. It was already becoming clear that the structure of local government was out of date. Tourist and amenity questions were attracting more public attention and action was needed. Altogether it was an un-promising script and it would have taken a strong Minister to make much of it. Some of these problems Noble tackled with more success than others.

He began by announcing that the abolition of industrial derating would be postponed, a popular move, but, to use the oft-derided cliché, this decision had been in the pipeline when he came to office. His first speech, in a debate on industry, was not impressive.[1] He had to endure some paternal remarks from Gaitskell, and the *Scotsman* commented unkindly on his performance that 'as a demonstration of

oratory to inspire, it failed. Mr Noble is in need of more practice.'
On subsequent appearances he held his own, but he was not a dominating speaker. Ministers' ability to defend themselves from the Despatch
Box has more than a superficial or temporary significance. That is
where reputations are made, and the media's views on Ministers'
future, or survival, are heavily coloured by exchanges on the floor of
the House. Civil servants in preparing briefs are very conscious of this,
but when the Minister rises to speak it is up to him, and his advisers are
aware that this is an art form of its own. It is significant that the few
career civil servants who have become Members of Parliament, and
the even smaller number who have become Ministers, have not shone
as orators.

In terms of tangible projects, Noble's main achievements included
the agreement on the Fort William Pulp Mill and the decision to
move the Post Office Savings Bank to Glasgow. He could regard them
as big feathers in his bonnet. The firm of Wiggins Teape had for some
years been interested in building a pulp mill which would use timber
from Highland plantations. There was no real alternative to Corpach,
near Fort William, as a site where an enterprise of this size could be
built, where adequate supplies of timber were available, and where
effluent difficulties could be overcome, but the Treasury had to be
convinced that government assistance on the scale required—a £10 m.
loan—was justified. This was the measure of Noble's success, although
the decision was first announced in the Chancellor's 1963 Budget
speech,[2] and the finance was provided by the Board of Trade. (Special
legislation was eventually required.) The pulp mill, expected to offer
employment for up to 750 at the plant, and a much larger number in
the forests that supplied it, was much the biggest concern to come to
the Highlands since the atomic energy establishment at Dounreay.

Competition from areas outside Scotland for the Post Office
Savings Bank (employment 6–7000) was severe, and it was widely
reported that Noble had intervened in Cabinet to secure the transfer to
Glasgow. The claims of Liverpool and Tees-side were strongly canvassed, and the Civil Service Clerical Association said that if they had
to move Glasgow would not be their choice. Successive governments
have found the dispersal of Departments, or large parts of them, from
Whitehall an almost intractable problem. No large organisation takes
kindly to being uprooted and civil servants, particularly in the junior
grades when large numbers are involved, view the prospect with
horror. But the arguments invariably advanced against a move do not

depend on personal hardship. They are much more respectable. It is alleged that dispersal is expensive (which it probably is), and leads to inefficiency (which is much more doubtful). If the normal case put forward by a Department threatened with dispersal were taken at face value, it would appear that all the staff affected had to be within immediate reach of Whitehall for daily discussion with Ministers, attendance at Parliament, or consultation with professional and other bodies whose headquarters are in London S.W.1. Much of this is nonsense, but faced with near intransigence Ministers have been reluctant to insist on moves, far less take the invidious decision on where the Department should be sent. The next Labour Government regarded dispersal more seriously, but the Savings Bank was the first, and for long the only, government organisation to be brought to Scotland.

The debate on the economy centred on the Government's attitude to the Toothill Report. The sequence of events is instructive. In August, 1962, the Scottish Council had an unproductive meeting with Erroll, the President of the Board of Trade. Noble was present. Erroll would not agree that the incentives under the Local Employment should be made more flexible, and did not accept the 'growth area' concept. There were complaints that the Government had shown no sign of the radical new approach required to promote stable economic growth. In January, 1963, the Scottish Council repeated that the diagnosis had been done and action was needed. In February the Council insisted on seeing the Prime Minister, who made mildly encouraging noises about Toothill. All this was widely reported in the press, and the Scottish Office was getting no credit. In March Noble announced a £10 m. stimulant—capital investment on the electricity network, roads, and a new reservoir. The press ungratefully described this as a 'dole'. In April the Chancellor introduced standard grants and loans for building and plant expenditure, on the lines of one of the main Toothill recommendations. The wry comment was that nothing had been done till the Government was alarmed at the rise in unemployment in the North-East of England. In August the Prime Minister said that a White Paper on Central Scotland would be published in the autumn. This document (Cmnd. 2188), described as 'a more positive approach to regional economic planning than any government in this country has yet attempted', was welcomed by the Scottish Council as a belated but fundamental change in government thinking.

In fact it went a long way to accept the Toothill thesis. The four

New Towns of East Kilbride, Glenrothes, Cumbernauld, and Livingston, and a possible further one at Irvine, along with the Grangemouth/Falkirk complex, were designated as major growth areas. Other areas were identified for future growth. Increased public investment on communications and on housing was foreshadowed. There was an assurance that the financial inducements in the growth areas would not be withdrawn while they were needed, thus meeting complaints of lack of continuity. Action to put the plan into effect would be phased and co-ordinated by the Scottish Development Group, comprising senior officials from the Scottish Office and Great Britain Departments and chaired by an Assistant Under-Secretary of State.

Much hard work had gone into the preparation of the White Paper, and Noble was entitled to claim that it was a distinct innovation. It set the pattern for similar plans produced over the next decade. But the reaction was disappointing. The press dismissed the Scottish Office's reluctant commitment to regional planning as an amalgam of current proposals which, thanks to the Treasury's (Great Britain) increase of 11 per cent for expenditure on public services, had been conveniently concentrated into a plan to modernise Central Scotland. A similar plan for the North-East of England was published at the same time, and the conclusion was that Scotland had not been allowed to keep her lead.

Noble continued to defend himself, and on 3rd December he told the House that Scottish applications for grants under the Local Employment Act had shown a dramatic increase.[3] The Scottish Council, who were now calling for more research contracts in Scotland as a counter to the South-East England plan which had recently been published, were given a grant of £93,000 to publicise the attractions of Central Scotland—but a similar payment was authorised for the North-East. On 15th September, 1964, Noble designated Irvine as the site of the next New Town. The announcement was made at a press conference on the progress report called 'Development and growth in Scotland, 1963-64' (Cmnd. 2440). Unfortunately this was on the very day that the date of the General Election was proclaimed, and, inevitably, the coincidence was remarked.

It is difficult to assess Noble's effectiveness in the economic planning struggle. The acceptance of the growth area doctrine and the processing of the detailed proposals were bound to take time. But most of the major decisions in these two years had been taken, and announced, by Great Britain Ministers. There was also a new tendency for the

Scottish Council to by-pass the Secretary of State and go direct to Whitehall. On the other hand Noble could say that he had succeeded in making his colleagues address their minds to Scottish problems. But, perhaps due to a failure in presentation, there was an unfortunate impression in the country, and certainly in the press, that Scotland's Minister was hopping on the touchline. Much the same is true of his relationship with the Scottish T.U.C., who had been campaigning for a new Scottish Development Authority. After alleging that Noble treated them 'like some small rural authority',[4] they too insisted on seeing the Prime Minister.

Noble made a valiant effort to allay Scottish apprehensions about the effect of the Beeching Report. In August, 1962, long before the sharpness of the Beeching axe was revealed, he maintained that there would be no railway closures in Scotland unless there was an adequate alternative. He stuck to this line when the Beeching proposals were published in March, 1963. In January, 1964, the Scottish Council again went to see the Prime Minister, who gave them the impression that the cuts might be delayed. Beeching promptly issued an unrepentant statement, and the *Scotsman* asked what Noble was doing, since the Prime Minister had said that it was his job to see that all Scottish interests were properly considered. In fact he was active in the Scottish cause. The Highland Panel strengthened his hand by saying publicly that they would resign if any Highland lines were closed without suitable alternative services. As it turned out, Marples, the Minister of Transport, announced the closure of only eight minor lines during Noble's time, but Beeching was still asserting that uneconomic lines must be closed, and Noble's successor inherited a crown of thorns. Noble, for his part, was able to demonstrate that no lines had been closed without his consent, but there was no confidence about the future. Noble was in a difficult position since it was inescapable that the ultimate decision lay not with him, but with the Minister of Transport.

The Secretary of State's White Paper on 'The Modernisation of Local Government in Scotland' (Cmnd. 2067) was published on 27th June, 1963. Its origins were diverse. The local government structure had not been reviewed for more than a generation and there were signs, notably in a speech by the Chairman of the Association of County Councils, that even the authorities themselves were aware of the need for change. The industrial developments at Bathgate and Linwood had shown that rigid adherence to local boundaries was the very devil, and the Scottish Office were busy drafting their White

Paper on Central Scotland which was bound to make severe demands on local authorities for its success. At one stage Noble had in mind to appoint a Royal Commission, but (as subsequent events confirmed) this would take time, and the case for reform was urgent. Then the embarrassing recommendations published by another Committee—nothing to do with local government—endorsed the view that instead of a time-wasting enquiry the Secretary of State should publish his own White Paper and start immediate consultations on its content. Noble decided to do this. Local government was one subject on which the Scottish Office could claim that they had all the necessary information at their disposal.

All the Scottish Departments, except for Agriculture, are concerned with local authority services. It could be argued that the supervision of local government is one of the *raisons d'être* of the Office. The relationship is an intimate one. All the principal local authority figures are well known at St Andrew's House, but this intimacy has its traumas. Departments may feel that town councils are being obstructive: conversely the councils resent interference from the mandarins on points of detail, and so on. After the last war it was even found necessary to set up a joint committee which solemnly pronounced that local authorities carried out their duties not only as agents of government Departments but as of right—a view that the Balfour Commission pompously observed was not always sufficiently present in the minds of those concerned. One odd consequence arises from Scottish local authorities dealing almost entirely with St Andrew's House, instead of with a number of departments as in England. Just because the Scottish Office is there, and so easily accessible, local authority officials tend to rely on it for advice more than happens with English authorities in their relationship with Whitehall. I pass no comment on the merits of this circumstance: but it exists. It is also the case that for most local authority functions the Scottish Office is the single paymaster, and in any major conflict the central Department will prevail. One would hope, however, that the Scottish Office do not treat the views of local authorities as cavalierly as was done during the debates on the Treaty of Union, when the Duke of Argyll proposed that representations from the burghs and the shires should be used for making kites.

Noble took great care with his White Paper. Both he and Lord Craigton, the Minister of State, were emphatic that it should be a document on which constructive discussions could take place, thus arriving in one move at the stage that would normally follow years of examination by a worthy Royal Commission. Briefly, in place of the two hundred or so authorities, of whom some had only a historic justification, the White Paper proposed a two-tier structure. The top tier would comprise the four cities, with their boundaries extended to take account of movements in population, and about fifteen counties based on amalgamations of existing authorities. The second tier would merge the burghs and their surrounding landward areas, and produce authorities with a population of about 40,000. Both tiers would be directly elected. The main functions would go to the top tier, but the second tier would retain housing. To combat apathy at local elections it was hoped that the top tier would offer an avenue to aspiring politicians, while parish-pumpers would find their satisfaction in the second one.

There were, of course, objections. The smaller councils did not shout with glee at their imminent demise. But the general reaction was favourable. The *Economist*, under a heading 'Scotland the Brave', commented

> Broadly, the nation-wide two-tier approach is the right one, and the emphasis on the economic functions of local authorities is even more right. Ideas, as well as people, have always been Scotland's most welcome gift to England.[5]

Four months later Noble disarmed the local authorities sufficiently to get them to agree to set up a Steering Committee and a Working Party of officials—a traditional pattern—to consider the scheme in detail. The Working Party's first report, published in June, 1964, came to broad agreement on the allocation of duties between the two tiers, with a few reservations, but the General Election intervened before they could pronounce on boundaries. Noble did not have time to finish his bold experiment, and the next government would have nothing to do with the White Paper proposals. J. G. Kellas, writing in 1975, observed that

> The Scottish Office was here ahead of the English departments and local authorities, and could have brought in a reformed system ten years before it will in fact be established.[6]

Signs of frenetic energy characterised much of Noble's other activities as Secretary of State. On 2nd November, 1962, the Mackenzie Committee, in a well reasoned report, recommended that the South of Scotland Electricity Board and the Hydro Board should be amalgamated. A fortnight later Noble was quick to assure the Scottish

Grand Committee that both Boards would continue as they were for at least another two years, and in July, 1963, he came out firmly against a merger, arguing that the preservation of two Boards was not incompatible with economical arrangements for generating and distributing electricity. This delighted the tribesmen who had been carrying the fiery cross round the Highlands, but there were thoughtful critics who doubted whether, since the main part of the Hydro Board's construction programme had been carried out, there was really any need for separate organisations.

In the autumn of 1963 Noble decided to seek new fields and lead a selling mission, with the emphasis on electronics, to the United States. The end product of these expeditions is never easy to identify, but this one, which avoided the well-worn paths to New York and Washington and concentrated on Los Angeles, San Francisco, and Chicago, was thoroughly prepared. The Scottish Office arranged a briefing with the heads of the United States firms which had factories in Scotland to ascertain their views of the merits and demerits of a Scottish location. While they had no complaints about the Scottish labour force, or the help they had received from the authorities, their main point was surprising. They suffered from a sense of isolation. Only fellow-Americans, it appeared, were prepared to talk 'shop' with them outside working hours.

Noble's venture into tourism proved ill-starred. The Countryside and Tourist Amenities (Scotland) Bill had been the main Scottish feature of the Queen's Speech at the beginning of the 1963–4 Session, and the Scottish Grand Committee, rather bemused by its radical nature, gave it approval in principle in December, 1963. The key proposal was to levy a modest *taxe de séjour* and spend the proceeds on tourist amenities which were not likely to be provided commercially. Noble had done well to get Cabinet approval, particularly since the Treasury strongly disliked hypothecating taxation for a specified purpose. Luckily Noble was able to point to a precedent in the betting levy. It was from the start a controversial scheme, as he recognised when he told the Grand Committee that the Scottish hôteliers had voted 117 to 42 against it. But only 24 per cent had even bothered to comment, and he concluded that the remaining 76 per cent were not greatly exercised at the prospect of paying the levy.

The opposition then became more vocal. The National Trust were petulant that the Bill did not include their cherished proposal to set up a countryside commission. The Scottish Tourist Board, a self-perpetuating body of men who had been eminent in other walks of life, were jealous lest the Council which would administer the levy would usurp their own position. The British Hotels and Restaurants Association, alarmed that a similar Bill might be enacted for England and Wales—this was not intended—were indignant. In face of this criticism, and the prospect of an early General Election, Noble abandoned the scheme, and on 19th February, 1964, he announced that the Bill would not proceed in its existing form.

Apart from making everyone look foolish, this was unfortunate on a number of counts. It did not exactly smack of firm government. Tourism has since become more of a growth industry, but no one has found another way of providing the amenities which attract visitors but do not pay for themselves. The more far-seeing hôteliers who knew that they would not be crippled by an annual levy of £2·50 (£1·50 after allowing for taxation) per bed felt that a chance had been lost. More significantly, if the Bill had been passed hotels could have made a good case for exemption from the Selective Employment Tax which the next government introduced and which had a detrimental effect on the tourist industry.

To take an objective view of Noble's time in office, the difficulties he met, and which were not all of his own making, should not be underrated. The Government was wavering—a circumstance which provokes Ministers into ill-considered and defiant assertion. Whitehall in its new-found enthusiasm for regional economic planning was paying more attention to other parts of Great Britain. There was a feeling that Scotland's requirements were being submerged in the wider picture. Only a Minister of ballast, judgment, and authority could have stemmed the tide.

NOTES

1 *Hansard*, 19th July, 1962. Vol. 663, col. 667.
2 *Hansard*, 3rd April, 1963. Vol. 675, col. 480.
3 *Hansard*, 3rd December, 1963. Vol. 685, col. 1100.
4 The *Scotsman*, 10th January, 1963.
5 The *Economist*, 28th June, 1963.
6 J. G. Kellas, *The Scottish Political System*. 2nd edition, Cambridge, 1975.

CHAPTER XVI

The Tawse

'How will the Scottish Office cope with the wrath of God?' Thus Miss Margaret Herbison, formerly Parliamentary Under-Secretary of State at the Scottish Office and later Minister of Pensions and National Insurance, on hearing that William Ross was to be the Secretary of State in the new Labour Government.

Ross had spent the last twenty years attacking Scottish Ministers and trying to hammer the Scottish Office, so the question was not a rhetorical one. In Chapter II I have described how incoming Ministers and civil servants look at each other and how mutual suspicion usually dissolves with the passage of time, but there is no point in pretending that relations between Ross and his advisers were uniformly harmonious. No one would believe it if I said that they were. It is not, however, part of this book to indulge the appetite for upstairs-downstairs revelations, and it will suffice to say that on some occasions the growth of respect and understanding takes longer than on others.

Two aspects of Ross's performance can be disposed of briefly. Since his election as Member for Kilmarnock after the war he had earned an unmistakable reputation as an abrasive speaker in the House, first from the back benches and latterly as Shadow Scottish spokesman. For much of the thirteen years of Conservative Government the Shadow Secretary of State had been the well-liked Tom Fraser. More recently Ross and James Hoy had shared the duties, but Hoy, in rather mysterious circumstances, left the Opposition front bench in March, 1963, and by then Ross had asserted an undisputed claim. Throughout his speeches in the House Ross saw no virtue in the Ministers who sat facing him. Noble he dismissed contemptuously as a 'kilted canary'. He made no concessions, and when he reached office he received few.

This enthusiasm for embroiling himself with the Opposition extended to his relationship with the media. The Wilson government, led by the Prime Minister, was obsessionally suspicious of the press, and was always convinced that it was not getting a fair deal. Ross did not look on reporters with affection. There was none of the easy informality which, say, Hector McNeil had cultivated. Instead, he bridled at the first whisper of dissent, and the atmosphere at press conferences was not improved by his habit of referring to his critics as 'bleaters'. Television crews, annoyed at his brusqueness, would react by shining the light in his eyes to produce a distorted image on the screen. The outcome of Ross's somewhat grim view of public relations was to give him a uniformly critical press, even when he had a good case.

These are the trappings, and in time they will be forgotten. The character of the man is more significant. A former schoolmaster, he served with some distinction with the army in India during the 1939–45 War. Austere, ascetic, he was a perfectionist with very high standards of his own, but he was not good at communication. He was in consequence a lonely figure, relying on his own judgment—frequently based on unremitting homework in the House of Commons Library while in Opposition. The more detailed information which was made available to him from official sources seldom affected his viewpoint. The 'wrath of God' suggests that he exemplified the more restrictive aspects of Calvinism. (There is an interesting metaphysical question whether Calvin had as punitive an effect on the Scottish genus as is sometimes supposed, or whether the Scots actively demand someone of Calvinist outlook.) In the long history of the Scottish Office it probably did the Department no harm to have a Minister who was implacably aware of his own rectitude and who was not slow to prescribe the scourge. From the start of his tenure the civil servants at St Andrew's House were aware that there had been a change of style and conducted themselves accordingly. One more word on Ross's general attitude. The diverse nature of the Secretary of State's duties makes a fair amount of delegation inescapable, and this was not greatly to Ross's liking, although he was fortunate to have two outstanding junior Ministers in Dickson Mabon, the ebullient, staccato debater, and Norman Buchan, intelligent and endowed with a sensitive political conscience. They did not always avoid the tawse.

A serious assessment of Ross's time at the Scottish Office, longer even than Maclay's, must depend on the measures he brought to the Statute Book, the major projects he secured for Scotland, his effect on the national well-being through economic planning, and his reaction to political developments.

In legislation the major Bills which Ross promoted were that creating the Highlands and Islands Development Board and the Social

Work (Scotland) Bill. Both were distinct innovations in Great Britain terms, but the idea that there should be a special development agency for the Highlands was not new. The Balfour Commission cast a scaly eye over the proposal and found that it could well lead to duplication and conflict of policy and effort. (The Highland Board's tourist campaign, which trod on the tender bunions of the Scottish Tourist Board, might be thought to support this reservation.) But the pressure for a new authority continued; the Board was promised in the Election Manifesto; it appeared in the Queen's Speech; at Second Reading the blood was strong, the heart was Highland, and Ross essayed an emotive speech.[1] By the autumn of 1965 the Board was in being.

There was plenty of criticism, both during the passage of the Bill and afterwards. The Board's powers to acquire land, carry on business, and provide services were thought to be alarmingly wide. It spawned staff on the orthodox Parkinson principle, and there were early aberrations such as its grant to help find the Loch Ness Monster. More significantly, as the Board took off like a hot-air balloon it was not clear that the members knew what they were meant to do. This is the charitable view of the romantic proposals for huge industrial develop-ment, new cities, etc.—to make people take the Highlands seriously, as the Chairman naïvely explained—and the demand for a new uni-versity. The Board was soon in dispute with Dickson Mabon when he appeared to advise concentration on smaller, more practical projects. There were teething troubles with the Board's membership, and Ross wisely decided to recruit Tom Fraser to provide a leavening of political experience.

The Board is financed by a grant-in-aid from the Scottish Office and it has proved a useful channel for injecting much needed capital into the Highlands. In the initial period up to November, 1971 it had dis-bursed £9·5 m. in grants and loans for over 1600 projects, and by 1974 the expenditure had risen to £20 m. As early as 1970 the Board's annual report could claim the promotion of 5000 new jobs. The larger developments have, in general, not materialised, and the Board has not been able to play a major part in relation to North Sea oil, but—and this is the real justification for its existence—it remains the one executive agency with a positive remit to attract development to its area.

Ross's vital contribution was not to persuade the Cabinet that a new organisation was needed (this was consistent with the current planning philosophy) but to obtain powers for it to spend public funds of its own volition. In the face of concerted attacks in its early years Ross stood by the Board and he is entitled to the credit for forging an effective instrument, one that has no exact parallel elsewhere.

Social work was another field where the Scottish Office led the field. Following the Kilbrandon Report in 1964 (Cmnd. 20360), Ross issued a White Paper on Social Work and the Community (Cmnd. 3065), and after discussion with the local authorities he introduced the Social Work (Scotland) Bill which was passed in 1968. As a result the services provided by different Departments in local authorities— children's, education, and welfare—together with the probation service, were brought within a single social work department under its own Director. Various official committees had wrestled with this subject, in Scotland and England, since the 1950s, but Ross eventually decided to go his own way despite English protests, and his Bill was more comprehensive that the later English one.

Ross also emerged successful from a brisk contest with Barbara Castle over the Transport Bill which she promoted in 1967. The Scottish Office approach was that since the Secretary of State was already responsible for roads in Scotland, and since he was concerned with the shipping services to the Western Isles provided by MacBrayne, as well as those to Orkney and Shetland, there was a logical case for his taking full charge of passenger road transport and ships through a single organisation. The press were aware that the Minister of Transport thought otherwise, but Ross prevailed and set up the Scottish Transport Group. We have not attempted to cover all Ross's legislative progress, but these examples are sufficient to show the dour, and sometimes successful, way in which he asserted a Scottish point of view.

In February, 1966, the Highland Board was anxious to claim that it had influenced the decision by the Minister of Technology that the new prototype fast reactor should be built at Dounreay. Certainly the Board lobbied the Minister, but a decision of this nature is not taken without prolonged infighting and Ross's personal intervention must have carried more weight. (There was no Secretary of State for Dorset to argue the claims of the alternative site at Winfrith.) If Dounreay was a win, and a justifiable one bearing in mind the large sums already invested on infrastructure there, the announcement that one of the three new aluminium smelters would go to Invergordon would be more accurately described as a draw. The decision to authorise not one smelter, for which there had been strong competition by the companies concerned, but three smaller, separate ones, may have been sound commercially. It may have made planning sense to divide smelter capacity so as to locate new plant in each of three development areas—Invergordon, the North-East of England, and Anglesey. There may have been some justification on economic or efficiency grounds, or on the simple need to keep all the options for the future. The contrary thought is that it was a political carve-up. Either way Ross kept his powder dry.

He did not, however, manage to bring other large government enterprises to Scotland when moves were mooted. The most disappointing failure was to secure the Royal Mint, which was due for dispersal from Woolwich. Here he had a fortuitous historical argument since the Treaty of Union committed the signatories to keep a Mint in Scotland. Cumbernauld could offer all the facilities required and was visited by the Mint Staff on reconnaissance. But the Mint went to Wales, as did the Vehicle Taxation unit of the Ministry of Transport, employing a large block of staff. It is not necessary to count heads to note that the Welsh influence in Wilson's Cabinet was strong. We come back inevitably to the question of clout, the weight which the Secretary of State carries with his Ministerial colleagues, individually and collectively. There can be no doubt that Ross enjoyed the Prime Minister's confidence, since he remained in office throughout various Cabinet reshuffles, but when it came to enlisting the support of other Ministers on matters like dispersal proposals the picture was less encouraging. The National Computer Centre, and the headquarters of the British Steel Corporation and the Land Commission, were but examples where his pleas went unanswered.

Regional economic planning was a prominent feature of the Wilson administration. Along with incomes policy, it was offered as the panacea for the country's economic ills. There was soon a full panoply of Planning Councils, serviced at the official level by Planning Boards, advised by economists, and buttressed by consultative panels, subgroups, etc. The Scottish Economic Planning Council was set up in February, 1965. (Three Councils for English regions and one for Wales were appointed at the same time.) The Scottish Council comprised industrialists, trade unionists, financiers, and members of local authorities. So much was common form.

The English Councils had *ad hoc* chairmen, but Ross decided that he would be the chairman of the Scottish Council, and regularly presided at its meetings. Apart from personalities, this was probably a mistake. The Secretary of State's presence imparted a degree of formality. Attitudes were struck, and frank discussion was inhibited. While Ross could speak with authority on government policy, he could not reveal Cabinet secrets, and the members, for their part, were inclined to speak from their own, sectional, interests. The result was a vigorous, but often unproductive, political dialogue, and those with long memories had an uneasy feeling that Woodburn's Economic Conference (Chapter XI) had been brought back from the mortuary.

The Council commissioned various studies and the Planning Board was instructed to prepare proposals for the development of the Scottish economy. But this could not be done in isolation from what was happening elsewhere. Meanwhile, in September, 1965, the Government issued its National Economic Plan (Cmnd. 2764) which bore all the marks of George Brown's optimistic belief in expansion. It was based on a 25 per cent increase in the national output by 1970, and though the initial jibe of a 'pipe dream of Utopia' can be discounted as hostile hyperbole nothing like this figure was attained. In January, 1966, another government statement designated the whole of Scotland, except for Edinburgh and Leith, as one of the new development areas, and the investment incentives were revised. Against this background, 'The Scottish Economy, 1965–70' (Cmnd. 2864) was approved by the Planning Council and published later in the same month.

Although the point is now largely academic, the Paper was a workmanlike document, better reasoned than those that emerged from the Councils in the South. There were two reasons for this. First, the Scottish Office, particularly J. H. McGuinness who made the subject his own, were now becoming skilled at producing this kind of artefact. They had been much involved in the Toothill Plan, and they had prepared the Central Scotland Plan under the last government. There were variations: the latest version was more refined; but in many respects the underlying approach was similar. Second, while other Departments and organisations contributed, this was primarily a Scottish Office document, and the fact that one Minister approved the constituent elements led to a more complete integration than was achieved in other Regional plans.

The main objectives set out in the Paper, described as 'a composite and interdependent scheme of policies and action', were the stemming of emigration and a cut in unemployment. Central Scotland and the Borders were selected for rapid development. The New Towns were to be the focal points and there would also be progress with the rehabilitation of derelict areas. A major development was envisaged near Galashiels. Public investment would continue until 1969–70 at a rate higher than throughout the rest of Great Britain, and would total about £2000 m. over the five years.

The public reaction was sceptical. The Plan was taken to be a tinkering with the previous Government's growth area policy, and a statement of what needed to be done rather than an outline for actual achievement. During the next five years there were inevitable complaints about lack of progress. It was alleged that the Planning Council was an amateur body trying to do a professional job. (This was a facile criticism: if it had been left to economists and the staff at St Andrew's House there would have been calls for more openness, more involvement, etc.) In December, 1969, however, the *Scotsman* commented sharply that Scotland was still losing jobs faster than new ones could be provided, with a net loss of 35,000 between 1964 and 1968.[2]

In view of Ross's personal commitment to the success of the Planning Council its activities should be examined more closely. In January, 1968, to mark its first three years, the Council claimed to have assisted the establishment of a major research centre for advanced engineering design, and the provision of container berths at Greenock. Not a formidable list, and these things might have happened in normal course. In May, 1970, reviewing the Council's work over the last five years, Ross referred to an increase of 19 per cent in industrial investment between 1961 and 1968, a narrowing in the wage gap with the rest of Great Britain, a drop in unemployment, and a substantial fall in net emigration from 47,000 in 1965–6 to 25,000 in 1968–9 and to 9200 in the first half of 1969–70. Plans for the Borders had, however, faltered due to opposition from the local authorities, determined litigation by a landowner, and the failure to stop the closure of the Edinburgh–Hawick–Carlisle railway line.

In retrospect, the Scottish public was probably led to expect too much from the Scottish Economic Planning Council. A critic, more unkind than most, quoted Roy Campbell:

> They use the snaffle and the curb all right,
> But where's the bloody horse?

But it should not be written off too lightly. Ross's personal involvement did, however, have one detrimental effect on the standing of the Secretary of State. The Council's plans were never more than partly realised, and this circumstance served to emphasise the limits within Scottish requirements influenced the Government's overall economic policy. The Selective Employment Tax is a case in point. Introduced in the 1966 Budget, it bore severely on the service industries, and in consequence on areas like the Highlands where these industries provided most of the employment. It was not in keeping with the Government's declared intention to aid regional growth, and Lord Bannerman complained in the Lords that 'this is a destructive, not selective employment tax. It is the crowning folly of legislation introduced for England and forced on Scotland.'³ The tax was increased in the 1968 and 1969 Budgets, and it was only after some bizarre arguments that the Treasury were persuaded to exempt the Scottish tourist industry, outside the Central Belt, from the imposition. The influence of the Planning Council was not obvious.

The same is true of the Government's acceptance of the Hunt Report proposals for incentive grants to 'gray' or intermediate areas which did not, on unemployment etc., grounds qualify for full development area status. The money was to be found at the expense of the existing development areas, of which Scotland was one. This was not the most damaging event in the 1965–70 period, but it supports the criticism that although the Secretary of State, advised by the Planning Council, had appeared to assume overt responsibility for bringing the Scottish economy into a better state of health, the most significant decisions were still taken elsewhere. The Government's grant to the Upper Clyde Shipbuilders is a further example. Under the Council's sponsorship much useful work was done in the preparation of detailed plans for various regions to serve as a framework for the future, but the glad confident morning of early 1965 was not recaptured.

As a diversion, Scotland could claim credit for an outstanding experiment in industrial relations. The Secretary of State was not personally responsible, but he was fully consulted about the scheme to rescue the Fairfield shipyard which was threatened with liquidation. Under the arrangements announced in December, 1965, Fairfield would be taken over by a consortium jointly financed by the Government, the trade unions, and private enterprise—all subject to direction by the industrialist (Sir) Iain Stewart. During Stewart's management remarkable progress was made in putting the whole complex business of labour relations on a new basis, and it was unfortunate that Stewart left Fairfield, and his experiment came to an end, under the later merger of the Clyde Shipyards. He had shown leadership of a very high order.

This Chapter has dealt at length with economic planning and industrial topics because they were the most prominent during Ross's time at the Scottish Office. His policies in other fields can be briefly mentioned. Environmentalists were pleased with his Bill which set up the Scottish Countryside Commission, a more effective measure than the corresponding English one. The teachers did not, however, find the former dominie sympathetic to their demands, and there were bitter disputes about pay. On local government reform, Ross jettisoned the work that had already been done, and a Royal Commission was appointed under Lord Wheatley. The Wheatley Commission reported in September, 1969, but Ross took the curious decision to defer the Government's White Paper on the recommendations till after the General Election. The Scottish Farmers' Union normally give the Secretary of State a polite hearing when he addresses them after the Annual Price Review, but Ross was not at ease in their company, as was evident on one occasion when the President had to delay proceedings to allow time for the removal of unfriendly placards.

Nothing had a more cataclysmic effect on Scottish politics in the 1960s than the Scottish National Party's victory at the Lanark by-election in November, 1967. There had been reports of an increase in S.N.P. membership, and they had been active at local government elections. Five years previously some psephologists had seen signs when William Wolfe came second at a by-election in West Lothian with 23 per cent of the vote, but nothing had prepared the country for Winifred Ewing's success in winning a seat where the Labour majority had been over 16,000. The rise of nationalism is discussed in Chapter XIX. One could argue that at this stage the S.N.P. triumph was as much a vote of protest against the two main parties, a cry of 'a pox on both your houses', a Scottish Orpington, as a demonstration of genuine Nationalist feeling. But Ross took it as a personal affront. He was spurred to denounce the Scottish Nationalists as the Scottish 'narks', or as a 'phoney' party, and to lard his speeches with patriotic phrases from Burns. (It is ironic that the Minister who made most effective use of Burns was not a Scot. Herbert Morrison used to call on his police escort, the admirable Sergeant Black who knew much of Burns by heart, to produce an apt quotation.)

The Hamilton by-election was the forerunner of a flurry of activity on the Home Rule front. For the Opposition, the Scottish Conservatives set up their Constitutional Committee in July, 1968, and in October the Queen's Speech promised consultation on the appointment of a Commission, although it was April, 1969, before the membership was announced. Ross continued to deride the Nationalists. Derision and contempt are legitimate weapons in the political armoury, but they are not necessarily effective in themselves. Ross took less trouble to expose the weaknesses, as he saw them, in the Nationalists' case by reference to his own, not inconsiderable achievements while in office, and many political commentators thought that his obdurate refusal to take the Nationalists seriously added to their numbers. The veteran Nationalist Arthur Donaldson went too far in saying that the Secretary of State was 'the best recruiting sergeant that we ever had',[4] but Ross's political reputation was not enhanced by his attitude to what still seemed a temporary phenomenon.

Ross went into Opposition after June, 1970, General Election, but returned in February, 1974 (Chapter XVIII). An interim assessment on his first period could not fault him for zeal. But despite his long period at the Scottish Office his influence on his Ministerial colleagues was not always apparent. (Winifred Ewing taunted him in the House for not being a member of the inner Cabinet, and in Opposition after 1970 he failed to secure a place on the Party's Parliamentary Committee, although he was later co-opted to fill a vacancy.) He had got authority to set up the Highland Development Board, but otherwise he would have found it hard to demonstrate that he had secured for Scotland anything that was not available in other Development Areas. The housing programme reached a record level, and emigration from Scotland declined. Both were admirable achievements, but unemployment remained higher than in the South and few large enterprises came to Scotland. Much of this was not within his control, but at times he had given the impression that it was. As a codicil to his first six years, the majority report of the Parliamentary Select Committee on Scottish Affairs (H.C. 267) at least by inference gave his administration a fairly clean bill, and had few suggestions for improvement. It is a fine balance.

In his first speech when he returned to the Opposition Front Bench Ross thundered against 'the Government of Edward the Unready'. He spoke in the same vein as he had done before he became a Minister.

NOTES

1 *Hansard*, 16th March, 1965. Vol. 708, col. 1079.
2 The *Scotsman*, 31st December, 1969.
3 *Hansard*, Lords, 6th December, 1967.
4 The *Scotsman*, 19th April, 1968.

CHAPTER XVII

The Ambassador

When governments change new managers take over the theatre, the principal actors are replaced and there is a different supporting cast, but the professionals and technicians remain in the wings. The scenario is rewritten, but the problems left behind by the last administration are still there. The civil servants loyally submit schedules of the most contentious issues, take instructions on the content of the next Queen's Speech, and apply themselves to undoing the work of their late masters. In 1970, for example, legislation was rapidly drafted to restore local education authorities' power to charge school fees, and British Standard Time was abolished. But as the new broom sweeps through the corridors there is sometimes the uncomfortable thought that this may not be the most businesslike way to do things. The traditional argument is that it is the consequence of adversary politics, and that it preserves the democratic process. The permanent staff provide continuity and impartial advice, and changes that are enacted are made in response to the decision of the country at the poll. Conversely, there is the heretical view that the citizens do not always benefit from this periodical *bouleversement*, and that the whole procedure is more aptly called the Great Game, the phrase used to connote the Imperial attitude to the Muscovites over India during the nineteenth century. In any event, the arrival of Gordon Campbell signalled the next permutation.

Campbell was a regular soldier by profession. Commissioned in the Royal Artillery, he commanded a field battery in the 15th Scottish Division during the 1939–45 War, and won two Military Crosses. A severe wound left him with a permanent disability, and in his time at the Scottish Office his close advisers greatly admired his fortitude in face of perpetual discomfort and frequent pain. He entered the Foreign Service in 1945, and had served in the U.K. delegation to the United Nations and in the Cabinet Office before James Stuart personally chose him to be his successor as the Member for Moray and Nairn. He had some time in the Whips' Office, becoming Scottish Whip in

1962, and was a Parliamentary Under-Secretary of State at the Scottish Office under Noble in 1963.

Campbell was also a diplomat, and diplomacy rather than confrontation was his method of proceeding. (He had been stationed in the Vienna Embassy when he received the invitation to stand for Parliament.) In essence he saw his rôle as Secretary of State as being that of the U.K. Government's Ambassador to Scotland. Let me explain. His Foreign Office training had left its stamp on him—evident in the way he acted as host to foreign royalty visiting Edinburgh, or in the elegant receptions at the new official residence in Bute House. More seriously, when deputations were dissatisfied, or indignant at the Government's response to their case, he remained courteous and invariably polite. But his diplomatic disposition went further than that. The Heath administration had an overall majority in the House and had secured 46·4 per cent of the U.K. vote. The Scottish figures were very different. There were now only 21 Scottish Conservative Members out of 71 (38 per cent of the vote), and for the time being the political climate in Scotland was adverse to the Government. It followed that in interpreting government policy the Secretary of State had to go warily. Campbell was not remiss in bringing Scottish grievances to the notice of his colleagues, for there was no more loyal or committed Scot, but he did so as an Ambassador reporting from his post. There had been a change of emphasis.

One of the principal problems that Campbell inherited was the report of the Wheatley Commission on local government. Ross and his advisers had spent much time in considering what should be done about it, but since incoming Ministers are not shown the files of the previous administration Campbell had to start again. By February, 1971, he was ready to publish his proposals, and his White Paper (Cmnd. 4583) accepted Wheatley in principle, but made some significant changes in detail. Campbell's tactics are of interest. Although the White Paper was described as 'a prescription for action and not a basis for negotiation', and indicated that the allocation of functions and the number of authorities were not negotiable, Campbell prudently made concessions to local demands both in his initial departures from Wheatley and during the passage of the Bill. In place of the existing two hundred authorities Wheatley proposed a two-tier structure, the top tier of seven 'regions'—including one for the huge West of Scotland area (2·5 m. people), and one for all the Highland counties— to undertake the most important duties of local government. The second layer of 37 districts, including the four cities, would have more demonstrably local functions, e.g. minor aspects of local planning, libraries, etc.

The pattern that finally emerged was somewhat different. Orkney and Shetland, and the Western Isles, were given separate status as 'island authorities'. The Borders and Fife (the latter only after prolonged debate) successfully asserted their claim to be regions on their own. The delicate social susceptibilities of several suburban areas round Glasgow were recognised by their removal from Glasgow to form individual districts. There were changes in the balance of functions between the two authorities. Housing became primarily a district responsibility—a decision that was sound politically, but scarcely helped the execution of the housing programme. The final picture comprised 9 regions, 3 island areas, and 53 districts. The timetable set out in the White Paper was realised, and the first elections to the new authorities took place in May, 1974.

Campbell was attacked, not least by his own supporters since the voting on amendments often cut across party lines, for some of the concessions he made. One may, however, applaud the tenacious way in which he guided the Bill through 42 Committee sittings. It is not so easy to be enthusiastic about the outcome. The spread of population, ranging from the congested Strathclyde area to the sparsely populated Highlands, makes it impossible to devise a structure that can be equally applicable over the whole country. Wheatley's Highland region would have stretched from Muckle Flugga in the Shetlands to the Mull of Kintyre. Campbell saw that this was impracticable and made different arrangements for the Islands and Argyll. But the Strathclyde behemoth remains.

If, on the cynical view, local government exists to provide services that private enterprises can never undertake at a profit, the Strathclyde regional authority is far too large to do the job properly. If, on the more respectable argument, local government should reflect the aspirations of the local inhabitants to run their own affairs, it is still too large. The proposal to create this leviathan was largely influenced by the apparent need to have one authority that could take, and administer, large-scale planning decisions. This was no doubt consistent with regional economic planning philosophy. But planning requirements of this dimension are so infrequent that they could have been met by the appointment of joint *ad hoc* bodies when the circumstances arose. There were precedents.

There is a further, equally damaging, criticism. The underlying objective in the reform was to effect a real transfer of power from the central department to local authorities. Wheatley argued the need to get away from the 'obsolete, irksome, and paternalistic' provisions that were said to stifle local initiative. The Treasury had, however, pointed to the conflict between the need for stricter control when local budgets were rising annually in huge leaps, largely at the taxpayer's expense, and giving the authorities more autonomy. Wheatley tried to conflate these conflicting desiderata by stating that 'It is when local government operates on the scale which its services demand that true local democracy emerges'—whatever that means. But the dilemma persists.

The new authorities have now been in operation for four years. Allowances can perhaps be made for the building of commodious new offices, or the creation of a hierarchy of highly-paid supervisory posts, though none of them would seem to be conducive of economy. But it would be difficult to find anyone who thought it sensible to produce such a monstrous imbalance as was done by handing the local administration of half the country to a single authority. Second thoughts might support the solution advanced by Ross and others in the House that Strathclyde should be split into four regions, with an overall authority to deal with strategic planning as necessary. (A former Lord Provost of Glasgow, Peter Meldrum, once told me that the best answer was to divide the Glasgow area into three. He justified this disarmingly on the ground that it would make for political peace. One segment would be inevitably Labour-controlled; one would be inherently Conservative; and the third would be a Tom Tiddler's Ground, open to contention.) It is significant that both pro- and anti-devolutionists are agreed that if a Scottish Assembly is created, in whatever form, its first task should be to dismantle the new local government structure.

There was no easy passage for the Housing (Financial Provisions) (Scotland) Act, 1972, and some local authorities refused to operate the standard rent scheme which was its main feature. Campbell patiently applied the statutory processes available to him, giving the recalcitrant authorities an opportunity to state their objections, holding enquiries, withholding housing subsidies, and eventually resorting to the courts. The 23 rebel councils were reduced to 14, on whom default orders were served, and in time only the burghs of Clydebank and Saltcoats persisted with their defiance. Clydebank Town Council earned its doctrinal martyrdom at the expense of two substantial fines before coming into line with government policy. Campbell's attitude was that his duty was to secure compliance with the law as it stood. (The next Labour Government, after making housing policy a main election issue, promptly froze existing rents.)

Campbell secured the inclusion in the 1973 Queen's Speech of Bills to allow crofters to become owner-occupiers of their crofts, and to reform the feu duty system. The General Election came before the necessary measures could be enacted, but Campbell had taken the initiative in grasping these thorny problems. The Crofters Bill, re-introduced in a slightly different form by the next Government, was an attempt to deal with land tenure difficulties that had long bedevilled those who were concerned with Highland affairs. It was recognised in the Highlands as the most important Bill on this subject since the Crofters Act passed in the last century, but as it contemplated a drastic change in the crofting way of life it also implied that hopes that the Crofters Commission would revive the isolated communities had failed.

Two controversial enquiries aroused public concern about the whole procedure for examining applications for planning permission. On one —the second runway for Turnhouse Airport—Campbell overruled the Reporter who held the enquiry and granted permission. It is often alleged that the Secretary of State's discretion is too wide and that he can too easily involve the 'national interest'. But no Minister will lightly disregard recommendations following a lengthy enquiry where the arguments are adduced by counsel, and those who criticise the mystique of town and country planning conveniently forget that the combined effect of the relevant statutes is to enable the Secretary of State to take a common-sense decision on the merits. As regards Turnhouse, despite local objections canvassed with religious fervour, the balance of opinion favoured Campbell's decision.

Wider issues arose on the proposal to construct an oil-drilling plat-form at Drumbuie on the Ross-shire coast. The site was held inalien-ably by the National Trust for Scotland, and the construction work, it was argued, would have a detrimental effect on the environment and the local community. But there was a brick in the riddle. It was declared government policy to speed up the extraction of North Sea oil. So, as the protracted enquiry dragged on, it was asked whether the Secretary of State could really be impartial. Campbell, who was a fair man, was fully conscious that this was more than a local dispute, and he was party to the decision announced in February, 1974, that the Government would itself take power in Parliament to acquire land urgently needed for the construction of oil platforms. The General Election followed almost immediately thereafter, and the next Government followed broadly the same principle with its Offshore Petroleum Development (Scotland) Bill. (Ross refused permission for work on the Drumbuie site, but allowed development to go ahead at near-by Kishorn. It needed a meticulous exercise of judgment.)

Neither Campbell's painstaking approach to other questions which he regarded as the basic business of the Scottish Office—a White Paper on the reorganisation of the administrative structure of the Health Service, another Paper on the Hunter Committee's proposals for freshwater fishing which had been dormant since 1965—nor his consultations on a new court system to replace the J.P. and burgh magistrates' courts diverted public attention for long from what was happening in the industrial field, in shipbuilding, steel, oil, and economic planning.

Campbell differed from his predecessor in his attitude to regional economic planning. Both the main parties were firmly committed to regional policies, the control of expansion in congested areas and the offer of inducements in development areas. There were periodical variations as both parties changed their minds about the form which the incentives should take, and they differed in the amount of state intervention which they were prepared to support. While endorsing the current regional policy, Campbell for his part did not think it necessary to claim a prime position for the Scottish Office. Instead, he saw his job as being to ensure that the Government's overall plans were framed in such a way that Scottish requirements fitted into them. As it affected the disposition of the Secretary of State this was more than a difference of degree. It was part of his Ambassadorial concept.

In December, 1970, Campbell was at pains to correct the impression that the Scottish Economic Planning Council was an executive, decision-making body, and its alleged key rôle in regenerating the Scottish economy receded into the background. To mark the change, 'Planning' was excised from its title which became the Scottish Economic Council, and George Younger, by now designated Parliamentary Under-Secretary of State for Development, was appointed Deputy Chairman. The Council might not be operating in the twilight, but its high noon had passed.

The 1972 Budget brought about several changes in regional policy.

Investment grants, which the Conservatives had previously thought too expensive for the jobs they created, were restored. There were to be building grants for projects in development areas, with a higher rate for the special areas with the highest unemployment. Conversely, free depreciation was to be allowed *passim*, so that the development areas' advantage was, in this respect, somewhat eroded. If these vicissitudes are hard for the reader to follow they were more irritating for the firms which had to find their way through the labyrinth. There is a fair criticism that they reflect bureaucratic advice that the mutations would have a more precise effect than was conceivably possible.

One thing was clear. While the new measures would apply to Scotland, they would do so only in parity with the other regions. At the same time it was announced that regional development offices, including a Scottish Industrial Development Office (S.I.D.O.) in Glasgow, would be set up with powers to give industrial grants without reference to Whitehall. But these new offices were to be responsible to a new Minister (Chataway) within the Department of Trade and Industry, and not to the Secretary of State. Ross at once denounced the creation of the S.I.D.O. as a 'downgrading of the Scottish Office', but Campbell was equally entitled to say that while Scotland would benefit from the new arrangements they did not affect powers which he had never had, or claimed to have. In an interview given after he left office Campbell said that, looking back, he had derived most satisfaction from getting the combination of regional measures in the 1972 Budget together with the appointment of the S.I.D.O.[1]

This self-effacing attitude was consistent with Campbell's underlying political philosophy, but no banners were waved to greet the arrival of the S.I.D.O., since it would have to compete with English regions. There was no obvious answer to the complaint that the Scottish Office had been diffident, if not remiss, in not claiming it, and the general view was that it would have come more rationally under the Secretary of State's jurisdiction. Critics soon found more fuel in the announcement in January, 1973, that there would be an Offshore Oil Supplies Office in Scotland, but again under the Department of Trade and Industry. Scotland, it was angrily alleged, could be entrusted with no more than a branch office under central supervision. Oil policy should be run in parallel with regional policy, but it was evident that the exploitation of oil resources was to be controlled from Whitehall. Nor were Campbell's opponents assuaged by the appointment of

Lord Polwarth, the Minister of State, to chair an advisory Oil Development Council for Scotland and to take special responsibility for oil. The Government was admittedly improvising in the unprecedented situation caused by North Sea oil, but it was far from clear how Polwarth's rôle would fit in with the Glasgow branch of the Offshore Oil Supplies Office, or with the Department of Trade and Industry. How, indeed? A jesting Pilate question.

A more fundamental query was where these *pas de bas* left the Secretary of State. Major decisions increasingly appeared to be outwith his control. It was John Davies, the Trade and Industry Minister, who announced the injection of £35 m. aid for Govan Shipbuilders, although Campbell's advocacy had much to do with it. But the new steel complex was destined for Tees-side, not Hunterston, as had been hoped. Had the balance of influence, if not of power, between the Secretary of State and Whitehall Ministers been altered by the concentration in the Department of Trade and Industry? Had the heightened status of the Industrial Minister been matched by a corresponding decline in the authority of the Secretary of State?

In an address to the Law Society of Scotland on 8th April, 1973, which attracted little attention at the time, Campbell explained his posture. 'The Secretary of State for Scotland is broadly the Minister for all domestic subjects except finance, the economy, and industry.'[2] To leave his audience in no doubt where he stood he made the same point three times during his speech. The matters for which he did not have responsibility were finance, the economy, and industrial affairs. One political commentator suggested that the Trade and Industry office in Glasgow harked back to Defoe's barb that Scotland no more required a Minister than Yorkshire (Chapter I). Campbell was not disturbed. He was not interested in acquiring the appearance of power for its own sake, or in asserting a nationalist claim for the sake of the facile popularity that would follow. He was an Ambassador and, as other members of the diplomatic corps have found, his motives and actions were often misunderstood.

With the Nationalists Campbell existed in an uneasy vacuum. Devolutionary proposals were awaiting the report of the Kilbrandon Commission, although the Conservatives, at their meeting at Perth in May, 1973, had appeared to renege on their own scheme of a Scottish Convention. But the portents were there. The Scottish National Party had secured 11 per cent of the Scottish poll in 1970, although only one of their candidates was returned. In the four by-elections held since then, however, they had fared better, polling 35, 30, 42, and 19 per cent of the votes cast, and at Govan (November, 1973) they turned a Labour majority of over 7000 into an S.N.P. one of 571. Campbell was eventually to suffer what he must have regarded as the final indignity of defeat by Winifred Ewing at the next General Election.

Campbell had never shown much relish for the sharp exchanges of debate in the House of Commons. At one time the Opposition tabled a motion criticising the 'silent Minister', but on his translation to the Lords he found the more rarefied atmosphere of the Upper House more congenial. There he has displayed oratorical gifts that were not always apparent while he was Secretary of State. An honest man, his strictly constitutional view of the duties of his office would have been more acceptable earlier, in the days of Gilmour and Collins, when government intervention was less pervasive. If that seems a mildly derogatory assessment, he would have been justified in praying in aid the views of Dr McCrone, the head of the Economics and Statistics Unit at the Scottish Office, who revealed in March, 1972, that the effect of regional policies over the previous ten years had been to produce a shortfall of at least 200,000 jobs in Scotland, and that to secure a measure of full employment would have required additional investment of about £200 m. a year.[3] That would have been beyond the scope of Scotland's Minister as Campbell, or anyone else, saw it.

NOTES

1 The *Scotsman*, 23rd April, 1974.
2 *Ibid.*, 10th April, 1973.
3 *Ibid.*, 17th March, 1972.

CHAPTER XVIII

Extra Prep

Ross returned to the Scottish Office in March, 1974, as the only Minister to be Secretary of State for a second term, although Adamson and Gilmour had both been Scottish Secretary in the twenties before the dignity of the office was enhanced. He remained as long as the Wilson administration lasted, and retired with Wilson to the back benches in April, 1976.

Ross had no doubt that the Scottish Nationalist Party now offered a real threat to the survival of the Labour Government and was soon denouncing them with characteristic energy. In April, 1974, he reminded the Scottish Trades Union Congress that the S.N.P. were an irrelevant and shoddy party which had disgraced the name of Scotland.[1] He was reproved by the press for what seemed an extravagant attack. Not abashed, Ross stuck to the same line and in February, 1976, he told the House of Commons that the S.N.P. were 'conning the people of Scotland into tartan chaos',[2] and that the S.N.P. slogans were 'founded in the politics of greed and selfishness'. One might have assumed that he had spent his time in Opposition studying the invectives against Catiline with which Cicero used to weary the Roman Senate.

The Kilbrandon Commission had reported shortly before the General Election, but the Government were not hastening to declare their attitude to it. A discussion document was issued in June, 1974, but it did not take the discussion much further. The Scottish Labour Party were meanwhile in some difficulty. In June their Council had voted against devolution, but the Scottish Labour M.P.s, whose calculations showed that at least thirteen Scottish seats were now threatened by the S.N.P., called for a special conference. This was duly held in August, and the Scottish Labour Party obediently reversing their earlier decision, voted for a devolutionary scheme, although they were emphatic that there was to be no proportional representation when it came to electing a Scottish Assembly.

Ross was by now a devolutionary dove, but, he reiterated, he was still a hard-liner so far as separation was concerned. In October, 1975, Harry Ewing was appointed as an additional Parliamentary Under-Secretary of State—bringing the number of Scottish Ministers up to six for the first time—to assist in dealing with devolutionary matters, and there were promises of a Bill in the next session of Parliament. This was followed by the publication in November of a White Paper on 'Our changing democracy: Devolution to Scotland and Wales'. Ross's hand could perhaps be seen in the extensive powers it proposed to retain for the Secretary of State, including a veto over the decisions of the new elected Assembly. But this was not the only reason why the White Paper failed to satisfy the devolutionists, or why it was greeted with a 'barrage of derision and denunciation'.[3] The subsequent intro-duction, and chequered progress of the Devolution Bill came after Ross's time at the Scottish Office. So much for the dominating political issue, as it emerged.

Two conclusions on Ross's attitude to the rising tide of nationalism seem inescapable. First, although he no doubt proceeded from a sincere conviction that the S.N.P. policy was not in the interests of the country, or his party, his capacity for lambasting its proponents did little to further an objective discussion of the merits. He did not share Walter Elliot's belief that the Scots had a native predilection for argu-ment. Second, though no one man could be held responsible for the growing success of the S.N.P. at the poll, his relentless opposition in the sixties prepared the soil in which the Nationalist seed grew. In the short term, until 1971 he was probably right in his assessment of the Nationalist upsurge that had flourished briefly at Hamilton in 1967. Later, he had reluctantly to accept the views of the devolutionists in his own party and support the proposals for a Scottish Assembly.

In the political temper of the time the Queen's Speech in October, 1974, foreshadowed no fewer than five Scottish Bills, dealing with the acquisition of sites for oil-related purposes, the appointment of district courts, local government finance, housing (to abolish mandatory rent increases), and the creation of a Scottish Development Agency.

Ross was anxious, not only to demonstrate the Government's con-cern in legislative terms but also to revive the rôle of Scotland's Minister in the industrial field. There were three positive steps. He took over the Department of Trade and Industry's Glasgow Office, which then became part of the Scottish Economic Planning Depart-ment (formed under Campbell in a minor reorganisation of the Scottish Office). Its functions included advice on industrial locations, the steering of industry, etc. The S.I.D.O. was also transferred to the Scottish Office, and in February, 1975, Ross announced a Bill to create a Scottish Development Agency, responsible to him and with an initial budget of £200m. Armed with these comprehensive, and over-lapping powers, Ross could say with manifest justification that he was Scotland's industrial Minister.

This remarkable accretion of powers was received with some bewilderment. It was asked whether a single instrument, rather than these multiple organisations, would not have made more sense. The officials who advised on machinery must bear the brunt of this criticism. It had all been far too hugger-mugger. Then it was suggested that the Scottish Development Agency was going to be a poor relation of the (Great Britain) National Enterprise Board, and there were fears that the N.E.B. would still control the most important developments. Most disappointing to Ross was the reaction that the new arrangements would merely facilitate an eventual transfer to the Scottish Assembly. But none of these criticisms should be allowed to detract from Ross's achievement in wresting control from Whitehall, belated though it was.

No such initiative marked Ross's approach to other domestic issues during his second term. Scotland was lagging far behind England in divorce reform, but Ross did not provide facilities for legislation. He was reluctant to accept the need for altering the obsolete licensing laws, and, not surprisingly, he was again involved in bitter disputes with the teachers about remuneration. On these matters the last word may be left with a Labour M.P., John Mackintosh. Writing in the *New Statesman*, he said

> The longstanding opposition of the Labour leadership in Scotland to such liberal causes as divorce law reform, reform of the licensing laws, and free contraceptive aids on the Health Service meant that the party had little appeal to other sections of the community, to the young or to the progressive elements in the professions.[4]

NOTES

1 The *Scotsman*, 20th April, 1974.
2 *Hansard*, 6th February, 1976. Vol. 904, col. 1500.
3 The *Scotsman*, 29th November, 1975.
4 *New Statesman*, 16th January, 1976.

CHAPTER XIX

The Cordial Union

'Hath not God', King James VI and I asked Parliament in 1604, 'first united these two Kingdoms both in Language, Religion, and similitude of manners?' It is a tenet among historians to give many of James VI's aphorisms at least a retrospective validity. Was this eulogy of the union of the monarchies a temporary aberration by the most learned fool in Christendom? Or, to pose the question differently, how does it come about that the electorate is now asked to contemplate the fission, if not of the Crown, of everything else? I make no claim to analyse the Scots' attitude towards the English since 1603, but, as there are no short-term objectives in constitutional matters, a bare outline of the historical perspective must precede an attempt to answer this conundrum. We can then assess how Scottish Ministers and their advisers have reacted over the last fifty years to assertions of nationalism.

Sir Thomas Craig, in his *Treatise on the Union of the British Realms* written in 1605 but not published till 1909, claimed that the union of the crowns was

> an effort to achieve a permanent reconciliation between two proud and spirited peoples, who from the cradle of their history have been animated by the most determined mutual rancour.[1]

His views may not have been entirely typical of Scottish sentiment at the time, but, as Professor Daiches has pointed out in his illuminating study, at the beginning of the seventeenth century, there were more Scots than Englishmen in favour of a complete union of the two countries.[2] It is not, however, the allegiance to a single monarchy but the Union of the Parliaments in 1707, the transfer of legislative power to Westminster, that Home Rulers have since called in question. The preamble to the Union, English anxiety about the succession to the throne, recurring fears of a French invasion, Scottish resentment at exclusion from English commercial markets, have been fully documented elsewhere, and I crave the indulgence of historians for this brief summary.

The Treaty of Union was not popular at the time. Defoe, the English propagandist, might break into doggerel rhyme in his *Review*:

Union's the Nation's life, and Peace the Soul,
Union preserves the Parts, and Peace the Whole.

But there were violent representations and riots while the Scottish Parliament discussed the Articles of the Treaty. The counties were opposed to it, and as the Earl of Seafield reported to Godolphin, 'A majoritie of a convention of boros have also addressed against it'. Whatever view one takes of the debates at the time, the far-seeing and at time prophetic speeches of Andrew Fletcher, or the devious antics of Peers who spoke on one side but were prepared to vote on the other, the final decision was taken on pragmatic grounds. The majority of Scots who favoured the Union did so for hard-headed commercial reasons. They contrasted the appearance, and prospects, of mercantile prosperity, south of the Border with their own stagnant economy. The Commissioners were bartering the Scottish Parliament and the security of the succession, for trading advantages and access to wider markets.

Though the Duke of Queensberry in his concluding speech on 9th March, 1707, had hoped that 'you will study to promote a cordial union with our neighbours', there was widespread suspicion. If anything could ensure the permanence of the new relationship it was, ironically, the 1745 Rebellion. Lowland Scots, alarmed at the spectre of being overrun by the Celtic, Catholic supporters of Prince Charles Edward, were willing to stomach their dislike of rule from the South, and those who criticised the Union were equated with Jacobites.

Throughout the first half of the eighteenth century it was not just the Scots who disliked the Union, realising Fletcher's fears of 'posting to London for Places and Pensions, by which, whatever Particular Men may get, the Nation must always be the Loser'. The English regarded the intruders with antipathy or scorn, as was later evidenced in John Wilkes's *North Briton*. But there followed a century when the benefits of free trade between the countries were more widely recognised. In 1854, David Masson, writing in the then influential *North British Review*, observed that

Increased quiet, increased commerce and wealth, increased liberty, increased civilisation—these have been the consequences to Scotland of the once detested Union.[3]

It was in the Victorian era that the idea of a 'British' nation became current. The Queen's affection, if not preference, for Presbyterians, her Highland retreat and retainers, might cause amusement at the Court of St James's, but Balmorality set a tone of its own.

Not that the Scots were universally content. No time, it was alleged, was found for Scottish legislation, and Scottish grievances were perpetually neglected at Westminster. The campaign for the creation of a Scottish Minister has been discussed in Chapter I. By 1856 it had reached such dimensions that *The Times* was moved to print a scathing attack on Scottish nationalism.

> Scotland has lost way. She remains motionless, relying on past achievements, boasting of great men that are dead and gone, repeating maxims that were discoveries once, but are mere platitudes now, and showing few signs of intellectual or moral vigour. . . .
>
> Hardly a single idea on political or social subjects comes in the present day from Scotland. . . .
>
> We south of the Tweed have risen to the conception of a United Kingdom; nay, more, of a British Empire, and every subject of the Queen finds here a career in which he may advance without fear of jealousy or prejudice. But in Edinburgh the cry, or at least the feeling, still is, Scotland for the Scotch. Yet the more Scotland has striven to be a nation, the more she has sunk to be a province.[4]

This was, however, the time when in the aftermath of the great Reform legislation the direction of government was changing. Increasingly it was concerned with the provision, or the supervision, of new domestic, and essentially local, services. This was the time when the case for a Scottish Assembly was strongest. It could—in the days before government became more involved in all the functions that affect the whole country and are now taken for granted, ranging from welfare benefits to economic planning—have been presented as a logical extension to the establishment of the Scottish Office. Even the Marquess of Bute, from the Olympian detachment of his antiquarian studies, saw the point. He wrote to Rosebery to urge that

> the internal legislation of Scotland ought to be committed to some nationally representative body, to meet, not in London, but in Edinburgh, if necessary at a different time to the Imperial Parliament; and which, if the title of Parliament were not given it, might at least deserve the scarcely less historic and honoured one of National Convention.[5]

It is arguable that the desirability, and the possibility, of setting up a separate Scottish legislature was at its highest during the period from

1886 to the First War, and that the case for, and the likelihood of, such a development has diminished ever since. An ingenuous view? It may be, but it is supported by the Liberal Party's commitment at the time, and by the frequency with which the Home Rule question engaged the attention of Parliament.

There was an understanding that Scottish Home Rule would have to be considered, but that it should wait till the more pressing Irish problem was settled. This took much longer than was expected, and Scottish M.P.s became increasingly impatient. The sequence is significant. The Scottish Home Rule Association was formed in 1886, with Dr G. B. Clark, M.P. for Caithness, as President and 12 other M.P.s among its members. By 1892 the Labour leaders Keir Hardie and Cunninghame-Graham had been recruited as Vice-Presidents. In 1889 Home Rule was brought to the vote, but lost by 200 votes to 79 —the Scots being 22 to 19 against it. In February, 1890, Clark moved an amendment to the Gracious Speech asking for a separate Scottish Parliament, but lost by 278 votes to 112.[6] Further motions for Home Rule within a federal system were brought forward in the 1890s. Westminster was wearying of Celtic debates, and in 1894 the Scottish Grand Committee was formed as a palliative to consider purely Scottish Bills. In 1908 a Bill introduced by Captain D. V. Pirie passed its first stage by 107 votes, the Scots this time being 41 to 9 in favour. But no further action was taken, and Sir Hugh Dalziel's Bill in 1911 met the same fate. In 1913, when the Irish Bill had been passed by the Commons, Sir W. H. Cowan returned to the charge, and after declaiming that 'A Scottish Office in London can never be other than an absurdity', asserted that 'We desire nothing but the power of local legislature and administration'.[7] From 1889 to the outbreak of the First War Scottish M.P.s kept up the pressure for some measure of Home Rule. But the support of the Liberal and Labour leaders meant that the Conservative and Unionist Members, who were equally hostile to Irish Home Rule, opposed the attempts to secure a separate Scottish Parliament.

It is, however, of interest that the Irish question moved both Churchill and Asquith to consider wider devolutionary proposals. In a Memorandum which he circulated to the Cabinet on 1st March, 1911, Churchill suggested the division of the United Kingdom into 'ten areas, having regard to geographical, racial, and historical considerations'. Each area would have its own legislative and administrative body, separately elected, and in Ireland, Scotland, and Wales they would be 'clothed with Parliamentary form so far as may be desirable in each case'.[8] Asquith, speaking on the Government of Ireland Bill in 1912, declared himself in favour of legislative devolution. The route towards a federal system seemed to be opening. But the War intervened.

At the 1918 Election there was still some flirting with Home Rule, and in 1919 a Speaker's Conference on Devolution was set up under Mr Speaker Lowther. The Conference Report (Cmd. 692) rehearsed previous arguments, and very diffidently produced two alternative schemes. No one was much enamoured of the Lowther Report, either at the time or later, and there seems to have been no attempt to follow it up. In effect, the picture after the 1914 War was radically changed. It is not difficult to see why. Concern with immediate post-war problems, the depression of the twenties, and the disintegration of the Liberal Party all contributed.

The chief proponents of Home Rule were now the members of the Independent Labour Party, but significantly the Scottish Trade Union leaders, who had supported it from 1918 onwards, had moved into opposition by their 1931 Congress. Parliament still fitfully debated the Scottish question, and in 1924 Tom Johnston made an emotional speech on the Government of Scotland Bill, invoking Robert Louis Stevenson and Burns,[9] but as we have already seen (Chapter IX), his general attitude to Home Rule was at best ambivalent. In the same debate Sir Henry Craik, uniquely a Scottish civil servant before he entered Parliament, made a good establishment speech.

> I would ask hon. Members who press for this Bill to remember that they have not a monopoly of love for their country, of patriotic feelings, or of heartfelt, innate attachment to every association of romance or of characteristic quality that we have had handed down from our ancestors in Scotland. . . .
>
> I am against the whole thing. It is mischievous from beginning to end.[10]

If the main parties were not entirely disenchanted with Home Rule in the interwar years, they were not wildly enthusiastic about featuring it as a main electoral issue. In this period nationalism found its most explicit expression in the Scottish literary renaissance. Writers, rather than politicians, kept the idea before the public. Meanwhile, the growth of Labour support in Clydeside was much more important politically, although both Liberal and Labour Parties remained nominally committed to various forms of Scottish devolution. It is to the latter part of this time that the Scottish National Party owes its origins.

There were already three different Nationalist cadres—the Scottish Home Rule Association, the Scottish National League, and the Scottish National Movement. They coalesced almost by accident in the aftermath of the Rectorial Election at Glasgow University in 1928, when the National Party of Scotland was formed, owing much to John MacCormick's initiative. MacCormick was an attractive figure, but a political innocent. In his autobiography he tells of the growth of his party, the merger with the more cautious Scottish Party to produce the Scottish National Party in 1934, and his own resignation after an internal disagreement in 1942. It is a strangely touching book, and as he describes his secret negotiations with Liberal leaders and plans to hold a great meeting of a Scottish Convention in 1939 (frustrated by the Munich crisis), it is reminiscent of a John Buchan novel.[11] He saw his triumphs in terms of winning Rectorial elections.

MacCormick's main political achievement was his direction of the Scottish Covenant Movement which held two well-attended assemblies in 1947 and 1948 and attracted 2m. signatures. But MacCormick and his followers were now attacking the Labour Government, and neither Attlee nor the Conservative Opposition showed them any sympathy. By the time the Balfour Commission had reported in 1954 (Chapter XIII) the Covenant's impetus was spent, although it was not formally disbanded. The leadership of the Nationalist forces now passed to the S.N.P. and its guiding genius Dr Robert MacIntyre.

To take a summary view of subsequent developments, there is much to be said for Professor Hanham's account. His thesis is that the great achievement of the S.N.P. from 1942 to 1964 was simply to have survived. Its survival had, however, been based on a very limited conception of nationalism. By shunning intellectuals, by concentrating on the smaller man, it deliberately set out to win the rank and file of the older political parties, rather than their leaders. It became emphatically the party of the little man, and its philosophy had just the right ring to make a direct appeal to the ordinary man in the street who had never taken an interest in politics. 'The S.N.P.', he concluded, 'is a grassroots political movement or it is nothing.'[12]

Whether or not one accepts Professor Hanham's view, it is clear that the S.N.P.'s impact was most unmistakably felt when it won the Hamilton by-election in 1967. Soon after, it had a signal success at local elections, winning 101 seats, 62 of them from Labour. At the 1970

General Election the reservations of the hard-liners who thought that the comet would soon burn itself out seemed to be vindicated when the S.N.P. lost Hamilton, and only one of its candidates was returned. A year later its local gains were wiped out. Then the S.N.P. found the fuel it had been looking for in North Sea oil. Concentrating on the slogan 'It's Scotland's Oil', in 1973 it won a by-election at Govan. In the 1974 General Election it won 7 seats in February and increased this to the present figure of 11 in October. We have seen in earlier chapters how the main parties reacted to the S.N.P.'s electoral advance.

In the political context oil is no more than a North Sea Bubble. Estimates fluctuate, but none suggest that there is an inexhaustible supply of oil beneath the ocean, and there are many Scots who feel unhappy at the claim that it belongs to Scotland. Strictly speaking, under the Treaty of Union it is not exclusively Scottish. The revenues from it are already heavily mortgaged to relieve Exchequer debts which Scotland shares. Moreover, if the oilfields had been found off the East Anglian coast, would the Scots have assented to a claim that it was English oil? These are viscous questions. Oil may account for much of the S.N.P.'s present support, but it does not explain the recurring resurgence of Scottish nationalism.

Within the ambit of this book only a summary explanation can be attempted, but the Nationalist disposition appears to have two main sources—one psychological, and the other pragmatic. Psychologically the weaker partner in the Union feels at a disadvantage. There is a latent fear that the Scots and their native traditions will be absorbed by their neighbour in the South, that they will be irrevocably Anglicised. But although the Scots have been subject to Anglicising influences since the days of Queen Margaret in the twelfth century, there have been few deliberate attempts since the Union to impose an English pattern. Scottish institutions, the law, the church, the educational system, have maintained their distinctive form. In practice, the English attitude to Scottish affairs is more marked by indifference. Scottish M.P.s are left to get on with their own legislation while English Members indicate their lack of concern in the most decisive way—by their absence. Sir Godfrey Collins was not the only Secretary of State to be dismayed to see the House emptying as he started a Scottish Debate. Gazing at the backs of his English colleagues as they scurried from the Chamber, he was not mollified by their later assurances that no personal affront was intended, but they had other, more pressing, business. The complaint of disinterest, which goes back to Trevelyan,

an early Scottish Secretary, is better founded than the one that Westminster has attempted to stifle Scottish aspirations.

The pragmatic reason for discontent is more easily identified. The
depression between the Wars left a legacy of bitterness in Scotland,
and the 'rationalisation' whereby English-based firms closed their
Scottish branches was not forgotten. Even in the improved conditions
after the 1939–45 War the contrast between unemployment rates in
Scotland and the South-east of England provokes questions whether
Scotland would not fare better with more autonomy. It is a matter of
judgment how strenuous have been the efforts to correct this imbalance. Certainly regional economic planning has been designed to
create a more favourable industrial climate in Scotland. But if Scottish
incomes are lower than in the South, public expenditure per head—
and the Scottish Office can mark much of this to their credit—is
higher. This may be dismissed as the consequence of misgovernment,
but an examination of the relevant Votes does not show a lack of
concern for Scottish needs.

How have successive Secretaries of State reacted to the expression
of Scottish nationalism? All, save one, have been Scots, patriotic Scots.
As geographical Ministers they can scarcely be faulted for their
commitment to furthering the Scottish cause. But as members of the
United Kingdom Government they have been subject to the political
facts of life, either in overall economic circumstances or in the standing
of their Party. Some have been more successful than others in overcoming these inhibitions. Woodburn, for example, was nearly submerged in the Attlee Government's eagerness to carry out nationalisation and social reform measures. Noble found the political tide running
against him. On the other hand, Johnston in the wartime coalition and
Stuart during MacMillan's affluence were able to secure many of their
objectives. What is surprising in retrospect is that the way in which
they have administered the original functions of the Scottish Office—
law and order, health, agriculture and education—has not attracted
any more vocal criticism than has been heard in England. The Scottish
health and legal aid services, to take two instances at random, are more
efficient in terms of cost benefit than in England. It is when public
agitation forces Scottish Ministers to appear to do what they have no
power to accomplish (e.g. in promoting economic growth) that they
adopt postures that arouse dissent. Maclay saw what was needed and
launched experiments in regional economic planning. Ross eventually
acquired executive authority to assist industry, but did so at a stage

which was, however unjustly, seen as a political device to disconcert the S.N.P.

We have dwelt incidentally, in the chapters on individual Ministers, on the attitude that they adopted to Home Rulers in general, and finally to the S.N.P. For long they relied on the orthodox theory that any political movement should be judged by its success at the ballot box, a convenient doctrine since General Elections are determined on a combination of United Kingdom issues. Until the seventies this appeared to be intermittently successful, and it was possible to cite the wider national interest against what could be defined as a narrow parochialism. Pre-war Scottish Ministers had a comparatively easy ride on nationalism as they built up the prestige of their office. Later, McNeil was more than a match for the Nationalists: Ross was, until latterly, too obdurate in his refusal to take them seriously. Throughout the whole of our fifty years, however, those who have been Secretary of State have relentlessly tried to exercise their geographical function to secure advantageous treatment for Scotland. They have been skilful—at times very skilful—in bartering their support for Cabinet colleagues' proposals in exchange for reciprocity on Scottish measures. It is regrettable that the public judge them by the number of visible projects, the strip mill or the smelter, that they have brought to Scotland.

If a Scottish Assembly comes into existence it is most probable that it will have to be financed by a block grant. The many abortive attempts to replace rating by a local income tax as the basis of local government revenue merely underline the hazards to be met by the proposition that there should be a separate Scottish fiscal system. But the block grant would undoubtedly be to Scotland's detriment. It has been the perpetual concern of Scottish Ministers to ensure that the Exchequer contribution on each individual service should take account of Scotland's geographical position and her different economic and social structure. They have also made much of the need to reduce emigration. All these arguments would be lost with a block grant. The Treasury could be relied on to fix the initial grant at no more than the sum of the existing ones. Thereafter it would be a sitting target when cuts in public expenditure were under review. It is also likely that the Assembly would spend the grant with some alacrity and count on public support to demand more. The unhappy friction that would follow needs no emphasis, but those who seek the pot of gold have found it to be a delusion ever since Chaucer's Pardoner's Tale.

Scottish Office officials have been attacked for hostility to the S.N.P. But they have to take their instructions from their political masters, and the charge of bias is not supported. Their attitude has been to report the views of the S.N.P., as of other pressure groups, when submitting proposals to Ministers. The rise of the S.N.P. has not strengthened their hand in Whitehall: it has made their job more difficult. In discussion with Whitehall Departments, particularly the Treasury, they have to rebut charges that what they are proposing is simply a sop to the Nationalists. This does not facilitate an objective discussion, and the end product is not always to Scotland's advantage. Civil servants are fully aware of the influence that their Ministers carry in Cabinet and frame their interdepartmental arguments accordingly. This is a delicate business, and the Scottish Office record is not a discreditable one, but it does not help when other Departments become weary of the sound of the pipes.

These paragraphs are written in the spring of 1978 when the House of Lords is busy applying surgery to the Devolution Bill and the referendum lies ahead. The future rôle of the Secretary of State is still far from clear, but it appears that the status of the historic office may be reduced to that of a superior liaison officer. He can hardly speak in Cabinet as Scotland's Minister if Scottish policy is to be formed and enacted by a Scottish Assembly. His power will be amputated, and an amputated limb is discarded and soon forgotten. Leaving aside the Party implications of retaining seats at Westminster, it is difficult to see that Scotland will be better served by a Scottish Assembly, which is the inevitable preliminary to complete separation, as well as by the top-heavy local government structure. There will be an excess of government. The S.N.P. case, according to Mrs Margo MacDonald, is that Scotland needs a Parliament in order to get jobs. Judging by the Westminster track record, one would not be too sanguine that these expectations will be fulfilled.

The final paradox is that the case for a geographical Minister in the U.K. Cabinet, not for a separate Assembly, is strengthened by our accession to the European Economic Community. The Community, to follow J. K. Galbraith's shrewd analysis, did not have its origins in a sudden access of economic and political enlightenment after the Second World War.[13] It came into being primarily because modern corporate and multinational organisations had made the old boundaries obsolete. If the British Government is to continue to represent British interests in face of E.E.C. pressure, and the underlying pressures that brought the Community about, it needs to be strengthened, not subjected to fission. So far as Scotland is concerned, this means the continuance of Scotland's Minister. Economic problems in Scotland are basically the same as in the rest of Great Britain, though they differ in degree. In order to cope with them, the gradual trend is towards assimilation, but Scotland's institutions, starting with the Scottish Office, are sufficiently resilient to withstand absorption. To be acceptable, government must be seen to adopt policies which are overtly favourable, or not unfavourable, to Scotland. That requires the protective presence of the Secretary of State.

These tentative conclusions appear to neglect the most important question of all, the one at the heart of the whole debate, namely the preservation of the Scottish ethos. How is the Flower of Scotland to flourish amid the Party managers' calculations of political advantage? The answer has nothing to do with oil, and is little affected by attempts to open a new debating chamber in the old Royal High School. Most Scots regard themselves as different from the English, and they will not deny themselves the intermittent luxury of disliking, resenting, or even despising their Southern neighbours. But this need not mean that they really wish to abjure the benefits of being part of a single United Kingdom. It is tempting to go back to Walter Scott's *Letters of Malachai Malagrowther*, written at the time of the banknote crisis in the 1820s. As a recent scholar has observed, Scott conjured up the picture of the Scotsman as a romantic realist, as one in whom conflicts between fact and fancy are reconciled by sheer force of character. 'In short, he taught Scotsmen to see themselves as men whose reason is on the side of the Union, and whose emotions are not, and in whose confusion lies their national confusion.'[14]

Is it a forlorn hope that the pre-war Scottish Renaissance can still find new inspiration within the cordial Union? The next time devolution comes before Parliament, and Scottish Members are asked to vote for the guillotine that will be required to pass the latest piece of gerrymandering, they might recall the last words of Lord Balmerino. When he mounted the scaffold to pay the penalty for his part in the Jacobite rebellion, he looked at his executioner and gave him this envoi.

'Take care wi' that damned axe. It might hurt someone.'

NOTES

1 Sir Thomas Craig, *De unione regnorum Britanniae tractatus*, ed. C. S. Terry. *Scottish Hist. Soc. Publications*, vol. lx. Edinburgh, 1909.
2 David Daiches, *Scotland and the Union*. London, 1977.
3 *North British Review*, vol. xxi, 1854.
4 *The Times*, 4th December, 1856.
5 *Rosebery Papers*, 3rd November, 1881. National Library of Scotland.
6 *Hansard*, 19th February, 1890. 3rd series, vol. cccxii, col. 1677.
7 *Hansard*, 30th May, 1913. Vol. lii, col. 471.
8 Cab. 37/105.
9 *Hansard*, 9th May, 1924. Vol. 173, col. 796.
10 *Hansard*, 9th May, 1924. Vol. 173, col. 838.
11 J. M. MacCormick, *The Flag in the Wind*. London, 1955.
12 H. J. Hanham, *Scottish Nationalism*. London, 1969.
13 *New Statesman*, 10th February, 1978.
14 *Government and Nationalism in Scotland*, ed. J. N. Wolfe. Edinburgh, 1969.

APPENDIX I

Secretaries of State for Scotland

1926   Rt. Hon. Sir John Gilmour, Bt., D.S.O.

1929   Rt. Hon. William Adamson.

1931   Rt. Hon. Sir Archibald Sinclair, Bt., K.T., C.M.G. (later Viscount Thurso).

1932   Rt. Hon. Sir Godfrey Collins, K.B.E., C.M.G.

1936   Rt. Hon. Walter Elliot, C.H., C.M.G.

1938   Rt. Hon. D. J. Colville (later Lord Clydesmuir).

1940   Rt. Hon. Ernest Brown, M.C.

1941   Rt. Hon. Thomas Johnston.

1945   Rt. Hon. The Earl of Rosebery, K.T., D.S.O., M.C.

1945   Rt. Hon. Joseph Westwood.

1947   Rt. Hon. Arthur Woodburn.

1950   Rt. Hon. Hector McNeil.

1951   Rt. Hon. James Stuart, C.H., M.V.O., M.C. (later Viscount Stuart of Findhorn).

1957   Rt. Hon. John S. Maclay, C.M.G. (later Viscount Muirshiel, K.T.).

1962   Rt. Hon. Michael A. C. Noble (later Lord Glenkinglass).

1964   Rt. Hon. William Ross, M.B.E.

1970   Rt. Hon. Gordon T. C. Campbell, M.C. (later Lord Campbell of Croy).

1974   Rt. Hon. William Ross, again.

1976   Rt. Hon. Bruce Millan.

Appendix II

The Chronology of the Scottish Office
Reproduced, with kind permission, from
The Scottish Political System, by J. G. Kellas.
2nd edition, Cambridge University Press, 1975.

1746   Office of Secretary of State for Scotland lapses; Lord Advocate thereafter chief Scottish minister.

1828   Home Secretary made formally responsible for Scottish affairs, but Lord Advocate in practice responsible.

1845   Board of Supervision for Poor Relief established (to 1894); thereafter Local Government Board for Scotland (to 1919).

1849   Fishery Board (established 1808) restricts operation to Scotland.

1857   General Board of Commissioners in Lunacy (to 1913); thereafter, General Board of Control (to 1962).

1872   Scotch Education Department (committee of Privy Council); 1918 renamed Scottish Education Department.

1877   Prisons Commission (to 1928).

1885   SCOTTISH OFFICE established, taking most Home Office functions, and education. Scottish Secretary responsible to Parliament for Scottish boards.

1886   Crofters Commission (to 1911, and from 1955).

1892   Secretary for Scotland in the Cabinet.

1897   Congested Districts Board (to 1911). Responsible for Highland re-settlement.

1911   Scottish Insurance Commissioners (to 1919). National Insurance.

1912   Scottish Board of Agriculture (to 1928).

1913   Highlands and Islands Medical Services Board (to 1919).

1919   Scottish Board of Health (to 1928), absorbs Insurance Commissioners, Highland Medical Board, and Local Government Board for Scotland. Parliamentary Under-Secretary for Health for Scotland created.

1926   Elevation of Secretary for Scotland to rank of a Principal Secretary of State. Parliamentary Under-Secretary for Health for Scotland becomes Parliamentary Under-Secretary of State for Scotland.

1929   Creation of Departments of Agriculture for Scotland, Health for Scotland and Prisons Department, replacing boards (1912, 1919 above) and Commission (1877, above).

1937   Gilmour Committee Report on Scottish Administration (Cmd. 5563) recommends Edinburgh-based Scottish Office, and tighter control of Scottish administration by Scottish Secretary.

1939   Opening of St Andrew's House, Edinburgh, and vesting of powers of
        Scottish Office (now four departments of Agriculture, Education,
        Health, and Home) directly in Secretary of State.

1939–   Piecemeal transfer of functions to and from the Scottish Office, and
1975   successive Scottish Office departmental reorganisations. Main additions:
        electricity, roads, some transport; increased activity in economic
        planning, agriculture, health, social work, Highland development,
        aspects of oil and industrial development. Main loss: social security
        (National Insurance).

        Present departments: Agriculture and Fisheries, Development, Home
        and Health, Education, Economic Planning.

        Two additional Under-Secretaries of State (1940, 1951); Minister of
        State (1951); Second Minister of State replaced one of the Under-
        Secretaries (1969–70), returns with three Under-Secretaries (1974–6).
        An additional Under-Secretary of State was appointed in 1975.

Selected Bibliography

Note. Unless otherwise stated all books were published in London

Memoirs of Walpole, vol. ii, Coxe. 1978.

Lord Cockburn, *Memorials of his Time*. Edinburgh, 1856.

W. C. Smith, *The Secretary for Scotland*. Edinburgh, 1885.

Sir Thomas Craig, *De unione regnorum Britanniae tractatus*, ed. C. S. Terry. Scottish Hist. Soc. Publications, vol. lx. Edinburgh, 1909.

G. F. Young, *The Medici*. 1910.

Thomas Johnston, *Our Scots Noble Families*. Glasgow, 1913.

A. V. Dicey and R. S. Rait, *Thoughts on the Union between England and Scotland*. 1920.

Walter Elliot, *Toryism and the Twentieth Century*. 1927.

Arthur Woodburn, *An Outline of Finance*. 1928.

Robert Munro (Lord Alness), *Looking Back: Fugitive Writings and Sayings*. Edinburgh, 1930.

A Scotsman's Heritage, essays by Walter Elliot, Lord Macmillan, *et al.* 1932.

Thomas Johnston, *Memories*. 1952.

David Keir, *The House of Collins*. 1952.

Lord Macmillan, *A Man of Law's Tale*. 1952.

Arthur Campbell Turner, *Scottish Home Rule*. Oxford, 1952.

Letters of Daniel Defoe, ed. Healey. Oxford, 1955.

J. M. MacCormick, *The Flag in the Wind*. 1955.

J. Steven Watson, *The Reign of George III 1760–1815*. Oxford, 1960.

Dame Edith Sitwell, *The Queens and the Hive*. 1962.

H. J. Hanham, 'The Creation of the Scottish Office, 1881-87', *Juridical Review*. 1965.

Gavin McCrone, *Scotland's Economic Progress*. 1965.

I. Budge and D. W. Urwin, *Scottish Political Behaviour*. 1966.

J. C. Beckett, *The Making of Modern Ireland 1603–1923*. 1966.

James Stuart, *Within the Fringe*. 1967.

J. G. Kellas, *Modern Scotland: the Nation since 1960*. 1968.

J. P. Mackintosh, *The Devolution of Power*. 1968.

H. J. Hanham, *Scottish Nationalism*. 1969.

Gavin McCrone, *Scotland's Future: the Economics of Nationalism*. Oxford, 1969.

Tom Jones, *Whitehall Diary*. 1969.

Penguin Book of Scottish Verse. 1970.

George Pottinger, *The Winning Counter*. 1971.

Nigel Fisher, *Iain MacLeod*. 1973.

Kenneth Young, *Harry, Lord Rosebery*. 1974.

J. G. Kellas, *The Scottish Political System*. Cambridge, 1975.

Lord Windlesham, *Politics in Practice*. 1975.

Sir John Colville, *Footprints in Time*. 1976.

William Ferguson, *Scotland's Relations with England: a Survey to 1707*. Edinburgh, 1977.

David Daiches, *Scotland and the Union*. 1977.

Index